THE IMAGERY
OF KEATS
AND SHELLEY

A Comparative Study

by

RICHARD HARTER FOGLE

THE UNIVERSITY OF NORTH CAROLINA PRESS
Chapel Hill

PREFACE

THIS STUDY employs comparison in order to define the characteristic qualities of two poets decidedly similar, and still more decidedly different. The "richness," "concreteness," and "intensity" of Keats are critical commonplaces; the "abstractness" and "evanescence" of Shelley are little less familiar. By setting them together one can test the truth of these generalizations and insofar as they seem to be reliable define their meaning more closely than is possible in isolation.

The approach through "imagery" is an expedient which somewhat simplifies a complex and elusive problem. For the moment it may perhaps be enough to say that I have tried to seize upon the advantages of a specific mode of attack while at the same time preserving a sense of the wholeness and meaning of poetry. I do not "murder to dissect"; it might be more modest and more exact to say that I do but murder in jest, provisionally. What I abstract in order to examine, in short, I try earnestly to restore.

No previous comparison of the imagery of Keats and Shelley has been attempted. Indeed, there is not to my knowledge any extensive comparative study of their poetry in existence. Nor in the separate scholarship of each poet can be found much study specifically of their imagery.

Among standard works upon Keats I have been most largely influenced by C. D. Thorpe's *The Mind of John*

Keats and J. M. Murry's *Keats and Shakespeare* and
Studies in Keats. Of more restricted studies, I am indebted to W. J. Bate's valuable monograph, *Negative
Capability*. Mr. Bate's more recent and exhaustive *The
Stylistic Development of Keats*, although important, is
unrelated to my purposes. Two unpublished doctoral
dissertations, Sverre Arestad's *A Study of Keats's Use of
Imagery* (University of Washington, 1938), and Dorothy
B. Van Ghent's *Image-Types and Antithetical Structure in
the Work of Keats* (University of California, 1942), have
anticipated my examination of Keats, but from points
of view so different from my own that I have been unable
to utilize them. Miss Van Ghent's reinterpretation of
Keats's poetry through *gestalt* psychology is, however,
both original and penetrating.

No detailed examination of Shelley's poetic imagery
has so far as I am aware been made. Herbert Read in his
Defense of Shelley has concerned himself with psycho-
analysis rather than poetry. William Empson, Allen
Tate, John Crowe Ransom, Cleanth Brooks, and other
contemporary critics, have analyzed the imagery of
single poems of Shelley, with results dismaying to
everyone. Carl Grabo has discussed the scientific and
metaphysical bases of Shelley's imagery in *A Newton
Among Poets*, *The Meaning of the Witch of Atlas*, and
The Magic Plant, but has not dealt with the literary
problem. Newman I. White's definitive biography and
his abridged *Portrait of Shelley* likewise emphasize the
scientific and philosophic sources.

In forming my views of the nature of poetic imagery
I have drawn from a number of authorities, among
whom should especially be named June E. Downey in

her *Creative Imagination*, J. M. Murry's *Countries of the Mind*, I. A. Richards' *Philosophy of Rhetoric*, and C. D. Thorpe's articles on empathy. Professor Erika von Erhardt-Siebold's careful studies of synaesthesia in the Romantic poets must be acknowledged, although my own investigation is wholly independent of them.

This book is devoted primarily to examination of the poetry itself of Keats and Shelley. It makes little use of biography, and in general ignores the problem of imaginal sources as irrelevant to its purpose. It is not, on the other hand, purist or exclusive in point of view. Poetry, in my opinion, cannot profitably be studied without some external frame of reference. A poem is not a solid, complete artifact, like a painting or sculpture; it cannot adequately be analyzed from a point of view wholly aesthetic, in terms of its design and its technique only. Criticism which attempts to deal with poetry in isolation is, I think, condemned to poverty and sterility.

My approach is therefore eclectic. It endeavors to preserve the wholeness of poetry, conceptual as well as emotional and sensuous, insofar as it is possible, while at the same time taking full advantage of the opportunities for concentration upon the poetic text which the approach through imagery offers. While adopting in different chapters different points of view, it strives to maintain at the core an entire, although sometimes implicit, self-consistency. It is expository and to a degree appreciative, in the belief that the "affective" vocabulary and attitude is entirely valid when it develops, as I hope it does here, organically from honest and painstaking analysis. It avoids for the most part the enuncia-

tion of judgments, preferring to emphasize the analytical and sympathetic functions of criticism and to keep its standards implicit.

It may possibly be objected that my treatment of the thought of Keats and Shelley takes too little account of the chronological development of their ideas. To such a charge I must, I believe, plead guilty. My justification is that I am above all concerned to add, so far as I am able, to the understanding and appreciation of their poetry, and that to this purpose all other considerations are subsidiary. Along with this general defense, I urge several more specific points in support of my procedure. As regards Keats the chronological method is inappropriate. His considerable poetry was written within a span of at most three years, from 1816 to 1819; his most significant letters cover a period little longer. Also, his poetic and intellectual progress is toward the refinement and development of ideas and theories present in his poetry and letters almost from the beginning. The early *Sleep and Poetry* contains in embryo all that appears in the late *Fall of Hyperion*; his most complete account of the poetic imagination, from which he never departed, occurs in a letter written in 1817. With Shelley, of course, the situation is somewhat different. In his career a slow but steady evolution from materialism to Platonic idealism is definitely traceable. In his poetry, however, certain elements are constant from first to last, and it is upon these elements that I attempt to fasten.

Some readers may also feel that the final chapter of this study, "Romantic Bards and Metaphysical Reviewers," lies somewhat outside the previously established pattern. With this point of view I can sympathize,

and yet advance considerations which for myself at least more than counterbalance the objections. Anyone who writes about Shelley nowadays must reckon with very powerful and general prejudices against his poetry, usually based upon little knowledge of it. Shelley scholars have nevertheless for the most part stuck to their last, declining to enter upon a fundamental critical argument. This is no doubt partly because they diagnose hostile criticism as a passing aberration and lack respect for the critics who have attacked him. I myself, however, have been impressed by the general intelligence and seriousness of such critics as T. S. Eliot, John Crowe Ransom, and Cleanth Brooks, while wholly denying their authority on Shelley and on Romantic poetry.

In view of the influence wielded by these critics, as well as of their significance, it seems well worthwhile to meet the attack, particularly on the grounds of poetic imagery where the New Critics are most at home. There have been, of course, such excellent defences of Shelley as C. S. Lewis's "Shelley, Dryden, and Mr. Eliot," but the nature of the present study may perhaps give it a special claim to speak.

The specific conclusions arrived at in Chapter Two are based upon a sampling procedure rather than a complete analysis of Keats's and Shelley's verse. If the method needs to be justified, one might appeal to the very widespread use of this technique now current in statistical investigations. In employing it I have made every effort to secure a truly representative body of material.

As working-texts I have used standard one-volume editions: for Keats, *John Keats: Complete Poems and Se-*

lected Letters, edited by Clarence D. Thorpe; and for Shelley, G. E. Woodberry's *The Complete Poetical Works of Percy Bysshe Shelley*.

Parts of this book have appeared in *College English*, *Publications of the Modern Language Association of America*, *Philological Quarterly*, *Modern Language Quarterly*, and *A Journal of English Literary History*. The final chapter, "English Bards and Metaphysical Reviewers," which originally appeared in *ELH*, has been completely revised, although its structure and its thesis remain the same.

I cannot adequately signalize my debt to Professor Clarence D. Thorpe, who advised in the first preparation of this book as a dissertation at the University of Michigan. I owe much also to the other members of my committee. Finally, I am indebted to the Tulane University Council on Research for aid in publication.

                                                                    R. H. F.

CONTENTS

THE IMAGERY OF KEATS AND SHELLEY

POETIC IMAGERY

I   In attempting to define poetic imagery we are faced at the outset with difficulties of terminology. "Imagery" is sometimes used as a synonym for "metaphor" in poetry; often, on the other hand, the two are considered as entirely distinct. To the psychologist and to many critics imagery in poetry is the expression of sense-experience, channelled through sight, hearing, smell, touch, and taste, through these channels impressed upon the mind, and set forth in verse in such fashion as to recall as vividly and faithfully as possible the original sensation. In these terms, a poetic image is the record of a single sensation.

If imagery is thought of as synonymous with metaphor, however, the single poetic image is a figure of speech involving comparison or likeness. And since "metaphor" is also ambiguous, used as it is for a single class as well as the entire species of figures, confusion is worse confounded.

Another source of possible misconception is the common identification of imagery with pictorial representation, which has misled many who have accepted the sensory view of imagery into overemphasizing the element of the visual and excluding other sensory factors.

3

While giving due heed to these objections to the word, I nevertheless employ it here in default of a better. In this study "imagery" will be used broadly to signify the principle of "figurativeness." "Metaphor" has undesirable associations with rhetoric and formal logic; it implies a kind of mechanical anatomizing which excludes from the analysis of poetry too much which ought to be considered. "Imagery," however, even with its misleading sensory connotations, comes closer to critical realities.[1]

II   Since poetic imagery is very frequently identified with the sensory element of poetry, it is necessary to explain the relationship of imagery, as it is here understood, to sensation. The prevalent modern academic opinion holds, with more or less qualification according to the holder, that sensuousness and concreteness is the peculiar and distinctive characteristic of poetry. To Robert P. Tristram Coffin poetry presents ". . . the clearest images, the most memorable of objects seen. But objects always. The things we can see, touch, hear, taste, and smell."[2]

1. ". . . though the suggestion of the word 'image' is dangerous, the word is necessary. For metaphor and simile belong to formal classification. The word 'image,' precisely because it is used to cover both metaphor and simile, can be used to point toward their fundamental identity; and if we can resolutely exclude from our minds the suggestion that the image is solely or even predominantly visual, and allow the word to share in the heightened and comprehensive significance with which its derivative 'imagination' has perforce been endowed—if we conceive the 'image' not as primary and independent, but as the most singular and potent instrument of the faculty of imagination—it is a more valuable word than those which it subsumes: metaphor and simile. To them clings something worse than false suggestion, a logical taint, an aura of irrelevancy."—John Middleton Murry, *Countries of the Mind*, p. 4.

2. *The Substance That Is Poetry*, p. 15.

In the opinion of Bliss Perry poetry is imagery and imagery is sensation, more or less refined by the transforming and modifying power of the mind through which images pass. The function of poetry is "to convey the 'sense' of things rather than the knowledge of things." The reader of poetry should concentrate his attention upon realizing the imagery as vividly as possible, as if, says Perry, "the image were not made of words at all, but were naked sense-stimulus."[3] Miss Edith Rickert presents the same attitude toward imagery in her *New Methods for the Study of Literature*,[4] a work intended to supply a complete rationale and method for the analysis of poetry in the classroom. To her it is "mental reproduction, without external stimulus except through words, of things seen, heard, touched, tasted, and smelled. . . . Imagery is a mode of expressing experience in the form of mental pictures."[5] More recently John Crowe Ransom has defined the poetic imagination as "an organ of knowledge, whose technique is images," and which "represents to the reflective mind the particularity of nature."[6]

The earliest and most influential modern exposition of this point of view is to be found in the *Speculations* of the brilliant T. E. Hulme, the father of Imagism.[7] Poetry, said Hulme

. . . is not a counter-language, but a visual concrete one. It is a compromise for a language of intuition which would hand over

3. *A Study of Poetry*, pp. 48, 94-95.
4. Chicago, 1927.
5. *Ibid.*, pp. 24, 27.
6. *The World's Body*, p. 157.
7. For the fullest account of Hulme's influence upon the Imagists see Glenn Hughes, *Imagism and the Imagists*, pp. 3-23.

sensations bodily. It always endeavours to arrest you, and to make you continuously see a physical thing, to prevent you gliding through an abstract process. It chooses fresh epithets and fresh metaphors, not so much because they are new, and we are tired of the old, but because the old cease to convey a physical thing and become abstract counters. . . . Visual meanings can only be transferred by the new bowl of metaphor; prose is an old pot that lets them leak out. Images in verse are not mere decoration, but the very essence of an intuitive language.[8]

The account of poetry offered by this interpretation of imagery is unsatisfactory. If poetry is "a compromise for a language of intuition which would hand over sensations bodily," then poetry has no real *raison d'être*, since it does badly what we can all do well. Why should we concern ourselves with second-hand representations of an intuition of things which we command at first hand? And, since words are not things, in what degree are they able "to convey a physical thing"? The method of approach advocated by Professor Perry and implied in the work of Miss Rickert and Hulme does not enrich poetry; it impoverishes it. It exhibits a single element for examination, while excluding all others. If the reader follows the advice of Perry and concentrates upon realizing the imagery as vividly as possible, "as if the image were not made of words at all, but were naked sense-stimulus," he is no longer concerning himself with poetry, for poetry is words. He is concentrating instead upon his own free imagery, aroused by the words before him but not necessarily helpful in interpreting them.

The tendency evident in all these writers to consider imagery as predominantly visual is also misleading. The assumption that the value of poetry lies in its power to

8. *Ibid.*, p. 135.

call up vivid visual imagery need only be examined briefly in order to demonstrate its lack of foundation. Psychologists have shown that neither all readers nor all poets are "visualizers"; and that lack of visual imagery does not necessarily imply lack of comprehension or poverty of mental and emotional processes.[9] In many instances excessive emphasis upon the visual can be a positive hindrance to our appreciation of poetry. I. A. Richards cites such an example in Lord Kames's comment upon a passage in Shakespeare.[10] For my own part I recall two famous lines from Shakespeare, "In cradle of the rude imperious surge," and "The multitudinous seas incarnadine." An attempt to visualize completely the imagery of either of these lines destroys them. The "cradle" is obviously ludicrous if dwelt upon and objectified; its force lies partly in the rocking motion common to the surge and the cradle, but chiefly in the conceptual and emotional associations which result from the interplay of the two elements of the figure. The calm domesticity of the one combines with the "rude imperiousness" and uncontrolled power of the other to produce pathos and menace; for the shipboy who is thus cradled, young as he is, is in imminent danger of falling, since he is asleep, into the sea which

9. "For many people the occurrence of a series of visual images is the normal mode of thought, and they naturally assume that such visualization is universal. But few mathematicians, musicians and philosophers, and not all poets, are visualizers; to some minds words themselves call up emotion as well as 'sense' directly, without the consciousness of any visual imagery, and this emotional response is in no way impoverished or restricted. . . . Hulme and Gourmont make the common error of supposing all symbols to be visual images. . . ."—Michael Roberts, *Critique of Poetry*, pp. 47–48, 49. See also T. H. Pear, "Imagery and Mentality," *British Journal of Psychology*, XIV, 291-99.

10. *The Philosophy of Rhetoric*, pp. 16-17.

cradles him and of perishing there. This is far from a complete account of the effect of the line, but it serves to show how inadequate and misleading a visual interpretation is likely to be. In the second example the visual element is somewhat more prominent; as in the first, however, by itself it explains nothing. Its power and meaning comes from the notion of blood behind it, symbolizing the horror and violence of the murder of Duncan. Something, too, should be attributed to the polysyllabic roll of the verse, with its murmurous reverberations of the ocean.

Attempts to define poetry as the vivid expression of sensation are unsound psychologically; from a purely literary point of view they fail to explain at all adequately the poetic fact. And, as Professor Richards points out, the terms "image" and "imagery" are likely through their associations to give rise to this misconception of the nature of poetry.[11] I employ them in this study, nevertheless, for the reason previously stated and because poetry is for the most part sensuous. This statement, if properly qualified, is not a contradiction of the foregoing argument. Poetry is more sensuous than prose because it is a richer, more meaningful, completer form of utterance than prose. Poetry offers us a balance

11. "The words 'figure' and 'image' are especially and additionally misleading here . . . they bring in a confusion with the sense in which an image is a copy or revival of a sense-perception of some sort, and so have made rhetoricians think that a figure of speech, an image, or imaginative comparison, must have something to do with the presence of images, in this other sense, in the mind's eye or the mind's ear. But, of course, it need not. No images of this sort need come in at any point. . . . We cannot too firmly recognize that how a figure of speech works has nothing necessarily to do with how any images, as copies or duplicates of sense-perceptions, may, for reader or writer, be backing up his words . . . the words can do almost anything without them, and we must put no assumption about their necessary presence into our general theory." —*Ibid.*, p. 98. See also I. A. Richards, *Principles of Literary Criticism*, pp. 122-24.

and equilibrium of concept, emotion, and sensation; prose does not. Poetry presents indivisible wholes of human consciousness, modified and ordered by the stringent requirements of form. Prose, aiming at a definite and concrete goal, generally suppresses everything inessential to its purpose; poetry, existing only to exhibit itself as an aesthetic object, aims only at completeness and perfection of form.

Consequently the sensational element in poetry must be considered. In itself, without reference to other modes, it is without significance. But literature, and of all literature especially poetry, is meaning; it is the organization of our consciousness of ourselves and of the world. The finest poetry provides for us the most perfect balance of the subjective and objective; the completest fusion.[12] The rôle of the senses, then, properly considered and dissociated from such crudities as the doctrine that poetry can hand over sensations bodily, is to aid in our perceptions of our environment; the sensuous is a mode of grasping the objective, without which the aesthetic balance would be imperfect.

Since poetry is a fabric woven inextricably from threads of concept, emotion, and sense, analysis of poetry must take all three into consideration, with the realization that they cannot be separated. Yet criticism

12. "Taste . . . will teach us to expect in its metaphorical use a certain reference of any given object to our own being, and not merely a distinct notion of the object as in itself, or in its independent properties. . . . By taste, therefore . . . we must be supposed to mean an intellectual perception of any object blended with a distinct reference to our own sensibility of pain or pleasure. . . . In this definition of taste . . . is involved the definition of fine arts, namely, as being such the chief and discriminative purpose of which is to gratify the taste,—that is, not merely to connect, but to combine and unite, a sense of immediate pleasure in ourselves, with the perception of external arrangement."—S. T. Coleridge, *Essays and Lectures on Shakespeare . . .*, pp. 352-53.

must have a vantage point from which to commence; a part must somehow be abstracted from the whole, with as little damage to its integrity as possible. Now, although the sensuous element in poetry is of itself the most dependent and the least important of the three which go to make up poetry, yet it is the most accessible to examination, and can tell us much about the other two. If it is understood that it has of itself no actual separate existence, it can be studied as symptomatic of the poet's general power of experiencing; a power necessary to the poetic whole. Poetry deficient in sensation is solipsistic, without grasp of actuality; poetry deficient in intellect and emotion is imagistic, without grasp of anything.

III   The principle of poetic imagery lies not in the sensuous, which is a part of the poetic experience, but in comparison, which subsumes the whole of the poetic experience. As I. A. Richards remarks of Hulme's theory of imagery,

What discourse 'always endeavours' to do is to make us apprehend, understand, gain a realizing sense of, take in, whatever it is that is being meant—which is not necessarily any physical thing. But if we say 'a realizing sense,' we must remember that this is not any 'sense' necessarily, such as sense-perception gives, but may be a feeling or a thought. What is essential is that we should really take in and become fully aware of—whatever it is.

. . . words cannot, and should not attempt to "hand over sensations bodily"; they have very much more important work to do. So far from verbal language being a "compromise for a language of intuition"—a thin, but better-than-nothing, substitute for real experience,—language, well used, is a *completion* and does what the intuitions of sensation by themselves cannot do. Words are the meeting

points at which regions of experience which can never combine in
sensation or intuition, come together. They are the occasion and the
means of that growth which is the mind's endless endeavour to
order itself.[13]

These "meeting points at which regions of experience
come together," by which the mind seeks to order itself,
are comparisons. Comparison is a bringing-together of
objects, concepts, or states of mind from different planes
of consciousness or being in such a manner that the
things so placed in contact with each other shall be seen
to possess an inner and essential similarity, as the whale
from the depths of the ocean is similar to the elephant
of the jungle, or as the shark is significantly termed
"the tiger of the sea."

Comparison, however, is not only a putting-together
of object and object, or concept and concept. It also
brings into close relationship object with concept, illu-
minates the abstract by means of the concrete, explains
the material by an abstraction and an abstraction by a
concept still more abstract. It realizes and objectifies a
feeling or mood by placing it beside a natural phenomenon, as in Verlaine's

> Il pleure dans mon coeur
> Comme il pleut sur la ville,

just as it works in a precisely opposite manner, by
attributing human qualities and emotions to natural
objects, as in Keats's lines:

> Those green-rob'd senators of mighty woods,
> Tall oaks, branch-charmed by the earnest stars,
> Dream, and so dream all night without a stir . . .

13. *The Philosophy of Rhetoric*, pp. 130-31.

Comparison fuses and confuses the perceptions of
the senses, finding analogies between their different
modes of action. Thus, in Baudelaire's

> Comme de longs échos qui de loin se confondent . . .
> Les parfums, les couleurs et les sons se repondent,

a common element is established among odor, color, and
sound. Or, wearing the neutral but fantastic dress of
the metaphysicals, it elaborately describes the physical
and psychic motions of a pair of lovers in terms of the
legs of a compass.[14]

Comparison is of course a universal principle of language; but it is peculiarly prevalent in poetry, which
for the most part avoids direct statement. We may say,
adapting Shakespeare, that poetic imagery seeks

> With windlasses and with assays of bias
> By indirections [to] find directions out,

or with Browning that it is "the oblique way of telling
truth," the only way to

> . . . do the thing shall breed the thought,
> Nor wrong the thought, missing the mediate word.[15]

That is to say that the richness, the concrete fullness of
aesthetic experience can be expressed only by indirection,
the resultant of the forces of two or more ideas in close
contact. This purpose and effect of imagery is in direct
contrast with the purpose and effect of simple statement,
which aims at saying *one* thing and avoids ambiguities
and overtones of meaning like the plague. For poetry
this ideal of simple oneness and clarity is too bald, too

14. John Donne, "A Valediction Forbidding Mourning."
15. *The Ring and the Book*, XII, 846f. Quoted by C. Willard Smith, *Browning's
Star-Imagery*, from which the suggestion has been taken.

utilitarian; it omits too much in its relentless pursuit of a severely limited object. To do justice to the largeness and complexity of experience poetry must follow the prescription of T. E. Hulme: "Never, never, never a simple statement. It has no effect. One must always have analogies, which make another world."[16]

Shelley's account of the life-cycle of a cloud is said to be entirely in accord with scientific fact, but obviously it would not recommend itself to a meteorologist. The imagery draws to itself too much which merely obscures the simple linear clarity of exposition.

> I am the daughter of earth and water,
> And the nursling of the sky,

proclaims Shelley's cloud. The scientist would certainly reject the irrelevant associations imported into the discussion by "daughter" and "nursling." To the poet, however, they are the essence of the passage.

Imagery is present whenever two things are put together in order that their relationships may be seen, provided that in these relationships the element of similarity is present.[17] As I. A. Richards has convincingly pointed out, however, imagery is not a simple matter of calling attention to resemblances. Comparison, he believes, "may be just a putting together of two things to let them work together; it may be a study of them both to see how they are like and how unlike one another; or it may be a process of calling attention to their likenesses or a method of drawing attention to

16. *Notes on Language and Style*, p. 18.

17. See Rosemond Tuve, "Imagery and Logic: Ramus and Metaphysical Poetics," *Journal of the History of Ideas*, III, 365-400, for a theory of imagery which places far more weight than does the present study upon the minute analysis of logical relationships.

certain aspects of the other.''[18] He calls attention also
to the "disparity element" in imagery, active as well
as the resemblance element.[19]

Professor Richards has rendered a valuable service to
criticism by demonstrating the rich and complex variety
of the thought-relationships of which imagery is capable. One may insist, however, while accepting and
profiting by his remarks, that the primary and determining factor of intelligible poetic imagery is likeness, without which no further relationship worthy the name can
exist at all. The disparities between two objects, for
example, are of significance only when we have been
impelled to bring them together by an anterior perception of their resemblances. Richards quotes Hamlet:
"What should such fellows as I do crawling between
earth and heaven?" in support of his contention that
disparities are as much operative in imagery as are likenesses. "When Hamlet uses the word *crawling* its force
comes not only from whatever resemblances to vermin
it brings in but at least equally from the differences
that resist and control the influences of their resemblances. The implication there is that man should not
so crawl."[20] True, in part; but the structure and the
very existence of the image depend upon the appropriateness of the idea of *crawling* to the idea of *man;* one
perceives immediately that in Hamlet's sense man can
so crawl. The disparities between the two notions are
secondary; they operate only after the primary resemblance has been established.

The conclusion to which Professor Richards' exam-

18. *The Philosophy of Rhetoric*, p. 120.
19. *Ibid.*, p. 127.
20. *Ibid.*, pp. 119, 127.

ination of the problem of imagery (in his terms, metaphor) leads him is not, I think, useful in the critical
analysis of poetry. He holds that the ordering faculty
which establishes the thought-relationships constitutive
of imagery exists only in the mind of the reader, not in
poetry itself. The mind is a connecting organ—"In all
interpretation we are filling in connections, and for
poetry, of course, our freedom to fill in—the absence of
explicitly stated intermediate steps—is a main source of
its powers." He quotes with approval this statement,
from William Empson's *Seven Types of Ambiguity:*

> Statements are made as if they were connected, and the reader is
> forced to consider their relations for himself. The reason why these
> statements should have been selected is left for him to invent; he
> will invent a variety of reasons and order them in his own mind.
> This is the essential fact about the poetic use of language.[21]

This stand is typical of the subjectivist, solipsistic
tendency evident in all Professor Richards' excellent
criticism. He is reluctant to permit to poetry any real
existence, as he is reluctant to attribute reality to anything outside the mind. This view is discouraging to
criticism, since it denies the significant existence of the
object which the critic contemplates. Unless the relationships which are poetic imagery possess objective
being, the problem itself disappears. In order to discuss
it with any confidence one must, in my opinion, believe
that these relationships existed first in the mind of the
poet and remain in his poetry, independent of its effect
upon the reader's mind.[22] A theory which places the

21. *Ibid.*, p. 125. See *Seven Types of Ambiguity*, p. 32.
22. For a detailed and authoritative refutation of the position of Richards see
René Wellek, "The Mode of Existence of a Literary Work of Art," *Southern Review*,
VII, pp. 735-54.

burden of organizing poetic materials upon the reader
instead of upon the poet is a slim basis for practical
criticism.

IV   The principle of comparison is not of itself
              sufficient to identify and distinguish poetic
imagery. It may justly be objected that comparison is
the universal mode of thought and language, and not
at all peculiar to poetry. Scientific discourse, it is true,
seeks oneness, a simple and austere clarity and fixity
of meaning incompatible with poetry. But all prose is
not scientific,[23] and even science is obliged to resort to
imagery to make itself comprehensible to the human
mind. Thus we have the "wave" theory of light; and
Sir James Jeans' explanation of "why the sky is blue"
in terms of an elaborate physical analogy.[24]

The real grounds for distinguishing the unique and
peculiar quality of poetic imagery as apart from the
imagery of prose are implicit, I believe, in Coleridge's
definition of poetry as "the production of a highly pleasurable whole, of which each part shall also communicate
for itself a distinct and conscious pleasure"; an end, he
says, which is attained "by the use of language natural
to us in a state of excitement."[25] In terms of imagery
this means that each image is to bear a weight of which
the prose image is free; it must not merely function as

23. "Poetry is not the proper antithesis to prose, but to science."—Coleridge,
op. cit., p. 9.

24. He compares for purposes of exposition light waves to sea waves, and
atmospheric dust to an iron pier. The light waves are diffracted by dust as are the sea
waves by the columns of the pier.—*The Stars in Their Courses*, pp. 25-26.

25. Coleridge, *op. cit.*, p. 10.

part of the whole, but must in itself be whole and perfect, able to bear the severest scrutiny.

A little consideration will show this to be true. A poet is judged by his imagery with a stringency and a closeness of analysis which no critic of prose would dream of applying. The prose writer stands or falls according to the effect of his whole work; the poet must face not only criticism of his total achievement, but of each individual part as well. In prose occasional crudities are forgiven, but poetry is always on its mettle. Theodore Dreiser is generally considered one of the most important novelists of the twentieth century; he is also considered one of the worst writers. What poet ever received the benefit of such a distinction?

The poetic image has, in fact, a greater degree of independence than the prose image. It has, as it were, a greater degree of self-awareness in proportion to the heavier demands made upon it; into it has gone more painstaking craftsmanship, a higher artistic finish. And here we must reckon also with the question which Coleridge raises of "excitement," or poetic emotion. It is a truism, I think, that emotion is the beginning and end of poetry in a sense unknown to prose. The poet is more excited about his subject than the writer of prose, he is called upon to sustain his excitement more consistently, and this excitement is of itself a value more nearly independent of what he is excited about than is the case in prose. This poetic state of heightened emotion makes itself felt in poetic imagery as a greater concentration upon all the terms of the image, just as do the demands of craftsmanship. Emotion gives every word a peculiar force and weight.

To illustrate the combined effects of self-conscious
artistry and poetic emotion upon imagery we may cite
Shelley's famous

> Life, like a dome of many-coloured glass
> Stains the white radiance of Eternity.

The quality of this figure lies in the concentrated richness
of its components and the complexity of their relations.
If one term were subordinated to the other, if any part
of the image were slighted in the interest of the whole,
the sum-total would be prosaic and commonplace. But
the attention and the emotion of the poet are fixed upon
all alike. "Life" is not subordinated to "Eternity" but
coequal; the "dome of many-coloured glass" is as important as "the white radiance." The dome is attractive
for its hint of smooth and symmetrical shape, for its
pleasant ecclesiastical associations; it is further meaningful through the physical-spiritual symbolism of its
reaching out toward Heaven or Eternity. The "many-
coloured glass" which "stains" is ambiguous in its implications. Glass is at once valuable and worthless. The
epithet "many-coloured" suggests pleasurable thoughts
at the same moment in which it condemns its own
triviality. "Stains" has a like variety of meaning; it
has the deep and mellow coloring of fine stained glass,
so that it consummates and enriches "white radiance"
just as it smirches its purity. And "white radiance" is
not only the Absolute, the goal of desire, perfect and
without alloy. It contains within itself also regret for
what is lost; a shudder at its own austere perfection.
Shelley is not propounding a single intellectual relationship between Life and Eternity, suppressing the indi-

dual identities of the parts in order to make a point.[26] e is offering to the reader a variety of relationships, d his expression of them is permeated by the emotion hich his perception of their possibilities has aroused him.

The sharp individuality, artistic economy, and in- nsity of emotion characteristic of the poetic image ay in part be attributed to the exacting formal require- ents of the poetic medium. The poet is forced to subdue is language to patterns of metre, rhythm, and in most stances rhyme. The effort to express his full meaning vithin the limits imposed by form is conducive in a enuine artist to the highest degree of intensity and oncentration; his imagery will possess a tensile power nd a distilled, essential quality not to be found in the ooser structures of prose.

The formal and aesthetic nature of poetry establishes he individual identity of poetic imagery in still another vay. It lends to imagery an aesthetic frame. Writing oetry is a dramatic and highly self-conscious act. When e sets pen to paper the poet adopts a special attitude oward life; an attitude reflected in imagery. Thus poetic magery is always on guard, always on its good be- havior; it is conscious always that it is not actuality, but an organization of actuality.

One further distinction should be drawn. Poetic im- agery is never "dead metaphor." Language is full of

26. See for a diametrically opposite account of this image I. A. Richards, *Principles of Literary Criticism*, pp. 239-40. Professor Richards considers it merely as an example of "scientific or prose use of metaphor," which is "illustrative or diagrammatical, pro- viding a concrete instance of a relation which would otherwise have to be stated in abstract terms." This is, I think, to omit consideration of the variety and the emotional qualities of Shelley's Life-Eternity comparison.

"dead" figurative expression, once alive, but now so staled and blunted by time and use that it remains unrealized and is mistaken for literal statement. Even the most artistic prose is not entirely free from dead metaphor, for prose is often impelled to seek for its purpose what is closest to hand; but good poetry must shun it like the plague. One unintended platitude, one stock-expression can destroy a poem. Poetic imagery is vital and fully realized in all its parts; in dead metaphor the parts merge and disappear, leaving only the general concept which they express. As Shelley has said, they "become through time, signs for portions or classes of thoughts instead of pictures of integral thoughts."[27]

V　　　　Imagery as here defined does not, unfortunately, lie wholly within the realm of objective classification. The problem of identifying individual figures of speech is comparatively simple—the broad principle of comparison underlies them all. An image may be a single word, and thus correspond to what is usually called a metaphor. It may be an explicit comparison with the two terms syntactically linked—a simile. It may be personification, a sub-species of metaphor: the attribution of human thoughts and qualities to inanimate objects, or the embodiment of abstract conceptions or states of mind in animate forms. It may, in fact, be any verbal figure of speech.

Even here there is a serious difficulty, as has been noted by I. A. Richards. Discussions of figurative lan-

27. "A Defence of Poetry," *Shelley's Literary and Philosophical Criticism*, ed. John Shawcross, p. 123.

guage are generally confused by an uncertainty as to exactly what is being discussed; a figure or image is sometimes thought of as one term, sometimes as another. Frequently it is considered to be both terms of a comparison. Professor Richards has offered a distinction which will help to clarify the situation: one term he calls the "tenor," the other the "vehicle." The relationship between them he describes as follows: the tenor is "the underlying idea or principal subject which the vehicle or figure means."[28]

This distinction between tenor and vehicle is valuable insofar as it supplies a new and sharper realization of the actual content of figures of speech. The general "figurative" principle, however, does not confine itself to individual figures or images. It is necessary to distinguish further between the "simple" image and the "complex" image, which is outside the scope of our usual investigations. How else are we to account for the typical lyric of the metaphysical poets, in which the poem itself is a single comparison composed of a number of smaller comparisons? Or how explain the structure of a Shakespearean sonnet, in which each quatrain presents an image analyzable into several component images? What of imagery as a recurring motif or theme in a play or narrative poem, like the ulcer-image which symbolizes the state of mind of Hamlet, the ominous and omnipresent theme of blood in *Macbeth*? The silence-images at the beginning of Keats's *Hyperion* present in brief the whole of the drama of the Titans, but their functions cannot be analyzed into tenors and vehicles save in the most general way.

28. *The Philosophy of Rhetoric*, p. 97.

The distinction between the simple and the complex image is generally made quite spontaneously in practice, but it has not been noticed in theory. This study will follow the usual practice of dealing with both under the single heading of "image," since both are determined by the principle of analogy and since no separate objective classification of "complex" images seems feasible. In order to establish a common basis for discussion, however, it is well to make clear that this distinction must be reckoned with.

The simple image, then, is a verbal comparison, a figure of speech. A complex image may be a fusion of simple images, a poem, a scene from a play, or even the play itself; it may be a recurring theme with a symbolic significance, like a Wagnerian leitmotiv. It is impossible to arrive at more than tentative conclusions about the nature and purpose of the complex image, other than saying generally that it is figurative in import. It appears most often as a theme woven into the texture of poetry; and its most typical use seems to be the objectification and projection into the concrete and physical of a mood, mental state, or meaning too subtle and rich for direct expression. It tends toward the unification of concept, emotion, and sensation within a single form or object; toward the definition and concretization of the indefinable and formless.

VI

Poetic imagery is to be defined broadly as analogy or comparison, having a special force and identity from the peculiarly aesthetic and concentrative form of poetry. It is to be judged accord-

ing to its creative power, the connotative richness of its content, and the harmonious unity and fusion of its elements.

The essential quality and function of imagery is a kind of creation; by the bringing-together of diverse objects, states of mind, or concepts new relationships are discovered, new connections between subject and object become apparent, new thought as it were springs into being, born of the fruitful mating of ideas and things apparently disparate and isolated from each other. Aristotle himself first bore witness to the creative power of imagery, as it works through analogy:

> . . . those words are pleasantest which give us *new* knowledge. Strange words have no meaning for us; common terms we know already; it is metaphor which gives us most of this pleasure. Thus, when the poet calls old age 'a dried stalk,' he gives us a new perception by means of the common *genus*; for both the things have lost their bloom.[29]

Elsewhere he calls the command of metaphor "the mark of genius, for to make good metaphors implies an eye for resemblances."[30]

John Middleton Murry terms imagery "the instinctive and necessary act of the mind exploring reality and ordering experience."[31] This exploratory and ordering quality of imagery is creative; it builds new structures of thought and orders experience in patterns hitherto undesigned.[32] Imagery is the living principle itself of language, by which our speech advances and is con-

29. *Rhetoric*, tr. Sir Richard Claverhouse Jebb, ed. J. E. Sandys, III, x, 2, p. 167.
30. *Poetics*, ed. S. H. Butcher, XXII, 9, p. 87.
31. *Op. cit.*, p. 2.
32. *Ibid.*, p. 9.

tinually revivified by the discovery and expression of
fresh analogies, which increase our knowledge of ourselves and of the world. Thus, to Shelley the poet is the
giver of language and of wisdom, for "the language of
poets is vitally metaphorical; that is, it marks the
before unapprehended relations of things and perpetuates
their apprehension."[33]

I am not prepared to discuss the question how far
poetic imagery may be said to provide us with new
knowledge of *truth*. "Creative" itself as applied to language is a metaphor which merely helps to explain a
phenomenon otherwise impossible of definition. While
avoiding the problem of the absolute truth of what
imagery reveals, however, one may at the same time
declare that imagery by offering to us new combinations
of objects and ideas presents us with new perceptions,
or new organizations of our perceptions. In this sense
it is creative.

Good imagery is richly evocative, various in the
implications of its meaning. It is complex, broad of
scope.[34] Other things being equal, the best imagery will
give us the most ideas, the most complex relationships,
the widest span of experience. The language of poetry
bears unusual weight, value, and significance[35] through
the interaction of thought and emotion with the concentrative requirements of form;[36] for poetry aims at

33. *Op. cit.*

34. "In general, rich imaginal content, a complex of various modes, contributes
enjoyment."—June E. Downey, *Creative Imagination*, p. 3.

35. The best explanation of what constitutes the value and power of poetic
language is in my opinion I. A. Richards' chapter on "The Interinanimation of Words"
in *The Philosophy of Rhetoric*.

36. "The images recognized by the consciousness of poets are those of experiences
and objects associated with feeling. The words employed to revive and transmit these

expressing indivisible wholes, conveying the fullest sense of experience, suppressing nothing relevant.

Complexity in itself, however, is not a value; it is the ordering of complexity which is important. The forcible juxtaposition of diverse elements does not constitute good imagery, as some modern critics have appeared to suppose.[37] The ideal image will present the most complete reconciliation of unity and diversity; it will express the fullest sense of life in its "rich, contingent materiality,"[38] controlled most consummately by the intellectual and imaginative power of the poet.[39]

---

images are usually described as 'concrete' or 'sensuous' in distinction from abstract or purely conceptual. They are 'experiential' words, arising out of bodily or spiritual contact with objects or ideas that have been personalized, colored with individual feeling. Such words have a 'fringe,' as psychologists say. They are rich in overtones of meaning; not bare, like words addressed to the sheer intelligence, but covered with veils of association, with tokens of past experience. They are like ships laden with cargoes, although the cargo varies with the texture and the history of each mind."
—Perry, *op. cit.*, p. 102.

37. E.g., Cleanth Brooks, *Modern Poetry and the Tradition*, p. 117.

38. In John Crowe Ransom's phrase.

39. Cf. Coleridge's famous definition of the poetic imagination, *Biographia Literaria*, ch. xiv.

IMAGERY OF SENSATION

I   A study of sense-imagery is of necessity subjective and introspective in method.[1] The student is certain to have physical and psychic peculiarities, imaginal idiosyncrasies which color his findings; it is highly improbable that any two persons could obtain identical results from examining the same passage of verse. To one the predominant sensory response from an image will be visual; to another tactual or organic. Readers are likely to be predisposed toward certain types of imagery. Miss June E. Downey, following Ribot, establishes a broad division between the plastic imagination, which demands concreteness, clarity, and order, and the diffluent or emotional imagination, which "would make things the symbols of vague infinities," dissolving what it touches "into a formless but creative chaos."[2] Robert Graves points out the general difficulties of classifying images according to their sensory appeal.[3] Individual responses vary too widely,

---

1. "Sense-imagery" means here the sensory content of *imagery* as it has been defined in the previous chapter. Thus the primary criterion for determining the individual image is the presence of comparison.

2. *Creative Imagination*, p. 2.

3. ". . . have we any statistics to show us what proportion of poetry lovers are what the psychologists designate as 'visiles,' or 'audiles,' or 'tactiles,' or 'motiles'?

in his opinion, to permit of valid conclusions about them.

Besides this imaginal variation of individuals, there is to be considered the variation within the individual reader himself. His reading will differ according to the time, the place, and his physical and mental state. If he is tired or distracted his response will vary from his response when he is fresh and alert. His general state of mind will also affect his reading; and this will obviously not be constant upon all occasions. Since a full examination of a given work cannot be carried out at one sitting, these considerations are important.

Furthermore the sensory content of images is frequently not simple but complex. In many instances a single image contains two or more sensory suggestions. When Keats describes a "venerable priest"

> *Begirt* with ministring looks . . .
>
> (*Endymion*, I, 149-50)

the image "begirt" is to me predominantly tactual, but it is visual as well,[4] and it is a nice question which aspect should be emphasized.

The problem of effective literary suggestion is another

And who will subdivide the visile satisfactorily into the *colour*-visile, the *black* and *white* visile, and mensuration visile, or similar categories? Or who will sub-divide the audible?"—*Poetic Unreason*, p. 264. Quoted from Michael Roberts, *Critique of Poetry*, p. 52.

4. This image affords a convenient illustration of the close relationship between concept, emotion, and sensation in poetry, and of the important but subsidiary rôle played by sensation. The meaning of the figure obviously does not lie in the physical qualities of "begirt," but it is almost indistinguishable from them. The "all-encompassing" and "closely-fitting" suggestions of the word aid in establishing the naturally venerable and sacerdotal aspect of the priest, inseparable from him as a human figure perceptible to the senses.

complication. The poet may conceivably attempt to express sensuous impressions and fail to convey them to the reader. In classifying sense-imagery we are consequently faced with the question, whether we should count only images whose sensuous content has actually been felt by us, or on the other hand include all images which could possibly have been felt as sensuous by the poet?

To Shelley's lines

> . . . the unnatural *thirst*
> For murder, rapine, violence and crime
> That still *consumed* thy being
>
> (*Queen Mab*, VI, 128-30)

I feel no sensory response, and assume that Shelley used "thirst" as a dead metaphor convenient for his purpose, without himself experiencing a physical sensation. But in so doing I assume a knowledge of Shelley's psychology and intentions which I do not actually possess. It seems safer, therefore, to omit consideration of *possible* sense-images and confine the discussion to those which are *effective*. Only thus, by confining himself to what he himself has experienced, can the reader be on safe ground.

The study of sense-imagery, then, has only a provisional reliability, bounded by the subjective limitations of the student. As a method of analyzing poetry it has, however, advantages which outweigh the disadvantages I have enumerated. Although admittedly subjective, the simple and definite process of classifying images according to their sensory content probably allows as little margin for individual variation as any

method which could be devised; and where disagreement is possible the grounds for it are in plain sight. Although readers are likely to differ at first over the sensuous characteristics of an image, close examination will generally bring about a *rapprochement*, in the absence of eccentric interpretations. If, for example, one reader classifies an image as tactual while another considers it visual, it is probable that both elements are present and that further consideration will reveal this fact to both readers.

In order to establish the sensuous characteristics of the poetry of Shelley and of Keats as accurately and reliably as the conditions of such a study permit, I have analyzed 1722 lines from Keats and 2318 lines from Shelley,[5] classifying all effective sense-images to be found in them under the headings visual, auditory, tactual, olfactory, gustatory, organic, kinesthetic, and motor. The poems from which these lines have been taken are as follows:

KEATS: *I Stood Tiptoe, Endymion* (I, 1-222), *Isabella* (1-104; 233-336), *Hyperion* (I, 1-103; 165-263), *The Eve of St. Agnes* (1-99; 208-324), *The Eve of St. Mark, La Belle Dame Sans Merci* (First Version), *Ode to Psyche, Ode to a Nightingale, Ode on a Grecian Urn, Ode on Melancholy, Lamia* (1-199), *To Autumn;*

SHELLEY: *Queen Mab* (I, 1-104; IV, 1-103), *Alastor* (1-106; 514-610), *Hymn to Intellectual Beauty, Ode to the West Wind, The Cloud, To a Skylark, Adonais* (271-495), *Prometheus Unbound* (II, iv, 1-110; II, v), *Lines Written Among the Euganean Hills* (1-205), *Lines* ("When the Lamp Is Shattered"), *Ode to Liberty* (1-185), *Stanzas Written in Dejection, Near Naples, The Witch of Atlas* (1-96; 264-364), *The Triumph of Life* (1-106; 334-438), *The Sensitive Plant* (I, 1-97; III, 1-113).

5. The number of lines taken from each poet is roughly proportionate to the amount of his poetic production.

This selection is representative of the two poets in all stages of their careers, although there is a preponderance of relatively late, mature work. I have mingled short poems with excerpts from longer works, in an effort to secure as wide a variety as possible. I have not attempted to select poems parallel in subject, save in the obvious case of Keats's *Nightingale* and Shelley's *Skylark*. On the whole I have striven to combine a search for representative work with a certain casualness of choice, so as to avoid weighting the evidence in favor of possible preconceptions.

The purpose of this analysis is in part to examine the validity of a generalization very common in Shelley and Keats criticism, so prevalent that to most of us the thought of Shelley immediately suggests poverty of the senses, vagueness, evanescence, and a dim infinitude, while with Keats we associate concreteness, solidity, and sensuous intensity. ". . .The highest beauties of Shelley's poetry," says Mr. Herbert Read, "are evanescent and imponderable—thought so tenuous and intuitive, that it has no visual equivalent; no positive impact. . . .The idea conveyed—the notional content—is almost negligible; the poetry exists in the suspension of meaning, in the avoidance of actuality."[6] In the opinion of Mr. F. R. Leavis, ". . . there is nothing to be grasped in his [Shelley's] poetry—no object offered for contemplation, no realized presence to persuade and move us by what it is. . . .The effect is of vanity and emptiness . . . as well as monotony."[7]

Keats, on the other hand, say the critics, is *par*

6. *In Defence of Shelley and Other Essays*, pp. 83-84.
7. *Revaluation*, pp. 210-11.

excellence a poet of the senses, of objects and images. In the words of Colvin, "Keats had a mind constitutionally unapt for abstract thinking. When he conceives or wishes to express general ideas, his only way of doing so is by calling up, from the multitudes of concrete images with which his memory and imagination are haunted, such as strike him. . . ."[8] M. R. Ridley finds the typical quality and highest value of Keats's poetry in his ability "to concentrate in one line or phrase the full rich essence of images."[9]

Professor Claude Lee Finney has made the most detailed comparison of which I am aware between the sensory characteristics of the poetry of Shelley and of Keats:

His [Shelley's] sensory system was unevenly developed. His poetic images sprang almost exclusively from visual, auditory, and motor sensations, which are the least sensuous of sensations. Intentionally as well as instinctively, he fled from the world of human life into a world of ideal abstractions, to which his imagination gave ethereal voice and motion. . . .

Keats, on the contrary, had an evenly developed sensory system. His poetry is not only rich in line, color, light and shade, and sound but it is also rich in images of the intimately physical sensations of taste, touch, smell, temperature, and pressure, and in images of the organic sensations, such as hunger and thirst, the most elementary but the most powerful of sensations. His imagery, accordingly, is both comprehensive and sensuous.[10]

This statement crystallizes the generally held critical opinion upon the subject. Shelley's sensations are comparatively weak, "the least sensuous of sensations." His poetry celebrates "a world of ideal abstractions." The

8. *John Keats*, p. 128.
9. *Keats' Craftsmanship*, p. 193.
10. *The Evolution of Keats's Poetry*, I, 154.

poetry of Keats, on the other hand, is rich in every type of sensuous imagery; it is the product of an evenly developed and comprehensive sensory system.

If this generalization is well founded, a line-by-line analysis should show a much larger proportion of effective sense imagery in Keats than in Shelley, and it should reveal in Shelley a marked unevenness of imaginal distribution, with almost no tactual, olfactory, gustatory, organic, or kinesthetic imagery appearing in his verse. In contrast, Keats's lines should demonstrate a remarkably even sensory development. What are the facts?

The facts disclose that Professor Finney's statement is generally, although not wholly, correct for Keats; but that for Shelley it is distinctly unreliable. In an examination of 2318 representative lines from Shelley and 1722 lines from Keats, I found 1781 effective sense images in the former, 1065 in the latter, or a ratio of images to lines of 76.8 per cent and 61.8 per cent, respectively. This method of calculation is perhaps somewhat crude; yet it gives a reliable notion of the comparative density of sensory imaginal content in the two poets. The difference is actually in favor of Shelley.

The distribution of images was as follows: visual, Shelley 39.5 per cent, Keats 40.1 per cent; auditory, Shelley 8.4 per cent, Keats 12.5 per cent; tactual, Shelley 14.8 per cent, Keats, 20.1 per cent; olfactory, Shelley 1.5 per cent, Keats 1.7 per cent; gustatory, Shelley .6 per cent, Keats 2.3 per cent; organic, Shelley 7.6 per cent, Keats 12.7 per cent; kinesthetic, Shelley 3.3 per cent, Keats 3.3 per cent; motor, Shelley 24.3 per cent, Keats 7.3 per cent.[11]

11. See charts, pp. 34 and 35.

These figures point the way to several significant onclusions. In the first place, they indicate that Shelley's images do *not* spring "almost exclusively from visual, auditory, and motor sensations, . . . the least sensuous of sensations." Some 72.2 per cent of his images are of these types: a percentage not greatly out of proportion to the 59.9 per cent of the sensuous and "evenly developed" Keats. In both visual and auditory imagery Shelley has actually a lesser percentage than Keats; the difference lies in the amount of motor imagery, in which Shelley is strong and Keats unusually weak. And one may, I think, question the assertion that motor sensations are weak in sensuous content.

There is comparatively little significant disparity to be found in regard to other types of sensation. Keats's 20.1 per cent in strong tactual imagery is very high, but Shelley with 14.8 per cent is not far behind. In the relatively weak olfactory sense their scores are practically identical. In gustatory imagery Keats is well in advance; but the sense of taste plays only a tiny part in the poetry of either. Keats enjoys a substantial superiority in strong organic imagery; they are even, however, in the equally strong kinesthetic.

In the light of this evidence the ordinary critical generalization that Shelley's poetry lacks sensuous force and richness seems definitely to be baseless. Compared with Keats, a poet whom all critics agree is distinguished by a high degree of concreteness and imaginal abundance, he suffers little if at all. He is not deficient in ability to perceive actuality through the channels of sense, as Mr. Read and Professor Leavis would have it; nor is his sensory equipment noticeably uneven, as Pro-

TABLE I

KEATS

	LINES	TOTALS	VIS.	AUD.	TACT.	OLF.	GUST.	ORG.	KIN.	M.
					IMAGES					
I Stood Tiptoe	242	110	40	18	24	1	2	10	7	8
Endymion	222	94	37	17	18	1		8	2	11
Isabella	207	126	41	16	26	2	5	21	5	10
Hyperion	201	141	61	17	23	3	1	20	5	11
Eve of St. Agnes	224	103	37	12	30	2	2	15	1	4
Eve of St. Mark	119	22	10	1	7			1	1	2
La Belle Dame Sans Merci (1st version)	48	8	6					1	1	
Ode to Psyche	67	68	30	12	16	3		4	1	2
Nightingale	80	81	27	12	12	3	2	13	1	11
Grecian Urn	50	47	22	9	7		1	5	2	1
Melancholy	30	57	20	3	10	2	6	10	5	1
Lamia	199	151	74	7	28		3	21	2	16
Autumn	33	57	23	9	13	1	2	6	2	1
TOTALS	1722	1065	428	133	214	18	24	135	35	78

TABLE II
SHELLEY

	LINES	TOTALS	VIS.	AUD.	TACT.	OLF.	GUST.	ORG.	KIN.	M.
Queen Mab	207	104	53	10	10	5	1	6	3	16
Alastor	200	125	48	20	13	2	7	8	5	22
Intellectual Beauty	84	43	17	7			1	1		17
The Cloud	84	111	42	5	22			7	5	30
To a Skylark	105	68	21	11	13	1		3		19
Adonais	234	213	84	13	37	2		19	13	45
Prometheus Unbound	220	156	63	16	12		1	18	8	38
When the Lamp...	32	33	13	6	5			2		7
Ode to Liberty	195	135	55	11	19			12	2	36
Dejection	45	25	6	3	4			3		9
Witch of Atlas	216	162	74	4	28			8	12	36
Triumph of Life	211	165	66	11	25	2		5	1	55
Sensitive Plant	210	210	73	14	42	15		19	5	42
West Wind	70	96	30	10	15			11	3	27
Euganean Hills	205	135	57	9	19			12	2	36
TOTALS	2318	1781	702	150	264	27	10	134	59	435

fessor Finney has declared. These judgments are impressionistic, not grounded in observation and evidence, and the fact that they represent a very widely held view of Shelley makes it the more necessary to demur against them.

In the following sections of this chapter—devoted respectively to visual imagery; tactual imagery; auditory, olfactory, and gustatory imagery; and organic, kinesthetic, and motor imagery—I shall endeavor to show more fully the importance of sense-perception in Shelley's poetry. One may speculate that the widespread misconception of its characteristics has arisen partly from the thinness and tenuity of the material with which he works, his clouds, mists, dews, water-scenes, etc.; so that his critics have confused his subject matter with his ability to handle it. Another interesting conjecture is that the amount and the power of his motor imagery has tended to conceal the presence of other sense-elements from his readers. These and other questions are worth consideration.

The purpose of this discussion is, however, not merely argumentative. In its preliminaries I have emphasized the problems of Shelley's imagery, perhaps somewhat to the neglect of Keats. This procedure is justifiable, I believe, since Shelley in this respect is far less well understood. In the remarks which follow, however, I shall hold more closely and impartially to the method of comparison and contrast, striving to throw light upon the characteristic sensory qualities of Keats as well as upon those of Shelley by placing them side by side for examination.

II   In their visual imagery Keats and Shelley differ less in degree than in kind. Images of sight occupy about the same position in the poetry of each: 40.1 per cent for the former, for the latter 39.5 per cent. The two poets, however, view the world in radically different ways. Keats is minute in observation, with an eye to every particular of every object;[12] Shelley, usually working on a panoramic scale, generalizes and reduces, in order that the details of his scenes may fit within a unity of the whole. Keats is naturalistic and representative, whereas Shelley more noticeably imposes his subjective conceptions upon what he sees. Shelley's vision is usually directed either up or down,[13] while Keats looks out before him, horizontally; he glances at the sky casually, albeit observantly, while Shelley's gaze is earnest and painful, as if he strove to pierce the atmosphere and arrive at some ultimate vision above the air itself. Paradoxically, Shelley the philosophical Monist[14] is frequently dualistic in the composition of his visual

12. "Nothing seemed to escape him [Keats], the song of a bird and the undernote of response from covert or hedge, the rustle of some animal, the changing of the green and brown lights and furtive shadows, the motions of the wind . . . and the wayfaring of the clouds; even the features and gestures of passing tramps, the colour of one woman's hair, the smile on one child's face, the furtive animalism below the deceptive humanity in many of the vagrants, even the hats, clothes, shoes. . . ."—Joseph Severn as recorded by William Sharp. Quoted by Sir Sidney Colvin, *John Keats*, pp. 79-80.

13. In this matter of physical point of view I owe the initial suggestion to a brief remark by G. Wilson Knight.—*The Starlit Dome*, p. 179.

14. "The view of life presented by the most refined deductions of the intellectual philosophy, is that of unity."—Shelley, "On Life," *Shelley's Literary and Philosophical Criticism*, p. 56. "Shelley found his way to a monistic theory of the universe in which matter and being—all the phenomenal world—are conceived of as but manifestations of thought."—Carl Grabo, *The Magic Plant*, p. 433. "This is the recurrent and central position with Shelley. The endless forms and concrete objects of this dull world are 'compelled' to take on whatever life and activity they possess by the power of the One Spirit."—Solomon F. Gingerich, *Essays in the Romantic Poets*, p. 225.

images; he paints two pictures, one above the other, with a neutral zone of emptiness between. Keats, on the other hand, imparts to his scenes a pervading unity which intellectually he would have hesitated to impose upon the world.

One may illustrate these assertions by reference to four early poems: *Queen Mab*, *I Stood Tiptoe*, *The Revolt of Islam*, and *Endymion;* and to two mature works, *Prometheus Bound* and *Hyperion*. In *Queen Mab* the journey of Ianthe in the chariot of the Fairy Queen begins on earth, traverses the universe itself, and ends *above* the universe, in the supernatural palace of the Queen. The airy travellers pass through "heaven's dark blue vault" (I, 209) "above the mountain's loftiest peak" (I, 216), from which point they behold far below "Tremendous Ocean . . . Calm as a slumbering babe" (I, 222-25). The chariot proceeds

> . . . through the midst of an immense concave
> Radiant with million constellations . . .
>
> (I, 232-33)

It moves on until

> Earth's distant orb appeared
> The smallest light that twinkles in the heaven;
> Whilst round the chariot's way
> Innumerable systems rolled . . .
>
> (I, 250-53)

Finally the travellers arrive at "Mab's ethereal palace" (II, 29), which although indescribable is yet "likest evening's vault" (II, 30). This palace rests on Heaven itself, as Heaven rests on the wave (II, 31-32); its "pearly battlements around" look "o'er the immense

of Heaven" (II, 39-40). Thus it is above and separate
from the limits of the physical universe. From this
height transcending height the Fairy opens before
Ianthe's vision a limitless prospect, in which matter,
space, and time have no meaning, and in which Earth
is an almost invisible point:

> Below lay stretched the universe!
> There, far as the remotest line
> That bounds imagination's flight,
> Countless and unending orbs
> In mazy motion intermingled . . .
>
> (II, 70-74)
>
> . . . .
>
> There was a little light
> That twinkled in the misty distance.
> None but a spirit's eye
> Might ken that rolling orb.
>
> (II, 83-86)

This vast panorama, constantly shifting in aspect
and focus until one ultimately reaches a point outside
it, presents a typical example of the spaciousness of
Shelley's scenes and of his visual dualism.[15] With it we
may contrast the scene described by Keats in a corres-
pondingly early poem, "I Stood Tiptoe." The poet
stands upon a *little* hill (l. 1), so that his eye surveys a
wide yet limited tract. "There was wide wand'ring for
the greediest eye," he says, "to peer about upon variety"
(ll. 15-16). He looks *about* him, not *above* him, as far as
the horizon. The sky is not to him an infinite space

---

15. I am aware of Shelley's very large indebtedness to Volney's *Ruins* in *Queen Mab*. See K. N. Cameron, "A Major Source of *The Revolt of Islam*," *PMLA*, LVI, 175-206; L. Kellner, "Shelley's *Queen Mab* und Volney's *Les Ruines*," *ES*, XXII, 9-40. *Queen Mab* is nevertheless representative of Shelley's typical visual qualities.

comprising within itself many planes, but "blue fields" (l. 10) and later a solid bowl, so fully realized as such by him that he refers to "the dwindled edgings of its brim." His imagination, however, does not work comfortably in even so definitely limited a territory as this before his physical eye. He is obliged to project his vision in fancy into the details of the scene (ll. 25-28), so as to observe them with greater particularity. Consequently he enumerates every flower, bush, and bird which the landscape about him might conceivably contain with a loving concentration of attention shown at its height in his amazing description of the minnows of the brook:

> . . . swarms of minnows show their little heads,
> Staying their wavy bodies 'gainst the streams
> To taste the luxury of sunny beams
> Temper'd with coolness. How they ever wrestle
> With their own sweet delight, and ever nestle
> Their silver bellies on the pebbly sand.
> If you but scantily hold out the hand,
> That very instant not one will remain;
> But turn your eye, and they are there again.
>
> (ll. 72-80)

Queen Mab and *I Stood Tiptoe* are admittedly unlike in subject matter; they have been selected not because of their parallels but because they represent extremes of difference. This instance of radical dissimilarity in the visual perceptions of Shelley and Keats might be dismissed if the same disparity in points of view were not to be found elsewhere. Shelley, however, has written no poem like *I Stood Tiptoe*, and nowhere in Keats is there to be found anything like the scale and sense of distance in *Queen Mab*, with its continual shifting of

ocus and perspective. Yet reference to a sky-journey
1 Keats closely analogous to the journey of Mab and
he Spirit of Ianthe will perhaps furnish still more con-
incing evidence.

In the fourth book of *Endymion* the hero ascends with
he Indian Maid into the sky on "two steeds jet-black"
l. 342). At first they ascend swiftly, flying "high as the
agles" (l. 348), and Keats conveys a sense of their
ising in "giddy air" (l. 355), "precipitous" (l. 358),
nd "towering" (l. 359). Soon, however, their flight
evels off and slows until

> Slowly they sail, slowly as icy isle
> Upon a calm sea drifting . . .
>
> (ll. 405-6)

nd instead of looking above and below them, like the
ˉairy and the Spirit in *Queen Mab*, Endymion, the lady,
ınd the two steeds fall asleep! Keats is not interested
n airy voyaging through immense distances (and in
ˉact, the distances do not appear to be great), but in the
sleepers and their dreams (ll. 398-484). After a long and
somnolent interval they advance once more "direct towards the Galaxy" (ll. 486-87). But even as they resume
.heir flight the moon appears (ll. 496-502); at the sight
the lady fades from view and her steed plummets to the
earth, whither Endymion soon follows. The abruptness
with which this journey concludes indicates that physically it is little realized by the poet; the visual imagery
gives little sense of the vast regions of sky which presumably it traversed.

A comparison of the settings in *Hyperion* and *Prometheus Unbound* will supply further evidence of these dif-

ferences in visual quality. Each poem is immense in conception; the personages are the Gods themselves, and the scene is bounded only by the artistic choice of the poet. Keats, however, lays his background in four separate places, highly localized and definitely delimited in space, while Shelley's "Ravine of Icy Rocks in the Indian Caucasus"[16] suggests cosmic distances of prospect in every direction. The scene shifts, of course, in *Prometheus Unbound* as well as in *Hyperion*, but in the former the backgrounds are lost in the spaces of the sky surrounding them.[17]

Let us contrast the openings of the two poems. At the commencement of *Hyperion* Saturn sits

> Deep in the shady sadness of a vale
> Far sunken from the healthy breath of morn,
> Far from the fiery noon, and eve's one star . . .
>
> (I, 1-3)

Keats thus at the outset explicitly limits his scene both vertically and horizontally; Saturn is shut in from the sky by a dense forest (I, 6-7), and from the earth by the walls of the vale. And this concentration and localization of vision instantly turns yet further in upon itself. Keats goes on to focus first upon the recumbent figure of Saturn, then upon his right hand (I, 18). A more circumscribed range for the eye could hardly be contrived.

16. Shelley's ravine undoubtedly comes directly from Aeschylus' "rocky gorge in Scythia" (Paul Elmer More's translation). Shelley's choice of models, however, in itself indicates the nature of his preferences, I think.

17. The scenes of *Prometheus Unbound* are laid as follows: I, A Ravine of Icy Rocks in the Indian Caucasus; II, i, a lovely Vale in the Indian Caucasus; II, ii, a Forest intermingled with Rocks and Caverns; II, iii, a Pinnacle of Rock among Mountains; II, v, . . . a Cloud on the Top of a Snowy Mountain; III, i, Heaven; III, iv, a Forest; IV, A part of the Forest near the Cave of Prometheus.

Throughout the remainder of the "scene" the visual interest lies chiefly in a motionless and statuesque tableau in which the goddess Thea kneels before the feet of Saturn.[18]

Prometheus, on the other hand, "Nailed to this wall of eagle-baffling mountain" (I, 20), looks out into a void peopled with the largest and simplest elements of Nature, Earth, Heaven, and Sea (I, 25-28), and animated only by crawling glaciers (I, 31), Earthquake-fiends (I, 37), and the genii of the storm (I, 42), contained within the slow and cosmic movement of day and night (I, 47). This vastness of scale is emphasized in the time-dimension; Prometheus has been bound to his rock "Three thousand years of sleep-unsheltered hours" (I, 12).

Keats's treatment of the palace of Hyperion (I, 166-305) gives further evidence of his visual definiteness and concreteness. The dwelling of the Sun God, like Hyperion himself, is huge, but bounded and delimited. Its outlines are plain; it is a celestial St. Mark's of domes and towers, a Byzantine cathedral (I, 218-23). Keats reduces his vast conceptions to a scale on which the physical eye can comprehend his images without difficulty. The sun itself, "The planet orb of fire," becomes a globe as solid and definite as the humanized symbolic sphere of a Book of Hours; it is laid tranquilly by for the night, "Spun round in sable curtaining of clouds"

18.   "One moon, with alteration slow, had shed
       Her silver seasons four upon the night,
       And still these two were postured motionless,
       Like natural sculpture in cathedral cavern;
       The frozen God still couchant on the earth,
       And the sad Goddess weeping at his feet" (I, 83-88).

(I, 271). To bring it further within the scope of human vision and sympathy Keats has endowed it with "two fair argent wings" (I, 284), which rise in salutation at the approach of Hyperion (I, 285–87).

Keats focusses his vision upon the palace itself;[19] he gives little notion of the space surrounding it. Hyperion, setting out from his sky-mansion to visit earth at the behest of Coelus, plunges from its eastern gates not into the distances of the heavens, but into a dense, dimensionless opacity:

> Then, with a slow incline of his broad breast,
> Like to a diver in the pearly seas,
> Forward he stoop'd over the airy shore,
> And plung'd all noiseless into the deep night.
>
> (I, 354-57)

We do not follow him in his journey; he appears to the reader again only when, his travels ended, he alights upon a mountain peak above his assembled brother Titans.

Shelley's palaces, on the other hand, are vantage points from which to gaze out into illimitable distance. Such is the dwelling of Queen Mab and such the temple in the *Revolt of Islam*, an edifice pictured significantly in terms of the wide heavens.[20] The ceiling of this "vast

19. One might notice here the definiteness and solidity of Keats's description of the banquet-room in another of his palaces—in *Lamia*. His use of detail is remarkable: the arch formed by the alternating palms and plantains (II, 125-30), with "jasper pannels" between the tree-stems; the *fifty* censers, each supported by a slender-footed tripod, with their fifty wreaths of smoke each reproduced by mirrors on the wall (II, 175-82); and the "*twelve* sphered tables," each *as high as the level of a man's breast* (II, 183-84).

20.   " 'Twas likest Heaven, ere yet day's purple stream
             Ebbs o'er the western forest, while the gleam
             Of the unrisen moon among the clouds

dome," obscured from view by "spell-inwoven clouds,"
is obviously emblematic of the night sky:

> Orb above orb, with starry shapes between,
> And horned moons, and meteors strange and fair,
> On night-black columns poised—one hollow hemisphere!
>
> (I, st. lii)

The image exemplifies Shelley's characteristically wide
range[21] and the upward direction of his gaze, as well as
his frequent visual dualism. The dome and the floor of
the palace are on different planes, separated by a neutral
zone of cloud.

I cite one further instance of the great disparity between the two poets in visual quality, direction, and
scope. Shelley finds a fruitful source of poetic inspiration
in the skylark, which soars vertically into the heavens
until it disappears; Keats is impelled to write some of
his finest verse by the nightingale, a dweller in trees,
which does not venture far above the ground. Hear
Shelley as he apostrophizes the lark:

> Higher still and higher
> From the earth thou springest
> Like a cloud of fire;
> The blue deep thou wingest,
> And singing still dost soar, and soaring ever singest.
>
> (*To a Skylark*, ll. 6-10)

Is gathering—when with many a golden beam
The thronging constellations rush in crowds,
Paving with fire the sky and the marmoreal floods" (I, st. xlix).
 21. The comprehensiveness of the vision of Shelley, and the concentration of
Keats, is apparent in their comments on art. Shelley takes in the whole picture impartially, while Keats turns his attention to the principal figure. Compare Shelley's
remarks on the paintings in an unnamed palace in Bologna (for example, Letter XV,
The Works of Percy Bysshe Shelley, ed. H. B. Forman, VIII, 49-56) to Keats on Alcibiades
in his galley (*The Letters of John Keats*, ed. M. B. Forman, p. 129. Hereafter to be referred
to as *Letters*).

The bird of Keats, likewise unseen, is hidden by thick foliage, not distance. It is near at hand. Shelley looks up at an object concealed from him by a thin veil of airy space—again the dualist image on different planes; Keats looks out horizontally upon the heavy, verdurous textures of the May night. Unable to pierce the darkness, in imagination he beholds a bower enclosed by leafy boughs[22] and numerously peopled with

> The grass, the thicket, and the fruit-tree wild;
> White hawthorn, and the pastoral eglantine;
>   And mid-May's eldest child,
> The coming musk-rose, full of dewy wine,
> The murmurous haunt of flies in summer eves.[23]

Shelley's visual imagery, as these examples show, is the product of an eye usually directed either up or down, and focussed on distance. Consequently he very frequently describes atmospheric phenomena and generalizes objects near at hand in order to harmonize them with his backgrounds.[24] The scope of Keats is far more limited; he concerns himself with describing the particulars of things close at hand. The insatiable eye of Shelley seeks always to pierce through, to go beyond physical possibility into the realm of the supernatural, while Keats is contented to remain within a set and

22. Dorothy B. Van Ghent in her interpretation, "The Nightingale" (Image-Types and Antithetical Structure in the Work of Keats), declares that the "covert" image is basic in Keats's poetry.

23. Derivative from the "roll-call of the flowers," beginning "Bring the rathe primrose that forsaken dies," in *Lycidas?* See Keats's *Staffa*, ll. 25-26. There is no mention of this parallel in R. D. Havens' *The Influence of Milton on English Poetry*, or in either H. B. Forman's or E. de Sélincourt's editions of Keats's poems.

24. The converse of this statement, that Shelley looks up because he is interested in atmospheric phenomena, might well be made. The acceptance of one, I think, need not invalidate the other.

predetermined boundary. The difference in the quality and the texture of their imagery is thus a matter of focussing, as it seems to me, and not of their respective holds on objective reality through visual perception. Keats is with Shakespeare as a great naturalistic poet of our tongue,[25] but he should not be used, as he too often is, as a stick with which to beat Shelley.

For Shelley, save occasionally in early work and a few hastily written lyrics, is firm in composition and vivid in visual realization. The frequent tenuousness of his chosen subjects and the sense of motion omnipresent in his poetry often mislead us into believing him cloudy of vision and wavering in technique. It should be noticed however, that his mists, dews, and cloud-patterns usually have clearly delineated contours; and we must not be diverted from perceiving the solidity and form of his frameworks by the sight of his occasional struggles to get out at the top of the frame.

Professor Knight has pointed out what he calls a "transverse technique" in *Queen Mab*, by means of which Shelley achieves a paradoxical impression of realism by subtle emphasis upon the thinness and bodilessness of the object he is describing.[26] I would hazard the opinion that in this technique, coupled with an opposing technique of reinforcement, lies the secret of the effect of Shelley's most characteristic imagery. He habitually pictures objects or phenomena almost inaccessible to the senses of the average man, and he emphasizes the evanescence and ethereality of these objects; but if we look we

25. See Matthew Arnold, "Keats," *Essays in Criticism*, p. 119; also John Middleton Murry, *Keats and Shakespeare*, pp. 4-12.
26. *Op. cit.*, p. 182.

shall usually find that he has strengthened and solidified his descriptions by reinforcing them with a thin but strong thread of steel, that his misty veils, his cloud-capped towers are firm of outline and composed of visible, even tangible, elements.

As early as *Queen Mab* this union of the solid and the ethereal is present in Shelley's verse, as appears from this description of the swift dash of the fairy's chariot through the yielding air:

> . . . rays of rapid light
> Parted around the chariot's swifter course.
> And fell, like ocean's feathery spray
> Dashed from the boiling surge
> Before a vessel's prow.

(I, 244-48)

The movement of the image is anticipated in "parted." The simple and indivisible element of light becomes visible and tangible as water; it takes on the quality of resistance. It is divided into its component parts, so that drops of light fall like spray before the impact of the onrushing chariot. The chariot itself becomes a ship beating up against a heavy sea. The two contrary elements of the image react upon each other in a strange manner; there is no fusion here, rather a rebounding and reinforcing of the opposing qualities of solidity and intangibility from contact with each other. Paradoxically, our sense of the ethereality of the chariot and the skyey strangeness of its flight through space becomes stronger because of the air-water, chariot-ship comparison.

A slighter illustration of this union of immateriality

 nd solidity may be drawn from one of Shelley's many
'woven'' images:

> . . . at the sound he turned
> And saw by the warm light of their own life
> Her glowing limbs beneath the sinuous *veil*
> Of *woven* wind . . .[27]

(Alastor, ll. 174-77)

This intimate linking of the notions of lightness and
 ntangibility suggested by *veil* and *wind* with the conno-
 ations of *woven* produces the same paradoxical effect.[28]

One could fill a volume with examples of this complex interplay of qualities in Shelley's visual imagery.
An analysis of two striking passages, the descriptions
of the Moon and the Earth in Act IV of *Prometheus
Unbound* will, however, adequately serve the present
purpose:

Ione

> I see a chariot like that thinnest boat
> In which the mother of the months is borne
> By ebbing night into her western cave,
> When she upsprings from interlunar dreams;
> O'er which is curved an orb-like canopy
> Of gentle darkness, and the hills and woods
> Distinctly seen through that dusk airy veil,
> Regard like shapes in an enchanter's glass;
> Its wheels are solid clouds, azure and gold,
> Such as the genii of the thunder-storm

27. Henry Sweet in his "Shelley's Nature Poetry" (*Shelley Society's Papers*), listed
almost fifty of these "woven" images.

28. Cf. *Prometheus Unbound*, II, i, 75-78:
> ". . . an atmosphere
> Which *wrapped* me in its all-dissolving power
> As the warm ether of the morning sun
> *Wraps* ere it drinks some cloud of wandering dew."

Pile on the floor of the illumined sea
When the sun rushes under it; they roll
And move and grow as with an inward wind:
Within it sits a wingéd infant—white
Its countenance, like the whiteness of bright snow,
Its plumes are as feathers of sunny frost,
Its limbs gleam white, through the wind-flowing folds
Of its white robe, woof of ethereal pearl,
Its hair is white, the brightness of white light
Scattered in strings; yet its two eyes are heavens
Of liquid darkness, which the Deity
Within seems pouring, as a storm is poured
From jagged clouds, out of their arrowy lashes,
Tempering the cold and radiant air around
With fire that is not brightness; in its hand
It sways a quivering moonbeam, from whose point
A guiding power directs the chariot's prow
Over its wheeléd clouds, which as they roll
Over the grass, and flowers, and waves, wake sounds
Sweet as a singing rain of silver dew.

Panthea

And from the other opening in the wood
Rushes, with loud and whirlwind harmony,
A sphere, which is as many thousand spheres;
Solid as crystal, yet through all its mass
Flow, as through empty space, music and light;
Ten thousand orbs involving and involved,
Purple and azure, white, green, and golden,
Sphere within sphere; and every space between
Peopled with unimaginable shapes,
Such as ghosts dream dwell in the lampless deep;
Yet each inter-transpicuous; and they whirl
Over each other with a thousand motions,
Upon a thousand sightless axles spinning,
And with the force of self-destroying swiftness,
Intensely, slowly, solemnly, roll on,

Kindling with mingled sounds, and many tones,
Intelligible words and music wild.
With mighty whirl the multitudinous orb
Grinds the bright brook into an azure mist
Of elemental subtlety, like light;
And the wild odor of the forest flowers
The music of the living grass and air,
The emerald light of leaf-entangled beams,
Round its intense yet self-conflicting speed
Seem kneaded into one aërial mass
Which drowns the sense. Within the orb itself,
Pillowed upon its alabaster arms,
Like to a child o'erwearied with sweet toil,
On its own folded wings and wavy hair
The Spirit of the Earth is laid asleep,
And you can see its little lips are moving,
Amid the changing light of their own smiles,
Like one who talks of what he loves in dream.

(*Prometheus Unbound*, IV, 206-68)

The imagery of this passage is so dazzling in its rush
and profusion that at first one is blinded; the sense of
light and motion overwhelms the mind's eye. Furthermore, the forms described by Shelley are so remote from
everyday life that it is difficult to find a frame of reference for them. The whiteness of the infant of the moon
is a little disquieting to eyes accustomed to different
flesh tones. Yet although these images are obviously
not naturalistic, their contours are clear and sharp. The
central images, the chariot of the Moon and the orb of
the Earth,[29] have simple but definite and fully realized
outlines.

29. "The original suggestion for this complicated image may well have been
from Canto xxviii of Dante's *Paradiso* or from Ezekiel's well-known vision of the
wheel."—Newman Ivey White, *Shelley*, II, 129.

Shelley's description of the moon-chariot typifies his method of mingling indefiniteness with firm line. The chariot is "like that *thinnest* boat" the new crescent moon, reduced by the light of dawn to a tiny silver line. Over this crescent shape is "an orb-like canopy of gentle darkness," within which are "hills and woods / Distinctly seen through that dusk airy veil." Indefiniteness is given an outline; a haze obscures objects which remain visible in defiance of it. The chariot's wheels are "*solid* clouds"—a startling paradox by which Shelley at once affirms and denies the objective reality of his image in a sudden imaginative flash. The solidity of these wheels is reinforced by "pile" and "floor" in the following lines; but what the poet offers with one hand he takes back with the other, for the "floor" is the surface of the sea at sunset, and the weighty material piled upon it is, once again, *cloud*.

The child within the chariot has plumes like "feathers of sunny frost," a delicate but definite figure which conveys not a picture of the wings but a notion of their essential quality. Its airy *robe* is *woof* of ethereal pearl. In the next image Shelley endows elemental light with sharply limned outlines:

> Its hair is white, the brightness of white light
> *Scattered* in *strings* . . .

In like manner, the analogy of the child's eyes with "heavens of liquid darkness" is extremely abstract, yet their effect is closely, strikingly portrayed. This "liquid darkness" is poured forth "as a storm is poured / From *jagged* clouds, out of their *arrowy* lashes." The two terms of the simile move together from point to point in

closest contact, despite the apparent initial incongruity of the comparison.

There is a still greater complexity and interplay of elements in the description of Earth. A multiplicity of swiftly moving forms and colors is contained within the simple, massive unity of the sphere, which is

> Solid as crystal, yet through all its mass
> Flow, as through empty space, music and light.

Within the primal sphere is a system of "Ten thousand orbs involving and involved . . . / Sphere within sphere," a relationship fluid yet constant, infinitely various yet ever the same. That Shelley's eye is on the object is manifested by his peopling "every space between . . . with unimaginable shapes"; his visual sense of design leaves nothing unaccounted for within the framework of the image. Here once more he combines indefiniteness with exactitude, a deliberate transcendence of sense-perception with the most careful respect for it. For these shapes are "unimaginable," they are "Such as *ghosts dream* dwell in the *lampless* deep"—one would say as deliberately inaccessible as possible to human vision—yet they are *intertranspicuous*, their limits and their relation to the pattern painstakingly defined.

The essential quality of these images, unity in variety, simplicity in complexity, is as it were crystallized in the lines

> With mighty whirl the *multitudinous orb*
> *Grinds* the bright brook into an *azure mist*
> Of *elemental subtlety*, like *light*,

in which "multitudinous" and "orb" interreact; the suggestion in "grinds" is sharply at variance with that

of "azure mist"; and "elemental" is forced into an intimate and paradoxical union with "subtlety."

In "The emerald light of leaf-entangled beams" Shelley characteristically attributes line and substance to a
phenomenon inherently difficult to resolve into its component parts for visual examination. The union of solidity and ethereality takes place once more in the
kneading of odors, music, and light "into one *aërial
mass.*" The figure of the sleeping Spirit of the Earth
opposes the human and naturalistic to the mathematical
and ultimate quality of the sphere and its immense
unities and offers an ironic comment upon it;[30] for as
its lips move in sleep Ione remarks that it is "mocking
the orb's harmony." This final word "harmony" epitomizes the passage; Shelley has enclosed a wilderness of
moving and conflicting objects in the single image of
the sphere and imposed upon them unity and system.

When one notices that Shelley has balanced simplicity of visual quality in the Moon against complexity
and variety in the Earth, appreciation of his skillful
workmanship progresses still further. The Moon is a
sharply outlined etching in black and white, the Earth
a full painting in which all the colors of the spectrum
are utilized, mingled and fused in many forms and
shapes. And if we realize that Shelley has set himself no
less a task than the representation of the Earth and
Moon in ultimate poetic terms, as they might be seen
by some vast, eternal, and intuitive onlooker, we must
concede his visual, intellectual, and artistic mastery of
his subject matter.

Unity and variety, solidity and evanescence, sim-

30. See Knight, *op. cit.*, p. 222.

plicity and complexity, stillness and motion, are all one in Shelley. The rapid flow of his swift-moving forms and essences is usually set in a motionless and solid frame. In that poem of his which most vividly conveys the feeling of fierce and breathless speed, the *Ode to the West Wind*, it is too seldom noticed that the wind moves beneath a solid dome, within which the scene is enclosed:

> . . . this closing night
> Will be the dome of a vast sepulchre,
> Vaulted with all thy *congregated* might
> Of vapors, from whose *solid* atmosphere
> Black rain, and fire, and hail will burst . . .
>
> (ll. 24-27)

These contrasting tendencies in Shelley's imagery may in part be attributed I believe, to what I have previously called his insatiable eye," coupled and sometimes at odds with his philosophical urge to impose unity upon the world. His thoroughgoing monism is responsible for his tendency toward generalization, for the vastness, the clarity, and the basic simplicity of his conceptions. Within the generous limits of these, however, his eye wanders from form to form, discarding one to rest momentarily upon another, and finally attempting to pass beyond "the dome of many-colored glass" in search of some ultimate reality beyond the range of mortal vision. He feels at once a sensuous delight in forms, colors, and motion and a desire to transcend to the realms of sense in search of the One.[31]

---

31. "The One remains, the many change and pass;
Heaven's light forever shines, Earth's shadows fly . . ." (*Adonais*, st. lii)

Shelley's scientific bent [32] also helps to account for his restless delight in a multiplicity of natural objects, and for his love of change, movement, and development.[33] To this scientific turn of mind we may perhaps assign as well another important characteristic of his visual imagery, its analytical quality. For Shelley reduces things to their component parts; his piercing[34] eye sees through the object of its gaze and anatomizes it. The elaborate interlocking system which makes up his sphere of Earth in *Prometheus Unbound*, and which the Spirit of Earth satirizes with his rhythmically moving lips, is analytical in conception. The thin, strong thread which usually reinforces even his haziest imagery exemplifies the same tendency. The scientific accuracy of that shimmering poem *The Cloud* is unassailable, as critics from Stopford Brooke to Carl Grabo have pointed out.[35] The series of dissolutions and rebirths through which the cloud passes are carefully differentiated processes, visualized separately. These swift transformations culminate in images of solid, simple, structural forms:

> From cape to cape, with a bridge-like shape
> Over a torrent sea,
> Sunbeam-proof, I hang like a *roof*,—
> The mountains its *columns* be

32. "Under slightly altered circumstances Shelley would have become a scientist . . . the teachings of science combine with Plato and the humanitarian French philosophers to compose Shelley's philosophy."—Carl Grabo, *A Newton Among Poets*, pp. 3-4. "What the hills were to the youth of Wordsworth, a chemical laboratory was to Shelley."—A. N. Whitehead, *Science and the Modern World*, p. 122. Quoted by Grabo.

33. "Shelley thinks of nature as changing, dissolving, transforming as it were at a fairy's touch."—Whitehead, *op. cit.*, p. 125.

34. Shelley uses the word *pierce*, *piercing*, etc., approximately sixty-one times in his verse.—F. S. Ellis, *A Lexical Concordance to the Poetical Works of Percy Bysshe Shelley*. Hereafter to be referred to as Ellis.

35. See Stopford Brooke, Introduction, *Selections from Shelley*, pp. xli-xlii.

> The triumphal *arch* through which I march
> With hurricane, fire, and snow,
> When the powers of the air are chained to my chair,
> Is the million-colored bow . . .[36]

(ll. 63-70)

These scenes are composed from separate parts, into which they are divisible. Shelley is not happy with complexity until he can resolve it into its components, or with actuality until he can perceive each shade of the subtle changes which it constantly undergoes.

In this respect Shelley differs profoundly from Keats, who sees particular things as wholes. Keats is content to accept things in their complexity, and he endeavors to express in his poetry the essence of this complexity, whereas Shelley strives to attain to a final simplicity by resolving wholes into their component parts. For this reason Keats's images are generally static and reposeful, as he concentrates intensely upon establishing the unique and peculiar quality of the object he contemplates, while Shelley's are restless and mobile. In *To Autumn*, for example, Keats deals with a subject notably conducive to philosophical moralizing about change and decay, the flux and dissolutions inherent in nature. Yet instead of linking the fine September day to the moving chain of the seasons, contrasting its failing beauty with the deathliness of winter and the eventual rebirth of spring, as would Shelley ("If Winter comes, can Spring be far behind?"), he isolates it, makes it a thing-in-itself.

He views the particular *sub specie aeternitatis*.[37] The

36. See further, ll. 77-84.
37. Cf. John Middleton Murry, "Beauty is Truth," *Studies in Keats: New and Old*, pp. 71-92.

essential quality of Autumn is, as it were, fixed in a motionless, eternal moment. To him the evening clouds are not a symbol of change, dissolution, and rebirth; he stays them forever, as if a motion picture were to be suddenly, permanently stopped in the midst of its movement:

> While barred clouds bloom the soft-dying day,
> And touch the stubble-plains with rosy hue . . .
>
> (ll. 25-26)

Likewise the four images in which he embodies Autumn all exemplify this timeless repose:

> Sometimes whoever seeks abroad may find
> Thee sitting careless on a granary floor,
> Thy hair soft-lifted by the winnowing wind;
> Or on a half reap'd furrow sound asleep,
> Drows'd with the fume of poppies, while thy hook
> Spares the next swath and all its twined flowers:
> And sometimes like a gleaner thou dost keep
> Steady thy laden head across a brook;
> Or by a cyder-press, with patient look
> Thou watchest the last oozings hours by hours.
>
> (ll. 13-22)

The intention is unmistakable; the poet obtains his effect by an almost hypnotic repetition of a single suggestion. The goddess[38] sits *careless* (of time and change, one may add), her hair *soft-lifted* by an almost imperceptible breeze, which is powerless to shake her statuesque composure. She lies sound asleep upon a *half-reaped* furrow,

---

38. I am aware that orthodox interpretation usually holds Autumn to be male, after the Latin Autumnus. Keats's personifications, however, seem to me to be without exception feminine; the "soft-lifted hair" in a man would be strangely epicene, in particular, and the gleaner with laden head is more likely to be a woman. Cf. Ruth amid the alien corn in the *Ode to a Nightingale*.

her hook sparing the next swath of grain; the movement of accident and circumstance is arbitrarily stilled. She is "drows'd with the fume of poppies," the flower of oblivion, which has transported her out of time into the eternal afternoon of the Lotos-Eaters. As a gleaner she keeps *steady* her laden head; a suggestion enforced by *patient* and *hours by hours* in the final image. If indeed time exists, or anything outside the charmed circle of her own unique identity, she steadfastly refuses to regard it.

The visual imagery of Keats is, then, for the most part synthetic, while Shelley's is analytical. One may say that Shelley's view of things is mechanical, Keats's organic. Keats's fondness for living, inseparable wholes is apparent in his success with human figures, in his grasp of their three dimensional roundness and fullness. Shelley, on the other hand, evinces little feeling for the human body;[39] his characteristic figures are frail apparitions, like the dream-maiden in *Alastor* (ll. 151-80), or his self-portrait in *Adonais* (ll. 271-98). The typical representation of the human form in Shelley gives a vague notion of "glowing limbs," seen through a veil.[40] His imagination is entirely at home with the simple and basic shapes of orbs, spheres, domes, and arches; but if we compare, let us say, the "frail forms" of the mountain-shepherds of *Adonais* to Keats's sculptural tableau of Saturn and Thea (*Hyperion*, I, 79-90) or the

39. For possible exceptions to this statement see *Queen Mab*, I, 12-44; *The Revolt of Islam*, VI, xxxv; and several passages in *The Cenci*, especially III, i, 1-28. *The Cenci* may be called the exception which proves the rule, for Shelley considered it quite uncharacteristic. See letter 23, *Peacock's Memoirs of Shelley*, ed. H. F. B. Brett-Smith, p. 193; *Trelawney's Recollections of the Last Days of Shelley and Byron*, p. 51.

40. E.g., *Prometheus Unbound*, II, v, 54-59; *The Witch of Atlas*, st. v.

tortured, gigantic figures of the Titan council-of-war (*Hyperion*, II, 19-78), we shall see a notable difference in effect.

III　　　In considering the manner in which Shelley and Keats represent the human body, we must reckon with the sense of touch as well as with sight. In Keats the tactual serves to strengthen and round out other types of sense-imagery. It merges and blends so closely with other sensations that it is often difficult to abstract for examination. The firmness and three-dimensional quality of Keats's human figures and personifications is in some degree to be accounted for by his power of reinforcing the impressions of the eye by other senses; very frequently by tactual imagery. This is one of the causes of the "sculptural" or "statuesque" tendency in Keats. [41]

The remarkably complete realization of warm, breathing flesh in his description in the *Ode to Psyche* of Cupid and Psyche in each other's arms is achieved by a concentration of tactual images, which subtly strengthen the central visual impression.

> They lay calm-breathing on the *bedded* grass;
> Their *arms embraced*, and their *pinions* too;
> Their *lips touch'd* not, but had not bade adieu,
> As if *disjoined* by *soft-handed* slumber . . .

> (ll. 15-18)

41. The sculptural quality of many of Keats's figures is most simply attributable, of course, to his familiarity with statuary, especially the Elgin Marbles, and his consequent ability to reproduce sculptural attitudes and shapes. Stephen A. Larrabee asserts that the characteristic quality of the Grecian figures in *Endymion* and *Hyperion* is their "stationing," which frequently recalls arrangements in the Elgin Marbles. See *English Bards and Grecian Marbles*, p. 221.

In like manner sight is enhanced by touch in *The Eve of St. Agnes:*

> The carved angels, ever eager-eyed,
> Star'd, where upon their heads the cornice rests,
> With hair blown back, and wings put cross-wise
>   on their breasts.
>
> (ll. 34-36)

Carved, the tangible weight of the cornice, and the feel of "wings put crosswise" all aid in establishing the effect of this vivid image. The same indirect suggestion of touch gives body and weight to the virgins of St. Agnes, who must *"couch supine* their *beauties*, lilly white" (l. 52).

In the *Ode on a Grecian Urn* one feels the "mad pursuit" and "struggle to escape" in a sensation of warmth ("Forever warm and still to be enjoyed," l. 26), and the scene of the sacrifice is projected into physical, three-dimensional being by the "silken flanks" of the heifer which stands before the altar. The function of tactual imagery in Keats is perhaps most plainly apparent, however, in a passage from an earlier poem, wrought with a technique less complex and more obvious: the description of the sleeping Adonis in *Endymion*, Bk. II.

> . . . on a *silken* couch of rosy pride,
> In midst of all, there lay a sleeping youth
> Of fondest beauty; fonder, in fair sooth,
> Than sighs could fathom, or contentment reach:
> And *coverlids* gold-tinted like the *peach*,
> Or ripe October's faded marigolds,
> *Fell sleek* about him in a thousand folds—
> Not hiding up an Apollonian curve
> Of neck and shoulder, nor the *tenting* swerve
> Of knee from knee, nor ankles pointing *light*;

> But rather, giving them to the *filled* sight
> Officiously. Sideway his face repos'd
> *On one white arm*, and *tenderly unclos'd*,
> *By tenderest pressure*, a faint *damask* mouth
> To slumbery pout, just as the morning south
> *Disparts* a *dew-lipp'd* rose. Above his head
> Four lily stalks did their white honours *wed*
> To make a coronal; and round him grew
> All *tendrils* green, of every bloom and hue,
> Together intertwin'd and *trammel'd* fresh:
> The vine of *glossy sprout*; the ivy *mesh*,
> Shading its Ethiop berries; and woodbine,
> Of *velvet* leaves and *bugle-blooms* divine;
> *Convolvulus* in streaked vases *flush* . . .

                                                    (ll. 392-415)

Keats is clearly striving to get an effect of sensuous
luxuriance, and he attains it in part by suggestions of
soft, silky surfaces, of light but sensuous pressures, of
tender but tenacious clingings. The couch on which
Adonis lies is *silken*; his coverlids are like the peach not
only in being gold-tinted, but in their soft and feathery
bloom as well—a bloom which is felt in the finger-tips.
They have a tangible weight; they *fall sleek*. The attitude
of Adonis is described in terms which reproduce the
actual pressures of his body. His knees in their "tenting
swerve" burden the couch more heavily than his ankles,
which his posture relieves of weight. The arm which
supports his head has forced his mouth to open slightly;
a *damask* mouth in feel as in hue, to the touch like a
dew-lipp'd rose, and to the eye as well. The flowers about
him cling together, *wed*, *intertwined*, *trammeled*, in *tendrils*
and in *mesh*. These flowers, woodbine of *velvet leaves* and
bugle-blooms and *flush convolvulus*, are soft, full, and
glossy.

One becomes aware in the later verses of this passage that Keats is using sound effects to heighten his tactual imagery. Rounded *l*'s and *r*'s occur too frequently to be accidental: in *tendrils, bloom, trammel'd, glossy sprout, velvet, bugle-blooms, Convolvulus, streak'd,* and *flush.* These words in their context produce the tactual sensations of rounded, yielding, yet firm surfaces.

We know that Keats had a theory about vowels. He sought harmony of sound through a system of careful variation and modulation. According to his friend Benjamin Bailey,

. . . one of Keats' favourite topics of conversation was the principle of melody in verse, which he believed to consist in the adroit management of open and close vowels. He had a theory that vowels could be as skilfully combined and interchanged as differing notes of music, and that all sense of monotony was to be avoided, except when expressive of a special purpose.[42]

So far as I know, however, Keats said nothing of a theory about consonants. Yet in the passage just examined there seems to be unmistakable evidence of a definite purpose: to express rich and luxuriant tactual feeling by a corresponding richness of consonantal sound. And Bailey's closing remark shows that Keats believed in the device of repeating sounds for a "special purpose." He employed this same device of consonantal repetition, I think, in his descriptions of physical love in *Endymion.*

These love scenes are unquestionably feeble and mawkish, as most critics of Keats have maintained. Yet as exercises in sense imagery they are extremely interesting, for in them he attempts the impossible task of transferring sensation as it were bodily into literature,

42. *Letters,* p. 108n.

of expressing sexual ecstasy directly in words. This he does mainly by the use of tactual images, buttressed with heavy consonantal sound. Endymion's encounter with his Dream Maiden in the jasmine bower is the most notable example:

> Enchantress! tell me by this soft embrace,
> By the most soft completion of thy face,
> Those lips, O slippery blisses, twinkling eyes,
> And by these tenderest, milky sovereignties—
> These tenderest . . .
>
> . . . .
>
> Revive, or these soft hours will hurry by
> In tranced dullness; speak, and let that spell
> Affright this lethargy! I cannot quell
> Its heavy pressure . . .
>
> (*Endymion*, II, 756ff.)

The triply-repeated "soft" is the key to the passage; Keats is trying to carry over the essential feeling of it directly, and because of this crude directness he fails. But by his repetition and interlacing of r's, l's, b's, and p's he does manage to convey something of the physical wholeness of the situation, despite the oft-mentioned horrors of "milky sovereignties" and "Those lips, O slippery blisses."[43]

43. See also the complaint of Alpheus to Arethusa, *Endymion*, II, 936-48:
> O Arethusa, peerless nymph! why fear
> Such tenderness as mine? Great Dian, why,
> Why didst thou hear her prayer? O that I
> Were rippling round her dainty fairness now,
> Circling about her waist, and striving how
> To entice her to a dive! then stealing in
> Between her luscious lips and eyelids thin.
> O that her shining hair was in the sun,
> And I distilling from it thence to run

This consonant device is utilized more subtly by Keats in late and mature poetry to underline rich sensuous experience. It heightens the vivid lassitude of a waking swoon in the *Ode on Indolence:*

> . . . Ripe was the drowsy hour;
> The blissful cloud of summer-indolence
> Benumb'd my eyes; my pulse grew less and less;
> Pain had no sting, and pleasure's wreath
>   no flower . . .
>
>   (ll. 15-18)

In *To Autumn* it aids in transferring to the reader the poet's sensations of the rounded, plumped-out fruits of warm September:

> To bend with apples the moss'd cottage-trees,
> And fill all fruit with ripeness to the core;
> To swell the gourd, and plump the hazel shells
> With a sweet kernel; to set budding more,
> And still more, later flowers for the bees,
> Until they think warm days will never cease,
> For Summer has o'er-brimm'd their clammy cells.[44]

At its best Keats's tactual imagery is exquisitely subtle and almost inseparable from conceptual and emotional perceptions. In answer to the somewhat rhetorical question of his friend Bailey, "Why should women suffer?" he writes, "These things are, and he who feels

---

> In amorous rillets down her shrinking form!
> To linger on her lily shoulders warm
> Between her kissing breasts, and every charm
> Touch raptur'd!—See how painfully I flow . . .

"Drunken from pleasure's nipple" (II, 869) is a brief but striking instance.

44. Note also, "It is as if the rose should pluck herself,
            Or the ripe plum finger its misty bloom. . ." (*Second Sonnet on Fame*)

how incompetent the most skyey Knight errantry its
[for *is*] to heal this bruised fairness is like a sensitive
leaf on the hot hand of thought."[45] The interplay between abstract and concrete, between intellect and
touch, is too swift in motion and complex in action
for one to follow it. This intuitional *feeling* into the
nature of things—or it might be called a stepping from
simple sensation to complex perception—is observable
also in the poet's account of the origin of *To Autumn:*

> How beautiful the season is now—How fine the air. A temperate
> sharpness about it. Really, without joking, chaste weather—Dian
> skies—I never lik'd stubble-fields so much as now—Aye better than
> the chilly green of the Spring. Somehow a stubble-plain looks warm
> in the same way that some pictures look warm—This struck me so
> much in my Sunday's walk that I composed upon it.[46]

The Eve of St. Mark had probably a similar beginning.
Keats remarked of it to his brother George and sister-
in-law Georgiana, "I think it will give you the Sensation of walking about an old county Town in a coolish
evening."[47] His comparison of the stubble-fields of Autumn to "the chilly green of the Spring" suggests that
he is thinking of the two poems as companion-pieces,
one evoking the feel of a cool spring evening, the other
the mellow warmth of September. This persuasion is
strengthened by Keats's manner of introducing *The Eve
of St. Mark,*

> . . . on the western window panes
> The *chilly* sunset faintly told
> Of *immatur'd, green* vallies *cold,*

45. *Letters*, p. 84.
46. *Ibid.*, p. 384.
47. *Ibid.*, p. 414.

> Of the *green, thorny, bloomless* hedge,
> Of Rivers new with spring tide sedge,
> Of Primroses by sheltered rills,
> And Da[i]sies on the *aguish* hills.
>
> (ll. 6-12)

Autumn is all ripeness, warmth, plumpness; Spring is immature, cold, and thorny. Its light is greenish, faint, and chilly; Autumn's is the rosy hue of barred clouds, which "*bloom* the soft-dying day" (ll. 25-26). Keats, it appears, has felt his way to the essential qualities of the seasons through delicate sensuous intuitions—especially through images of touch.

The tactual imagery of Shelley is less organic than Keats's. It does not, like Keats's, blend inseparably with the total meaning of his poetry. Like his visual imagery, it is to some degree generalized, but it is firm and definite. Like his visual imagery it is a solid background, a framework—sometimes a network—behind his foreground of evanescence, change, and motion. Shelley's cloud-capped towers generally have firm bases; his visionary Athens, for example, in the *Ode to Liberty:*

> Athens arose; a city such as vision
> Builds from the purple *crags* and silver *towers*
> Of *battlemented* cloud, as in derision
> Of kingliest *masonry*: the ocean *floors*
> *Pave* it; the evening sky *pavilions* it;
> Its portals are inhabited
> By thunder-zoned winds . . .
>
> (ll. 61-67)

Here is the characteristic Shelleyan interplay of airiness and solidity, yielding and resistance. Athens to Shelley's imagination is evanescent as cloud, fleeting as sunset; but

his clouds and sunsets possess a paradoxical firmness of actuality with which he is unable or unwilling to invest so familiar a phenomenon as the human body.[48] His tactual imagery is simple, architectural, and strong.[49]

A notable instance of the use of a tactual image to give body and firmness is "The emerald light of leaf-entangled beams," from *Prometheus Unbound*, with its suggestion of hardness in "emerald" and of resistance in "leaf-entangled." This image is repeated in the "inter-tangled lines of light" (l. 197) of *The Witch of Atlas*, from which comes also one of Shelley's most tensile networks:

> The plant grew strong and green; the snowy flower
> Fell, and the long and gourd-like fruit began
> To turn the light and dew by inward power
> To its own *substance*; *woven tracery* ran
> Of *light firm texture, ribbed* and *branching*, o'er
> The *solid rind*, like a leaf's *veined* fan . . .
>
> (ll. 257-62)

In *The Starlit Dome* Professor Knight remarks a "valuable distinction" to be made in discussing Keats's imagery. "He does not," says he, "offer much that is unpleasing to the tactile sense: the jagged or rough plays small part."[50] This is, I think, true; and I agree that it is valuable, although I am constrained to point

48. Since Shelley was passionately fond of sculpture (see his "Critical Notices of the Sculpture in the Florence Gallery") his lack of feeling for the human body is rather surprising. His interest, however, was rather in its expression of the ideal than of the living particular form. "[To Shelley] sculpture expressed the indestructible order of the universe, the abstract, intellectual beauty."—Larrabee, *op. cit.*, p. 188.

49. Shelley uses *floor* or *floors* in a figurative sense nineteen times; *pave* and its variants forty times; *pavilion* and variants about twenty times. *Dome*, his favorite architectural image, occurs fifty-three times in his poetry.—Ellis.

50. *Op. cit.*, p. 260.

out one instance in which the poet threw himself wholeheartedly into enforcing upon the reader a suggestion
both "unpleasing" and "jagged":

> Instead of thrones, hard flint they sat upon,
> Couches of rugged stone, and slaty ridge
> Stubborn'd with iron.
>
> *(Hyperion*, II, 15-17)

This does not, however, affect the general validity of
the statement. More typical are Keats's "velvet summer
song" (*Endymion*, IV, 297), his "jellies soother than the
creamy curd" (*The Eve of St. Agnes*, l. 266), and his
"wealth of globed peonies" (*Ode on Melancholy*, l. 17).
The point to be made here is that there is in this respect
a remarkable difference between Keats and Shelley.

Shelley uses rough-edged, "jagged" images with
great frequency. The tactual feeling in his

> . . . serpents, *bony chains*, twisted around
> The *iron crags*, or within heaps of dust
> To which the tortuous strength of their last pangs
> Had *crushed* the *iron crags* . . .
>
> *(Prometheus Unbound*, IV, 305-8)

has an acerbity duplicated in many other passages. The
boat of the poet in *Alastor* flees through "dark and *ruffled*
waters" (l. 319), is swept by the whirlwind "Through
the white *ridges* of the *chaféd* sea" (l. 322), and dashes
on into a cleft of the mountains where "The *crags* closed
round with black and *jagged* arms" (l. 359). At the
close of *Alastor* the poet, his journey at an end, lies down
to die beneath a *horned* moon resting on *jagged* hills
(l. 649). Shelley's mountains are usually thus sharp and
angular, and many of his longer poems have a mountain-

ous background.[51] The pinnace of the Witch of Atlas, like the boat of the poet in *Alastor*, passes beside rugged cliffs,

> By many a star-surrounded *pyramid*
> Of *icy crag cleaving* the purple sky
>
> (ll. 310-11)

and into a haven

> . . . around which the solid vapors hoar,
> Based on the level waters, to the sky
> Lifted their *dreadful crags*, and, like a shore
> Of *wintry mountains*, inaccessibly
> Hemmed in, with *rifts* and *precipices* gray
> And hanging *crags*, many a cove and bay.
>
> (ll. 387-92)

Beyond this haven

> . . . the outer lake beneath the *lash*
> Of the wind's *scourge* foamed like a wounded thing,
> And the incessant *hail* with *stony clash*
> *Ploughed up* the waters . . .
>
> (ll. 393-96)

Shelley's sensitivity to harsh, sharp touch-images is

51. One should remember in distinguishing between the smooth surfaces of Keats and the angularities of Shelley that the former had seen only the Scotch Highlands, a little more than a year before the end of his brief poetic career; while the more widely travelled Shelley was familiar with the Swiss Alps as early as 1814. This fact does not, however, in itself explain Shelley's fondness for the rough-edged and sharp. In his letters to Peacock from Switzerland he notably concentrates upon images of this kind. See, for example, his description of the glacier of Montanvert: "On all sides precipitous mountains, the abodes of unrelenting frost, surround this vale: their sides are banked up with ice and snow, broken, heaped high, and exhibiting terrific chasms. The summits are sharp and naked pinnacles, whose overhanging steepness will not even permit snow to rest upon them. Lines of dazzling ice occupy here and there their perpendicular rifts, and shine through the driving vapours with inexpressible brilliance: they pierce the clouds like things not belonging to this earth."—Letter 4, *Peacock's Memoirs of Shelley*, p. 111.

perhaps most definitively realized in the soliloquy of
Prometheus, *Prometheus Unbound*, Act I:

> The crawling *glaciers pierce* me with the *spears*
> Of their *moon-freezing crystals*; the *bright chains*
> *Eat* with their *burning cold into* my bones.
> Heaven's winged hound, polluting from thy lips
> His *beak* in poison not his own, *tears up*
> My heart . . .
>
> . . . .
>
> . . . the Earthquake-fiends are charged
> To *wrench* the *rivets* from my quivering wounds
> When the rocks *split* and close again behind;
> While from their loud abysses howling throng
> The genii of the storm, urging the rage
> Of whirlwind, and *afflict* me with *keen* hail.

> (ll. 31-43)

The Titan's agony is the pain of cutting, of tearing, of
splitting, reinforced by the sensations of cold which
merge with the ungentle touch of the knife. He is pierced
by the spears of the glaciers, whether only by the intense
cold of the glacial air or actually by the sharp edges of
their "moon-freezing crystals" as well. The "bright
chains" which eat into his bones do so in physical fact,
as well as figuratively by their burning cold. And in
like manner the "keen hail" afflicts him, piercing his
flesh with knife-like edges as well as knife-like chill.

In treatment of sensations of heat and cold Shelley is
generally, as in the Prometheus soliloquy, harsh, keen-
edged, and painful. Cold to him is piercing and agoniz-
ing; it is an enemy to man.[52] To Keats, however, cold
is usually pleasurable; he accepts it, even delights in it.

52. Shelley's dislike of cold is well known, and too generally commented upon,
I think, to require documentation.

As with other sensations, his experience of it is complex
and deep. Sometimes he describes it in terms of its
opposite, heat, striving by this paradox to express his
feeling of its essential quality, as in

> Let the red wine within the goblet *boil*,
> Cold as a bubbling well . . .
>
> (*Hyperion*, III, 18-19)

or the *Ode to a Nightingale*, wherein wine is both cold
and warm also; its essence is "the warm South," "Cool'd
a long age in the deep-delved earth." Coolness is sweet
to him: in *I Stood Tiptoe*, for example, the air is cooling
(l. 2), May flowers are "moist, cool, and green," (ll.
29-33), the minnows "taste the luxury of sunny beams /
Tempered with coolness" (ll. 73-74), the ripples "cool
themselves among the em'rald tresses" of reeds (ll.
81-82), and ethereal breezes cool the fevered sleep of
the languid sick. There are similar instances of Keats's
pleasure in *Endymion:* Proserpine takes refuge from
"Hell, obscure and hot," to dabble "on the cool and
sluicy sands" (I, 943-46); Endymion is refreshed by the
touch of spray from waterfalls, "Alive and dazzling
cool" (II, 609); and he lingers in his journey through
the underworld to enjoy the "cool wonder" of a sub-
terranean grotto (II, 878-85). In later poems the "cool-
rooted" flowers of the *Ode to Psyche* recall the May
flowers of *I Stood Tiptoe*, while in the *Ode on Indolence*
occurs the most compactly sensuous of all Keats's cool-
ness-images, "*cool-bedded* in the flowery grass."

Even his more uncompromising sensations of cold
are pleasurable. To hark back to the reference in Keats's
"Autumn-letter" to the "chilly green of Spring," and

n *The Eve of St. Mark* to the "chilly sunset" which
aintly tells of "unmatur'd green vallies cold," this chill
s to the poet the very essence of his experiencing of
Spring, and pleasurable for its associations with the
"green" and the faint sunlight which help to make up
he sum of his experience of it. Pleasurable also is Keats's
most elaborate description of cold, in the opening stanzas of *The Eve of St. Agnes.* The winter evening is, indeed,
"bitter chill," and yet this chill is so portrayed as to
be an object of aesthetic regard, without the pain of
direct sensation.

> St. Agnes' Eve—Ah, bitter chill it was!
> The owl, for all his feathers, was a-cold;
> The hare limp'd trembling through the frozen grass,
> And silent was the flock in woolly fold:
> Numb were the Beadsman's fingers, while he told
> His rosary, and while his frosted breath,
> Like pious incense from a censer old,
> Seem'd taking flight for heaven, without a death.
>
> (ll. 1-8)

.   .   .   .

> The sculptur'd dead, on each side, seem to freeze.

.   .   .   .

> Knights, ladies, praying in dumb orat'ries
> He passeth by; and his weak spirit fails
> To think how they may ache in icy hoods and mails.
>
> (ll. 14-18)

Cold is in every line; the verse of the slow Spenserian
stanzas lingers and hangs upon it. It is cumulative, furthermore, the impression gaining by repetition in intensity and climaxed by the Beadsman's imaginative
attribution of his feelings to "the sculptur'd dead." The

result, however, is aesthetic pleasure, arising from contemplation of a perfectly conceived and executed poetic effect. One participates in the misery of the owl, the limping hare, the silent sheep, and the shivering Beadsman, as each figure in turn is presented to the imagination; but misdirected sympathy disappears as the evening scene forms itself into a whole. These images function as parts of a totality far removed from the impact of raw, immediate sensation, a restrained and muted countertheme to the warm, youthful love of Madeline and Porphyro.

In contrast, Shelley's images of cold are sharper, more direct in impact, and somehow "harder." Their characteristics are plain as early as the youthful *Queen Mab*, in which he envisions a scene

> Where silence undisturbed might watch alone—
> So cold, so bright, so still . . .

(IV, 18-19)

and where

> . . . the sulphurous smoke
> Before the icy wind slow rolls away,
> And the bright beams of frosty morning dance
> Along the spangling snow.

(IV, 59-62)

In Shelley cold is akin to hard surfaces, impervious brightness, sharp-faulted mountains, stillness. It is somehow deathly. The background of the fatal drama of *Alastor* is the "icy caves" of the Caucasus (l. 143), and the "icy summits" of its "ethereal cliffs"(ll. 351-52). Cold, as we have noted, is part of the agony of Prometheus, tied to his

> . . . wall of eagle-baffling mountain,
> Black, *wintry*, *dead*, unmeasured . . .
>
> (*Prometheus Unbound*, I, 20-21)

Among the plagues which rain down upon him are "alternate frost and fire," and "cutting hail" (I, 266-70).[53] Sensations of hardness and sharpness are further evident in "The crystal-wingéd snow" which clings about him in "the moony night" (I, 383-84), and in the "keen ice" which attacks the "linked sleep" of Ione and Panthea. Cold is associated with the needle-like sharpness of peaks in

> . . . far on high the keen sky-cleaving mountains
> From icy spires of sunlike radiance fling
> The dawn . . .
>
> (II, iii, 28-30)

In *Prometheus Unbound* cold is a symbol of reaction and death. The deliverance from this winter and death is the thaw and the avalanche of spring:

> Hark! the rushing snow!
> The sun-awakened avalanche! whose mass,
> Thrice sifted by the storm, had gathered there
> Flake after flake, in heaven-defying minds
> As thought by thought is piled, till some great truth
> Is loosened, and the nations echo round . . .
>
> (II, iii, 36-41)

While the touch of Prometheus endows the Earth with a spring-like warmth, so that she joyfully exclaims

> . . . through my withered, old, and icy frame
> The warmth of an immortal youth shoots down . . .
>
> (III, iii, 88-89)

53. Cf. above, p. 71.

In a sense the action of *Prometheus Unbound* is a symbolic struggle between Cold, representing Evil, Reaction, and Death; and Warmth, the emblem of Good, Life, and Liberation.[54] Warmth conquers through the life-giving touch of Prometheus the Fire-Bringer.

In sum, Shelley describes cold as if he hates it like an enemy, the Principle of Evil in a kind of Manichaean dualism of existence, while Keats accepts it as a pleasurable part of the wholeness of sensational experience. In Shelley it is bitter, piercing, painful; in Keats it is rounded and, as it were, humanized by his acceptance of it.

Keats's images of heat, like his cold-images, are in the great majority of instances agreeable to the sense. Typically they suggest a mellow, genial warmth. We have already noticed the pervasive warmth of *To Autumn*, and in *Hyperion* and the *Ode to a Nightingale* the sunny warmth imprisoned in the cold body of wine. In these two latter examples heat and cold are fused in a single impression. Keats also *tempers* one feeling with another in such images as the minnows in *I Stood Tiptoe*, who

> . . . taste the luxury of sunny beams
> Temper'd with coolness

and in the exquisite modulation of

> . . . rain-scented eglantine
> Gave temperate sweets to that well-wooing sun;

54. Shelley loved and thrived upon heat. He wrote *The Cenci*, for example, at the Villa Valsovano near Leghorn, on a terrace at the top of the house, where "the dazzling sunlight and heat made it almost intolerable to every other; but Shelley basked in both. . . ."—Mary Shelley, Note to *The Cenci*, quoted in *The Complete Poetical Works of Percy Bysshe Shelley*, ed. G. E. Woodberry, p. 207.

> The lark was lost in him; cold springs had run
> To warm their chilliest bubbles in the grass . . .
>
> (*Endymion*, I, 100-3)

or in *The Fall of Hyperion* "the small warm rain" which "Melts out the frozen incense from all flowers" (I, 98-99).

Keats does not, like Shelley, contrast and oppose to each other heat and cold as Evil and Good, but accepts them as equally good, interesting, and desirable. The warmth of young love in *The Eve of St. Agnes*, with its "full-blown rose" (l. 136) and "warm unnerved arm" (l. 280) does not clash with the chill, "pallid moonshine" (l. 200) of the winter night, but blends and harmonizes contrapuntally with it. In a grimmer context, on one of the few occasions in which Keats portrays heat and cold at their fierce extremes, the two merge together:

> . . . with a pang
> As hot as death's is chill, with fierce convulse.
>
> (*Hyperion*, III, 128-29)

He often describes love as warmth. In *Isabella* Lorenzo compares the favors of his mistress to a "summer clime," amid which he will

> . . . taste the blossoms that unfold
> In its ripe warmth . . .
>
> (ll. 66-67)

The enjoyment of love requited and fulfilled is "like a lusty flower in June's caress" (l. 72). In *Lamia* the god Hermes feels at the mere thought of his wood nymph a "celestial heat" which burns "from his winged heels

to either ear" (I, 22-23); at her sight he burns once more
for "one warm, flush'd moment" (I, 129-30). Impetu-
ously he approaches her, and she cowers before him,

> . . . self-folding like a flower
> That faints into itself at evening hour:
> But the God fostering her chilled hand
> She felt the warmth, her eyelids open'd bland,
> And, like new flowers at morning song of bees,
> Bloom'd, and gave up her honey to the lees.
>
> (I, 138-43)

Shelley, except for his use of warmth to symbolize
spiritual regeneration, is characteristically sharp of edge
in his heat-imagery. He goes to extremes; his heat is
burning, mordant.[55] He feels it intensely; his realization
of it goes far toward enlivening the eighteenth-century
conventionality of some of *Queen Mab*'s feebler moments,
such as

> . . . the burning plains
> Where Libyan monsters yell
>
> (II, 216-17)

and

> Those deserts of immeasurable sand,
> Whose age-collected fervors scarce allowed
> A bird to live, a blade of grass to spring,
> Where the shrill chirp of the green lizard's love
> Broke on the sultry silentness alone . . .
>
> (VIII, 70-74)

To turn to verse fully representative of Shelley at the
height of his powers, reference to the treatment of heat
in *Prometheus Unbound* sufficiently exemplifies his quality.

55. See above, p. 71.

In Act I Prometheus prophesies that the Omnipotence of Jupiter will be

> . . . a crown of *pain*
> To cling *like burning gold* round thy dissolving brain!
>
> (I, 290-91)

The Titan on his rock suffers as keenly from heat as from cold. At night he endures the myriad onslaught of "the crystal-winged snow," and by day the sun "*splits* his *parched* skin" (I, 383-85). "Alternate frost and *fire*" *eat* into him (I, 268-69), an idea repeated in II, iv, 53-55, wherein "alternating *shafts* of frost and fire" drive the "shelterless, pale tribes" of humanity to mountain caves. The vision of Prometheus, induced in him by the suggestions of Furies, of martyrs to Christianity "*impaled* in *lingering fire*" (I, 612), is powerful and unpleasant, as is the image of Thetis oppressed by the "*quick* flames" and *penetrating* presence of Jupiter in III, i, 36-39. In all these examples a common sharpness and penetrative quality is present, vividly and imaginatively expressed.

IV   The auditory images of Keats are often soft, almost always full-toned and sweet. In his verse there are no dissonances; at his loudest he sings effortlessly, with "full-throated ease." In Shelley's sound-images, on the other hand, one can clearly distinguish between pleasant and unpleasant, and the unpleasant is more fully realized. Keats, like Milton, is "organ-toned," while Shelley has frequently a violin-like stridency.[56] The "shrill, keen joyance" of the sky-

---

56. Many of Shelley's friends have left on record comments about the shrillness

lark strikes Shelley's most characteristic note; the essential sound of Keats has the smoothness of the "solemn tubes" which accompany the ceremonious opening of Hyperion's palace-door (*Hyperion*, I, 206).

At the lower end of Keats's register are sounds so faint that they barely rise above silence and in their passing serve only to enforce it. Such is the

> . . . little noiseless noise among the leaves,
> Born of the very sigh that silence heaves

of *I Stood Tiptoe* (ll. 11-12), and in *Hyperion* the

> . . . one gradual solitary gust
> Which comes upon the silence and dies off
> As if the ebbing air had but one wave . . .[57]

> (I, 76-78)

Soft humming and buzzing noises are frequent in Keats; for him nature has no discordances. The "impatient doves" of the chariot of Venus in *Endymion* set up a "hum celestial" (II, 580-81). To Keats the buzz of bees is full and mellow, strained through honey:

> . . . take thence a skim
> Of mealy sweets, which myriads of bees
> Buzz from their honied wings . . .

> (*Endymion*, II, 994-96)

---

of his voice. Peacock, for example, remarks, "This defect he certainly had; but it was chiefly observable when he spoke under excitement. Then his voice was not only dissonant, like a jarring string, but he spoke in sharp fourths, the most unpleasing sequence of sound that can fall on the human ear."—*Op. cit.*, p. 16.

57. In *The Eve of St. Agnes* Porphyro's vigil in the closet of Madeline's chamber occasions an impressive silence-image of a somewhat different nature:

> . . . then from the closet [he] crept,
> Noiseless as fear in a wide wilderness. . . (ll. 249-50)

Shriller insects he constrains to sing in soft minors. In the *Nightingale* the murmurous hum of flies blends with the quiet of summer evening (l. 50). The final stanza of *To Autumn* renders most completely the smooth, full harmony of the Keatsian sound-instrument, in its symphonic blending of various keys.)

> Then in a wailful choir the small gnats mourn
> Among the river sallows, borne aloft
> Or sinking as the light wind lives or dies;
> And full-grown lambs loud bleat from hilly bourn;
> Hedge-crickets sing; and now with treble soft
> The red-breast whistles from a garden-croft;
> And gathering swallows twitter in the skies.

Gnats, lambs, and crickets are creatures far from mellifluous by nature, but in Keats they become so, through the subtle influence of his characteristic tone.

There are few storms, few troubled seas in Keats; his winds are gentle and low-toned.[58] The voice of his Nature is sweet and muted. Not so with Shelley, who is fond of describing the catastrophic and goes in for tempests, earthquakes, and wild waters. The "whirlpools and waves" of *Alastor*, which "rage and resound forever" about the base of the Caucasus (l. 357), cannot be duplicated from the poetry of Keats. The roar of thunder also is often to be heard in Shelley's verse (*Queen Mab*, IV, 27-28; *Alastor*, l. 343; *The Cloud*, ll.

---

58. For exceptions see the sonnet *On the Sea*, and the description of the voice of Enceladus in *Hyperion*, II, 305-07:

> The ponderous syllables, like sullen waves
> In the half-glutted hollows of reef-rocks,
> Came booming thus . . .

The tone of these passages, however, is deep, not harsh or shrill. There is a certain tranquillity about them. One might also recall the storm in *The Eve of St. Agnes*.

19-20). He strikes a shriller note with not infrequent "howls" and "yells" (*Queen Mab*, II, 217, VIII, 81; *Alastor*, ll. 565; *Prometheus Unbound*, I, 41, 95, 434, 449),[59] and occasionally a tone of plangent and rough-voiced agony, as in

> . . . a low and yet dreadful groan
> Quite unsuppressed is tearing up the heart
> Of the good Titan, as storms tear the deep,
> And beasts hear the sea moan in inland caves.
>
> (*Prometheus Unbound*, I, 578-81)

Shelley's more agreeable auditory images are numerous but less fully realized than his discordances. He throws out general suggestions, often alluring but sometimes vague and conventional. His references to music, for example, are very numerous[60]—far more so than Keats's—but they are more generalized, less weighty. His music is sweet, but elemental and unindividualized; it is thin. Keats's musical effects are more full-toned and various, as well as more self-consciously finished. In Shelley's *Prometheus Unbound*, for example, one finds references to "a sea profound of ever-spreading sound" (III, i, 84), and "The ocean-like enchantment of strong sound" (IV, 203), fraught with a vagueness typical of the poet in this regard. Keats is generally far more sensuous and far more elaborate, as is evidenced by such a set bravura piece as his invocation to Music in *Isabella:*

> O Melancholy, linger here awhile!
> O Music, Music, breathe despondingly!

59. This may be a legacy of Shelley's juvenile love of Gothic romance. The poems scattered through his own *St. Irvyne* are copiously supplied with yelling ghosts, yelling night-ravens, howling mountain-winds, raving storms, groaning demons, and shrieking owls.

60. There are approximately 133 of them.—Ellis.

> O Echo, Echo, from some sombre isle,
> Unknown, Lethean, sigh to us—O sigh
>
> . . . .
>
> Moan hither, all ye syllables of woe
> From the deep throat of sad Melpomene!
> Through bronzed lyre in tragic order go,
> And touch the strings into a mystery;
> Sound mournfully upon the winds and low . . .[61]

> > (ll. 433-36, 441-45)

The studied repetition of *m*'s, the interlacing of dark *o* sounds in

> O Ech*o*, Ech*o*, from some s*o*mbre isle,
> Unkn*o*wn . . .

and

> M*o*an hither, all ye syllables of w*o*e
> From the deep thr*o*at of sad Melpomene,

imitate onomatopoetically the deep and mournful note of the "bronzed lyre."

Keats's rather infrequent olfactory images are rounded, heavy, and pervasive. The lovers' "bower of hyacinth and musk" of *Isabella* (l. 86), the "embalmed darkness" and "soft incense" of the *Nightingale*, are representative of their characteristic soft and oppressive pungency. Incense, with its sacerdotal and ritual connotations, evidently appealed strongly to his senses and imagination. Its heavy fumes overcloud the brilliant banquet-scene in *Lamia:*

61. See also the "earnest trumpet" and "kissing cymbals" of *Endymion*, IV, 197-98; the "silver, snarling trumpets" and Music with "golden tongue," "yearning like a God in pain" of *The Eve of St. Agnes* (ll. 20, 31, 56); the "Voices of soft proclaim, and silver stir / Of strings in hollow shells" and the "solemn tubes / Blown by the serious Zephyrs" of *Hyperion* (I, 130-31, 205-8); and in *Lamia* "The soft, lute-fingered Muses" and "Deaf to his throbbing throat's long, long melodious moan" (I, 73-75).

Before each lucid pannel fuming stood
A censer fed with myrrh and spiced wood,

.   .   .   .

. . . fifty wreaths of smoke
From fifty censers their light voyage took
To the high roof, still mimick'd as they rose
Along the mirror'd walls by twin-clouds odorous.

(ll. 175-82)

In *The Eve of St. Agnes* Keats compares the frosted breath
of the shivering Beadsman to "pious incense from a
censer old" (l. 7). The sacrificial fire in the temple of
The Fall of Hyperion sends forth "Maian incense," which
spreads around—

Forgetfulness of everything but bliss,
And clouded all the altar with soft smoke.

(I, 104-5)

Keats offers before the neglected shrine of Psyche "incense sweet / From swinged censer teeming" (*Ode to
Psyche*, ll. 46-47). The lonely godhead of Hyperion is
fed with incense:

Blazing Hyperion on his orbed fire
Still sat, still snuff'd the incense, teeming up
From man to the sun's God.[62]

(I, 166-68)

This latter conception of Hyperion alone in his palace
of the sun, still godlike but filled with premonitions of
disaster, calls forth Keats's most vivid and pungent odor
image:

62. Keats's use of "teem" is indicative of the kind of effect he sought. The word
is pervasive, weighty, and intense. Besides these instances of its use in *Hyperion* and
the *Ode to Psyche* note also the "feast / Teeming with odours" in *Lamia*, II, 132-33.

> . . . when he would taste the spicy wreaths
> Of incense, breath'd aloft from sacred hills,
> Instead of sweets, his ample palate took
> Savour of poisonous brass and metal sick.
>
> (I, 186-89)

Shelley's olfactory images, somewhat more numerous than those of Keats, are more generalized, lighter, and as a whole less sensuous. The flower odors of *The Sensitive Plant*, the

> . . . jessamine faint, and the sweet tube rose
> The sweetest flower for scent that blows
>
> (I, 37-38)

and "clouds faint with the fragrance they bear" (I, 89), like the "champak odors. . . / Like sweet thoughts in a dream" of *The Indian Serenade*, have a vague ecstasy of sense and emotion typical of his more agreeable images of smell. His use of generalized words like "odour" and "fragrance" is significantly frequent.[63]

In Shelley's olfactory imagery there is, however, a powerfully realized strain of the sinister. The smell of pestilence and decay not infrequently arises from his verse. In his description of Plague in *The Revolt of Islam* he takes full advantage of the opportunities provided by his subject:

> . . . the thirsting air did claim
> All moisture, and a rotting vapor passed
> From the unburied dead, invisible and fast.
>
> . . . .
> . . . . Each well

63. "Fragrant" and "fragrance" occur twenty-two times in Shelley's poetry; "odour," "odours," "odorous," and their compounds sixty-seven times.—Ellis.

>   Was choked with rotting corpses, and became
>   A caldron of green mist . . .
>
>   (X, 115-17, 181-83)

The odors which pervade the dying garden in *The Sensitive Plant* are strikingly and unpleasantly forceful and imaginative in conception. Weeds stifle the air with their rank lushness:

>   . . . the dock, and henbane, and hemlock dank,
>   Stretched out its long and hollow shank,
>   And stifled the air till the dead wind stank.
>
>   (III, 55-57)

The Lady of the garden lies dead amid her dying flowers, and from her unburied body a "smell, cold, oppressive and dank" seeps "through the pores of the coffin plank" (III, 11-12). Above this scene of death wanders a "northern whirlwind," "Like a wolf that had smelt a dead child out" (III, 106-7).[64]

The olfactory imagery of the two poets presents the same set of contrasting qualities as do their auditory images. Keats is heavier, more concrete, and more uniformly agreeable to the sense. Shelley is not lacking in ability to portray sensation, but his most vivid olfactory descriptions are repulsive, while his pleasurable images convey merely a vague emotional ecstasy. The unity of Keats's sensory perceptions of the world contrasts with the sharp dualism of pleasant-unpleasant in Shelley. Difference of subject matter no doubt plays some part in determining this difference, although most probably choice of subject is in itself related to sense-preference.

---

64. Cf. *Prometheus Unbound*, I, 339-40:
>   "The hope of torturing him smells like a heap
>   Of corpses after battle."

But if we compare Keats's treatment of the mouldering
head of the murdered Lorenzo

> (Then in a silken scarf—sweet with the dews
>   Of precious flowers pluck'd in Araby,
>   And divine liquids come with odorous ooze
>   Through the cold serpent-pipe refreshfully,—
>   She wrapp'd it up . . .
>
>   [*Isabella*, ll. 409-13])

with Shelley in any parallel situation,[65] the fundamental
contrast remains. With Keats the "wormy circumstance," the raw fact of putrefying flesh, is hidden in
silken fabrics, and the smell of death overpowered by
sweet odors; Shelley, as we have seen, had a more direct
method of describing the body's decay.

This contrast also obtains in the matter of gustatory
imagery, although here the evidence is slight. In such
passages as can be found to bear upon the question the
difference in quality and emphasis is marked. In life
Shelley was a vegetarian, despite his occasional indul-
gence in the "well-peppered mutton-chops" of Peacock's
prescription.[66] He had little taste for food and drink.[67]

---

65. The closest parallel, ironically enough, is a passage in *Adonais:*
> "The leprous corpse, touched by this spirit tender
>   Exhales itself in flowers of gentle breath;
>   Like incarnations of the stars, when splendor
>   Is changed to fragrance, they illumine death
>   And mock the merry worm that wakes beneath" (ll. 172-76).

Shelley's emphasis, I think, is rather on the "leprous corpse" and the "merry worm"
than upon the "flowers of gentle breath."

66. Peacock, *op. cit.*, pp. 38-39, 54-55. See *Queen Mab*, VIII, especially the superbly
ridiculous
> ". . . no longer now
>   He [Man] slays the lamb that looks him in the face,
>   And horribly devours his mangled flesh . . ." (VIII, 211-13).

67. Haydon describes Shelley somewhat cholerically as a "hectic, spare, weakly

Keats, on the other hand, while neither glutton nor epicure,[68] was apparently accustomed to dine with both discrimination and enjoyment.[69] This difference is in some degree indicated in their poetry.

Keats's love of wine finds its definitive expression in the richly sensuous *Ode to a Nightingale*, in which he calls for "a draught of vintage," a "beaker full of the warm South, / Full of the true, the blushful Hippocrene" (ll. 11-18). In the *Ode on Melancholy* he uses the pleasure of tasting both literally and figuratively to signify an extreme and dangerous height of physical enjoyment. Melancholy is visible in her proper form to him only

> . . . whose strenuous tongue
> Can burst joy's grape against his palate fine
>
> (ll. 27-28)

His description of the repast set out by Porphyro in *The Eve of St. Agnes* is a companion-piece to the passage in praise of wine in the *Nightingale:*

> . . . a heap
> Of candied apple, quince, and plum, and gourd;

---

yet intellectual creature . . . carving a bit of brocoli or cabbage on his plate, as if it had been the substantial wing of a chicken."—*The Autobiography and Memoirs of Benjamin Robert Haydon*, ed. Tom Taylor, I, 253.

68. See the old canard of Haydon's, which has made a considerable impression: ". . . he flew to dissipation as a relief. . . . For six weeks he was scarcely sober, and—to show what a man does to gratify his appetites when once they get the better of him— once covered his tongue and throat as far as he could reach with cayenne pepper in order to appreciate the 'delicious coldness of claret in all its glory'—his own expression."—*Ibid.*, I, 302.

69. ". . . now I like Claret whenever I can have Claret I must drink it,—'tis the only palate affair I am at all sensuous in. . . . I said this same Claret is the only palate-passion I have I forgot game—I must plead guilty to the breast of a Partridge, the back of a hare, the backbone of a grouse, the wing and side of a Pheasant and a Woodcock *passim*."—*Letters*, p. 302.

> With jellies soother than the creamy curd,
> And lucent syrops, tinct with cinnamon;
> Manna and dates, in argosy transferr'd
> From Fez; and spiced dainties, every one,
> From silken Samarcand to cedar'd Lebanon.
>
> (ll. 262-68)

Keats's use of "honey" exemplifies the lingering, luxurious sensuousness of his gustatory imagery. Desiring in *I Stood Tiptoe* to honor the nuptials of Endymion and Cynthia, he asks the boon of

> . . . three words of *honey*, that I might
> Tell but one wonder of thy bridal night!
>
> (ll. 209-10)

Bliss he describes in *Endymion* as "a breathless *honey*-feel" (I, 903). He mentions the

> . . . mealy sweets, which myriads of bees
> Buzz from their *honied* wings . . .
>
> (II, 996-97)

To him there is no joy

> . . . so sweet as drowsy noons,
> And evenings steep'd in *honied* indolence.
>
> (*Ode on Indolence*, ll. 36-37)

While he conveys to the reader the paradoxical sweetness of the serpent-woman Lamia's voice in a like image:

> Her voice was serpent, but the words she spake
> Came, as through bubbling *honey*, for Love's sake
>
> (*Lamia*, I, 64-65)

The heavily sensuous significance with which Keats freights the more abstract "sweets" is also to be re-

marked as typical. His "mealy sweets" (*Endymion*, II,
995), his "temperate sweets of that well-wooing sun"
(*Endymion*, I, 100), his "spire of teeming sweets"
(*Endymion*, I, 223-24), "each sweet / Wherewith the
seasonable month endows / The grass, the thicket, and
the fruit-tree wild" (*Nightingale*, ll. 43-45), and "The
day is gone, and all its sweets are gone" (*The Day is
Gone*, l. 1), have all of them the smack of actual and
luxurious sensation.

In contrast, Shelley's infrequent gustatory images
are generally either unrealized or disagreeable. Eating
and drinking in his poetry are undisguisedly metaphorical. Such suggestions as are conveyed by

> . . . the warm ether of the morning sun
> Wraps ere it drinks some cloud of wandering dew
> > (*Prometheus Unbound*, II, i, 87-88)

or

> Even as a vapor fed with golden beams
> That ministered on sunlight . . .
> > (*Alastor*, ll. 663-64)

make no appeal, to speak conservatively, to human
appetites. Images with a dash of the sinister, although
chiefly abstract, possess a somewhat greater power of
evocation, however, as in the case of figures like

> . . . Ruin calls
> His brother Death! A rare and regal prey
> He hath prepared, prowling around the world;
> Glutted with which thou mayst repose . . .
> > (*Alastor*, ll. 618-21)

and

> . . . Oh, that God,
> Profuse of poisons, would concede the chalice
> Which but one living man has drained . . .[70]
>
> > (*Alastor*, ll. 675-77)

V   In his organic imagery Keats is massive, smooth, and almost slumberous.[71] One of his more usual effects is the hypnotic. The opening of the *Ode to a Nightingale* is perhaps the most accessible and unmistakable example of the Keatsian spell, wrought by a subtle use of organic effects to relax the critical faculties of the reader and leave him helplessly receptive to the poet's suggestions:[72]

> My heart aches, and a drowsy numbness pains
> My sense, as though of hemlock I had drunk,
> Or emptied some dull opiate to the drains
> One minute past, and Lethe-wards had sunk. . . .

The almost hypnotic quality of these lines is the result of a close combination of sound and meaning. The concentration of the intense words *aches*, *numbness*, and *pains*, the suggestive power of *drowsy*, join with the half-hidden undersong[73] of assonance in *numbness*, *drunk*, *some*, *dull*, *one*, and *sunk* to overpower the reader. This same effect is notably present also in

70. Shelley uses poison-images ninety-four times in his poetry (Ellis); in Keats I can recall only one striking instance, "Turning to poison while the bee-mouth sips." —*Ode on Melancholy*, l. 24.

71. Cf. Keats's definition of poetry as "might half slumb'ring on its own right arm."—*Sleep and Poetry*, l. 237.

72. See M. R. Ridley, *Keats' Craftsmanship*, pp. 217-18.

73.   "Soft went the music the soft air along,
      While fluent Greek a vowel'd undersong
      Kept up among the guests . . ." (*Lamia*, II, 199-201).

> . . . *Ripe* was the *drowsy hour*
> The *blissful cloud* of *summer-indolence*
> *Benumb'd* my eyes; my *pulse* grew *less* and *less*
> *Pain* had no *sting*, and *pleasure's* wreath no *flower* . . .
>
> (*Ode on Indolence*, ll. 15-18)

as it is in the first stanza of the *Ode on Melancholy:*

> Make not your rosary of *yew*-berries,
> Nor let the beetle, nor the *death-moth* be
> Your *mournful* Psyche, nor the *downy owl*
> A partner in your *sorrow's* mysteries;
> For shade to shade will *come too drowsily*,
> And *drown* the *wakeful anguish* of the *soul*.[74]
>
> (ll. 5-10)

Many of Keats's organic images work through sensations of throbbing or vibrating. In his earlier verse on two occasions he imitates the beat of the pulse in a tour-de-force of technique: once in the incomplete line of the second sonnet to Haydon,

> These, these will give the world another heart,
> And other pulses. Hear ye not the hum
> Of mighty workings?—

in which, to my fancy at least, the verse is finished off by a triple pulsation,[75] suggesting also the throb of a great dynamo; and in the crude but vivid

> . . . His poor temples beat
> To the very tune of love—how sweet, sweet, sweet.
>
> (*Endymion*, II, 764-65)

Music in Keats often vibrates, in verses like the onomatopoetic

---

74. Cf. "What *misery* most *drowningly* doth sing" (*Endymion*, II, 281-82), and "Or I shall *drowse* beside thee, so my soul doth *ache* . . ." (*The Eve of St. Agnes*, l. 279).

75. The omission of the remainder of the line was at Haydon's suggestion.

> The earnest trumpet spake, and silver thrills
> From kissing cymbals made a merry din,
>
> > (*Endymion*, IV, 194-95)

and in *Hyperion*,

> Voices of soft proclaim, and silver stir
> Of strings in hollow shells
>
> > (I, 130-31),

and

> Leave the dinn'd air vibrating silverly
>
> > (II, 128).

Shelley's organic images have neither the hypnotic spell nor the powerful throb and beat of which Keats was master. They are lighter, less closely wedded to the subconscious workings of muscles and nerves. They are not, however, without force and poignancy. His images of pain, for example, are simple, direct, and deeply felt. Such are the anguished cry of Prometheus ringing over the peaks of Caucasus,

> Ah me! alas, pain, pain ever, forever!

and his own outburst in the *Ode to the West Wind*,

> I fall upon the thorns of life! I bleed!
>
> > (l. 54)

Many of Shelley's most powerful organic images have a sinister strain, the dark tinge which has been earlier noted in other connections. One could cite many examples, but two from the ordeal of Prometheus will suffice to illustrate their quality. The Furies, applying to the Titan a species of mental torture before the real commencement of their grim business, suggest under guise of inquiry:

Thou thinkest we will rend thee bone from bone
And nerve from nerve, working like fire within

.   .   .   .

That we will be dread thought beneath thy brain,
And foul desire round thine astonished heart,
And blood within thy labyrinthine veins
Crawling like agony?

(*Prometheus Unbound*, I, 475-76, 488-91)

In keeping with the breadth of scope and vastness of prospect characteristic of his visual imagery, Shelley has many images of swift and vertiginous falling and rising. There is a hint of this in the mere epithet "eagle-baffling" (*Prometheus Unbound*, I, 20), and in the famous "Pinnacled dim in the intense inane" (IV, 204), with their strong suggestions of dizzying altitude. His description of the skylark's flight is an excellent example:

Higher still and higher
From the earth thou springest
Like a cloud of fire
The blue deep thou wingest
And singing still dost soar, and soaring ever singest.

In the golden lightning
Of the sunken sun,
O'er which clouds are bright'ning
Thou dost float and run
Like an unbodied joy whose race is just begun.

These two stanzas are filled with a swiftly rising and swooping movement evoked partly by meaning and in part by sound. The verses have a rocking, alternating movement, from the heavy terminal pauses of the short lines and the long caesural pause in the final Alexan-

drines. This movement of sound induces in the reader an unusual receptivity to the suggestions of flight in *springest, wingest, soar, float,* and *run.* The rocking motion is accentuated by the parallelism of *singing-soar, soaring-singest;* and by the alternatives *float* and *run,* which balance the swift spasmodic striking-out of feet with a smooth leveling-off of poised wings. The net result is a decided organic sensation of vertiginous flight.

Shelley's rising images are complemented by images of falling. The "Song of the Spirits" from *Prometheus Unbound,* for example, calls up feelings of a dizzying vertical downward plunging.

> To the deep, to the deep,
> Down, down
>
> . . . .
>
> While the sound whirls around,
> Down, down!
>
> . . . .
>
> In the depth of the deep
> Down, down!
>
> (II, iv, 54ff.)

In Shelley kinesthetic impulses mingle with organic in frequent images of tearing, rending, cleaving, piercing, shattering, bursting, breaking, etc.[76] These are peculiarly swift of action, forceful but fleeting in their effect, so that sensation is soon past, although momentarily violent. I quote from *A Vision of the Sea* a passage unusually rich in Shelley's characteristic kinesthetic imagery. It is a vigorous account of a shipwreck:

76. In Shelley's poetry *tearing* occurs 63 times, *rending* 38, *cleaving* 50, *piercing* 60, *shattering* 25, *bursting* 96, *breaking* 107, and the archaic *riving* 24 times.—Ellis. This calculation includes all grammatical forms of these words, but not their compounds.

> . . . now down the sweep
> Of the *wind-cloven* wave to the *chasm* of the deep
> It sinks . . .
> . . . the surf, like a chaos of stars, like a rout
> Of death-flames, like whirlpools of fire-flowing iron,
> With splendor and terror the black ship environ
> Or, like sulphur-flakes *hurled* from a mine of pale fire
> In fountains *spout* o'er it . . .
>
> .   .   .   .
>
> . . . *piercing* the sky from the floor of the sea
> The great ship seems *splitting*! it *cracks* like a tree
> While an earthquake is *splintering* its root, e'er the blast
> Of the whirlwind that *stripped* it of branches has passed.
> The intense thunder-balls which are raining from heaven
> Have *shattered* its mast, and it stands black and *riven*
>
> > (ll. 13ff.)

Typical also of Shelley's swift energy is this excerpt from *Prometheus Unbound*, filled with images of gripping, squeezing, splitting, and crushing:

> . . . prodigious shapes
> *Huddled* in gray annihilation, *split*,
> *Jammed* in the *hard*, black deep, and over these
> The anatomies of unknown wingéd things,
> And fishes which were isles of living scale,
> And serpents, *bony chains*, *twisted* around
> The *iron crags*, or within heaps of dust
> To which the *tortuous strength* of their last *pangs*
> Had *crushed* the *iron crags*; and over these
> The *jagged* alligator, and the might
> Of *earth-convulsing* behemoth . . .
>
> > (IV, 400-10)

In contrast to these swift and spasmodic images, which take instantaneous effect and instantaneously pass away, the kinesthetic in Keats evolves slowly, with

every element displayed in turn. Keats's technique is concentration and packed richness of sensation; he carries out his suggestions to the full. The kinesthetic imagery of Shelley strikes with a tingling shock, whereas Keats's images insinuate themselves slowly into our muscles and nerves until they finally rise to a crescendo of terrible effort. This slowness of development is evident even in the condensed violence of such a line as

> While Fate seem'd strangled in my nervous grasp,
>> (*Hyperion*, I, 105)

with its intensification of *strangled* by *nervous* and *grasp*. A more extensive example is

> At this, through all his bulk an *agony*
> *Crept gradual, from the feet unto the crown,*
> Like a *lithe serpent vast* and *muscular*
> *Making slow way*, with *head* and *neck convulsed*
> From *over-strained* might
>> (*Hyperion*, I, 259-63)

Keats is not content with the first image, in itself detailed and explicit, but enlarges and develops it by a second yet more concrete.[77]

Keats, it may be said without exaggeration, is of all poets the most leisurely in movement, Shelley among the swiftest. Keats has little motor imagery, while Shelley is astoundingly rich in it.[78] The fierce and fiery movement of Shelley finds adequate utterance as early as *Queen Mab*, in

77. Keats's search for fullness of sensation is apparent even in brief expressions like "smother'd up" (*Hyperion*, I, 106) and "pleasant smotherings" (*I Stood Tiptoe*, l. 132), rich alike in sound and sensuous feeling.

78. See charts, pp. 34-35.

> Whose *flashing* spokes, instinct with infinite life,
> *Bicker* and *burn* to gain their destined goal.[79]

(VIII, 152-53)

The flight of the poet in *Alastor* across the world, the dizzying transformations of *The Cloud*, the vertical climb of the skylark, the flashing apparitions of *Prometheus Unbound*, have a speed of motion almost omnipresent in Shelley.[80]

The melody itself of Shelley's verse is very often swift of pace, with light accents and unprecedented use of three-syllabled feet. Sound and meaning move in breathless unison in such verses as

> On the brink of the night and the morning
> My coursers are wont to respire;
> But the earth has just whispered a warning
> That their flight must be swifter than fire;
> They shall drink the hot speed of desire![81]

(*Prometheus Unbound*, II, v, 1-5)

and in the swift, light patter of

> Who, soothed to false repose by the fanning plumes above,
> And the music-stirring motion of its soft and busy feet,
> Dream visions of aërial joy, and call the monster, Love,
> And wake and find the shadow pain, as he whom now we greet.

(*Prometheus Unbound*, I, 777-80)

Keats, in contrast, is most himself in stately iambics,

79. Cf. ". . . O storm of death,
    Whose sightless speed divides this sullen night!" (*Alastor*, ll. 609-10)
80. He uses *speed* 73 times, *swift* 164, *sweep* 81, *rush* 55, *spring* 58, *fly* 144, *fast* 80, *flee* and *fled* 159 times.—Ellis.
81. Cf. "Others, with burning eyes, lean forth, and drink
    With eager lips the wind of their own speed . . ." (*Prometheus Unbound*, II, v, 135-36)

so packed and concentrated that they sometimes move
heavily: for example

> To bend with apples the moss'd cottage-trees,
> And fill all fruit with ripeness to the core;
> To swell the gourd, and plump the hazel-shells
> With a sweet kernel, to set budding more,
> And still more, later flowers for the bees . . .
>
> *(To Autumn,* ll. 5-9)

Almost every word has weight, even the articles and
prepositions. The stresses are not only heavy, but remarkably even of distribution; Keats's iambs are sometimes very like spondees,[82] a tendency which obviously
hinders movement.

Keats is often entirely static. The motionless Saturn
at the beginning of *Hyperion;* Autumn "sitting careless"
on her granary floor, or asleep on her furrow; Cupid and
Psyche in each other's arms; the silent and deserted town
of the *Ode on a Grecian Urn*—these are the very fabric of
his verse. Set in motion he is slow, smooth, and massive.
The slow settling to earth of the car of Venus (*Endymion,*
II, 516-25), the silent sail of the chariot of "mother
Cybele" with four maned lions haling "the sluggish

82. E.g., in

> "Bright star, would I were stedfast as thou art—
>   Not in lone splendour hung aloft the night . . ."
>
> "O soft embalmer of the still midnight . . ." (*To Sleep*)
>
> "And no birds sing . . ." (*La Belle Dame Sans Merci*)
>
> "Mid hush'd, cool-rooted flowers, fragrant-eyed . . ."
> "From chain-swung censer teeming . . ." (*Ode to Psyche*)
>
> "One morn before me were three figures seen . . ." (*Ode on Indolence*)
>
> "My heart aches, and a drowsy numbness pains . . ." (*Nightingale*)
>
> "No, no, go not to Lethe, neither twist
>   Wolf's-bane, tight-rooted, for its poisonous wine . . ." (*Ode on Melancholy*)

wheels'' (*Endymion*, II, 639-49), the gradual, indolent bursting of the foam on a "lengthened," rolling wave (*Endymion*, II, 347-50), the measured and dream-like pacing of the three figures Love, Ambition, and Poesy in the *Ode on Indolence*, are typically representative of his motor qualities. The nature of Shelley's motor imagery, on the other hand, is best exemplified by the fiery speed of the *Ode to the West Wind*:

> Thou on whose stream, mid the steep sky's commotion,
> Loose clouds like earth's decaying leaves are shed,
> Shook from the tangled boughs of Heaven and Ocean,
> Angels of rain and lightning . . .

(ll. 15-18)

SYNAESTHETIC IMAGERY

I   The function of all poetic imagery is to
           order, relate, and unify disparate modes of
physical, mental, and emotional experience. Synaesthesia is a particular species of imagery which purposes
chiefly to establish relationships between the different
modes of sensation, finding, for example, analogies between color and music, music and odor, odor and color.[1]
Baudelaire in his sonnet "Correspondances" at once
describes and exemplifies the aim of the synaesthetic
image as he sees it:

> Comme de longs échos qui de loin se confondent
> Dans une ténébreuse et profonde unité,
> Vaste comme la nuit et comme la clarté,
> Les parfums, les couleurs et les sons se répondent.
> Il est des parfums frais comme des chairs d'enfants,
> Doux comme les hautbois, verts comme les prairies;
> Et d'autres, corrompus, riches et triomphants,

[1]. Professor June E. Downey, writing primarily from the point of view of the
psychologist, distinguishes between "true" or psychological synaesthesia, "in which
sensations of a given sensory quality regularly and uniformly arouse sensations of
another sensory tone," and "coloured thinking or the employment of sense-analogies
in a figurative or reflective way."—*Creative Imagination*, p. 95. See also "Literary
Synesthesia," *The Journal of Philosophy, Psychology, and Scientific Methods*, IX, 490.
She concludes that poetic synaesthesia is generally not "true" synaesthesia. The
distinction is of little significance here.

Ayant l'expansion des choses infinies,
Comme l'ambre, le musc, le benjoin et l'encens,
Qui chantent les transports de l'esprit et des sens.

Scents, colours, and sounds melt and mingle with each other like far-off, fading echoes, perfumes are "fresh as the flesh of babes," "sweet as oboes," "green as meadows." The ultimate result is unity of sensation, vast, shadowy, and profound.

As Baudelaire's sonnet demonstrates, synaesthetic sense-transference is likely to be sudden and startling; it often cuts sharply across conventional patterns of feeling. Precisely the same effect is sometimes achieved by the swift merging of sensation and concept, however, in such an image as Marvell's "metaphysical"

Annihilating all that's made
To a *green thought*, in a green shade.

(*The Garden*)

Consequently this instantaneous fusion of the concrete and abstract will be considered in the present study, with some stretching of the privileges of definition, to be synaesthetic.

The literary value and significance of synaesthesia has been somewhat variously appraised. In the opinion of Irving Babbitt it is a symptom of a general confusion of the arts, originally fathered upon the world, with other monstrous progeny, by Rousseauist Romanticism.[2] Edmund Wilson cites it without comment in his *Axel's Castle* as an aspect of the extreme and indefinite sub-

2. ". . . it is merely a special aspect of a more general malady, of that excess of sentimental and scientific naturalism from which, if my diagnosis is correct, the occidental world is now suffering."—*The New Laokoon*, p. 185.

jectivity characteristic of Symbolist poetry.[3] Professor Cleanth Brooks, a lover of strangeness and heterogeneity in imagery, approves it as a species of metaphysical "wit."[4]

Modern synaesthesia, on which the remarks of Messrs. Babbitt, Wilson, and Brooks are based, stems mainly from the Symbolists and their precursor Poe.[5] It most frequently takes the form of "color-audition," or "tonal vision," in which sounds and colors are interchangeable. As a form of poetic imagery it is distinguished by its high degree of self-awareness and by the speed and surprise of its action; it is a literary artifice effective when sufficiently sudden in impact and *outré* in the terms of the analogy which it proposes. For the most part it works by swift but controlled violence, as in Francis Thompson's striking comparison of the rays of the setting sun with the blaring and clang of brasses:

> Thy visible music-blasts make deaf the sky,
> Thy cymbals clang to fire the Occident,
> Thou dost thy dying so triumphally:
> I *see* the crimson blaring of thy shawms!
>
> (*Ode to the Setting Sun*)

Although in theory a wholly legitimate extension of the principles which govern all imagery, poetic synaes-

---

3. P. 13. Wilson, like Babbitt, traces the synaesthetic tendency to Romanticism.

4. "It [synaesthesia] was never a characteristic of the Romantic poets. It represents a movement in the direction of metaphysical poetry."—*Modern Poetry and the Tradition*, p. 56.

5. See Poe's "Colloquy of Monos and Una" in which "taste and smell were inextricably confounded and became one sentiment, abnormal and intense. The rays of light of the candles set in the death-chamber affected me only as sound." Note also his "Haunted Palace," with its *flowing banners, winged odors, ramparts plumed and pallid,* and *sparkling echoes.*

thesia as it is practised by moderns is open to attack
from several directions. Its more serious manifestations,
in Baudelaire, Rimbaud, and others, diverge too far
from normal experience; they are involved, as Professor
Babbitt has said, in a "hopeless subjectivity."[6] No general agreement is possible about the appropriateness and
truth of the correspondences between different modes
of sense which the poet attempts to establish. Rimbaud's
well-known sonnet on the vowels,

> A black, E white, I red, U green, O blue,
> Vowels; some day I shall reveal your birth:
> A, black velvet swarm of flies that over earth
> Buzz to the foulest stench, abyss of hue
> Sombre; E frank with smoke and fierce intents,
> Spears of proud glaciers, white kings, blossom-dips . . .[7]

is expressive of perceptions too eccentric to be acceptable. Furthermore, even if one should admit the verity
of Rimbaud's color-vowel tone analogies, the fact remains that his attempted unification of sense-impressions
is not in itself a significant organization of experience.
It is lacking in conceptual and emotional depth of meaning, and tells us nothing of importance about our relations with actuality.[8] The limitations of synaesthesia
are unintentionally exposed in Huysmans' novel, *À
Rebours*. Huysmans reduces it to absurdity by carrying
it to its logical extreme. His hero, the exquisite Des
Esseintes, has a cupboard filled with assorted liqueurs,

6. *Op. cit.*, p. 182.

7. Quoted from Joseph T. Shipley, *The Quest for Literature*, p. 484.

8. The elaborate treatment of synaesthesia by such a contemporary poet as
John Gould Fletcher (see his Preface to *Goblins and Pagodas*, p. xx, and his various
"Symphonies" in color) in my opinion simply emphasizes its intrinsic triviality when
viewed as an independent and autonomous artistic principle.

each of which he has designated with the name of an orchestral instrument. The liqueurs correspond in taste to the tone of the instruments: curaçao to the clarinet, kümmel to the oboe, mint and anisette to the flute, etc.[9] By judiciously imbibing, Des Esseintes is able to play for himself elaborate symphonies.

Synaesthetic imagery in Shelley and Keats is generally less startling, less eccentric, and less self-conscious than the synaesthesia of the moderns. It works more quietly, blending itself with its background so as to remain unseen unless it is closely examined. It is less daringly subjective. Even the idealist Shelley would have refused to go as far as the Symbolist in trusting to his own perceptions; both Shelley and Keats display more deference toward average, normal experience than do their later rivals. Finally, the synaesthesia of Shelley and Keats is a means to an end, not an end in itself as it is to Rimbaud and Baudelaire. In all probability neither of the two Romantics recognized synaesthesia as an individual psychological phenomenon, so that for them sense-analogy was merely one of a number of effective poetic methods. They do not emphasize the single synaesthetic image as such, but merge it with larger complexes of concept and emotion. Its function is with them not to call attention to itself, but to aid in carrying out the purposes of the poem in which it occurs.

9. Cf. Babbitt, *op. cit.*, pp. 178-84.

II   Synaesthesia in Keats is a natural con-
          comitant of other qualities of his poetry.
Keats's verse is extraordinarily rich in sense-images, and
his sense-imagery is very full and comprehensive.[10] He
has at his command an unexampled abundance of vivid
sensory images. Therefore he slips readily from one order
of sensation to another when it suits his poetic purpose,
like a master improviser who transposes his theme into
a different key. Strong sensation is thus made to reinforce weak by his unusually powerful faculty of association; an odor-image may in a flash of associational
intuition be transformed into an image of weight, or
a sound-image take on the added sense of touch. Furthermore, synaesthesia is unusually fusional and swift in
action, and Keats's poetry is fusional and compact in the
highest degree, the more so as it gains in maturity. The
"intensity" of his verse is a result of intense compression, like a molten ore sublimed by enormous pressures.[11]

The synaesthetic imagery of Keats is almost always
actuated by a desire to attain the fullest possible sensuous effect. It frequently appears as a tendency to ally
sense-images with the sense of touch in order to make
them stronger and more concrete.[12] Whatever combina-

---

10. "The imagery of Keats's poetry has two notable characteristics. In the first
place, it is comprehensive, having images of all the sensations of the sensory system—
sensations of sight, hearing, touch, temperature, pressure, taste, smell, motor sensations, hunger, thirst, lust, etc. In the second place, it is sensuous, being rich in images
of the intimately physical sensations of touch, temperature, pressure, taste, smell,
and the internal sensations."—Claude Lee Finney, *The Evolution of Keats's Poetry*, II, 548.

11. M. R. Ridley has recorded in his *Keats' Craftsmanship* the history of the poet's
constant effort to attain the greatest possible compression and force in expressions
See also W. J. Bate, *Negative Capability*, pp. 53ff., on the relationship between Keats'.
tendency toward intense condensation and his "fusion of the senses."

12. *Ibid.*, p. 54.

tion of sensations he may happen to employ, however, he invariably invokes a stronger sense to reinforce a comparatively weak one.

Keats's pursuit of rich, full sensuous effects is incidental to a more arduous quest, his search for fullness and completeness of meaning. Sensation, powerful though it is in Keats's poetry, is but a single element in a highly complex unity. Consequently his fusions and transferences of sensation are incidental to his deeper, more complex syntheses of poetic experience, in which intellect, sense, and emotion are inseparably interwoven. His synaesthetic imagery is an outward manifestation of his intuitive sense of the Oneness of things, of the relationships between widely separate and dissimilar phenomena, of the intimate kinship of man and nature.[13] The secret of many of his sense-analogies lies in his unrivalled ability to absorb, sympathize with, and humanize natural objects, with effortless and instinctive ease.

Thus in the early *I Stood Tiptoe* he fuses sensation with emotion, the aesthetics of poetry with the aesthetics of nature:

> In the calm grandeur of a sober line,
> We see the waving of the mountain pine;

13. "He was immediately aware, through all his gifted senses, of the close interknitting of man, body, mind, and soul, with the green world of which he is a part. Reading, when he writes of spring, of autumn, one seems to be, not observing, but experiencing the quickening of spring, the ripening of autumn. That idea of oneness in all life, of organic relationship between all manifestations of life, toward which the natural philosophy of the time was groping, was with Keats . . . a sensation, as well as an instinct, an intuition. He was one in whom . . . there was immediate consciousness of the 'one life within us and abroad,' a physical as well as an emotional and spiritual awareness."—Margaret Sherwood, *Undercurrents of Influence in English Romantic Poetry*, p. 215.

> And when a tale is beautifully staid,
> We feel the safety of a hawthorn glade:
> When it is moving on luxurious wings,
> The soul is lost in pleasant smotherings . . .
>
> (ll. 127-32)

Strong personification, the sense of the humanity-nature relationship, is largely responsible for a sudden transition from hearing to motion in the image of the "meek and forlorn flower" in the same poem, so fixed upon its reflection in the water that

> *Deaf* to light Zephyrus it would not *move* . . .
>
> (l. 175)

Zephyrus is both the wind and a humanized deity, so that his coercive motor power is at the same time a kind of vocal persuasion. The image is complex; for the wind in actuality possesses the property of audibility as well as of motion and pressure.

Another kind of "humanization" occurs in

> . . . the *pillowy silkiness* that rests
> Full in the *speculation* of the stars
>
> (ll. 188-89)

verses characteristic of the "luxurious" early Keats. The cold, unearthly remoteness of the heavens takes on warm and sensuous personality by virtue of the fusion of tactual images of softness and fullness with the faint, almost abstract visual image "speculation."

In *Endymion* Keats synaesthetically endows light with breathing, throbbing sentience:

> . . . as the sunset peeps into a wood
> So saw he *panting light* . . .
>
> (II, 382-83)

It pulsates in regular bursts, and to this organic pulsation is added the further sensuous attribute of sound.[14] This interfusion of divergent senses at first seems forced, but in its setting it proves to be natural and functional. Endymion, following the light through "winding alleys," comes upon a group of slumbering Cupids. The general impression of sunlight resolves itself into living, breathing forms, and the unapproachable non-humanness of the sun's rays merges with the warm intimacy of human bodies.

This fusion of remote and forbidding natural phenomena with warm and intimate sensations of the body is more skillfully managed in one of the remarkable Alexandrines of *Lamia*,

> While, like held breath, the stars drew in their panting fires,
> (I, 300)

in which organic, visual, kinesthetic, and tactual images

14. A striking use of organic imagery in Keats to give sensuous tone is, "What misery most *drowningly* doth *sing* / In lone Endymion's ear . . ." (II, 281-82). Endymion's mood is revealed intuitively by the strongly organic "drowningly." This word is "intense"; Keats is suddenly bringing all his force to bear in a single concentrated effort. It is more direct and less subtle than Keats's mature imagery. He is trying to gain his effect by assertion rather than suggestion, and "drowningly" seems startling and a little out of keeping in its rather sentimental context. This attempt to get at the essence of physical experience by direct assertion seems to me closely related to his early use of abstract nouns to express the powerfully sensuous—such locutions as *dewiness, freshnesses, deliciousness, leafiness, flutterings, smotherings*. Of these Ernest de Sélincourt says, "His desire to place upon record his appreciation of nature and his enthusiasm for the beautiful has outrun his power of accurate portrayal, and he substitutes for that vivid delineation of significant detail which brings a whole picture before the mind terms which merely convey a vague and formless impression of it." —Appendix C, *The Poems of John Keats*, p. 600. This is excellent comment, but the fundamental point, in my opinion, is that these abstractions are attempts at compression and intensity which do not come off. Keats is too impatiently trying to strike to the heart of experience by methods too crude and direct; he is seeking to isolate the quality of sensuousness instead of setting forth the evidence of the senses.

combine. The cementing agent is Keats's power of personification, which in this instance synthesizes man and
nature, the organic and the inorganic, so quietly and
inevitably that the magnitude of the feat is likely to
pass unnoticed. The magniloquent boast of the young
Apollo in *Hyperion* produces a similar effect:

> . . . Point me out the way
> To any one particular beauteous star,
> And I will flit into it with my lyre,
> And make its silvery spendour pant with bliss.

(III, 99-102)

The impersonal forms of astronomy grow poetic and
warmly emotional under the magic touch of Keats's
mythologizing hand.

Synaesthesia in the poetry of Keats is generally compressive, complexly associational, functional, and unobtrusive. His sense-analogies are for the most part prepared for and explained by their contexts. In one of his
not infrequent references to wine, for example, pleasure
in its chill is synaesthetically allied to delight in its
rich coloring:

> . . . Here is wine,
> Alive with sparkles—never, I aver,
> Since Ariadne was a vintager,
> So *cool* a *purple* . . .

(*Endymion*, II, 441-44)

"Cool" is a quality of "purple," but "purple" is in
part merely a metaphor for "wine," so that the figure
balances precariously, ready to slip in two different
directions. This relationship of "cool-wine" as well as
"cool-purple" lends to the image a common-sense veri-

similitude which renders it easily acceptable, and lessens the surprise of the fusion of visual and tactual sensations. The synaesthetic effect results in some degree from intensely compressed expression.

Similarly complex are Endymion's impressions of water-spray in his journey through the underworld. The spray rises before him "Alive, and *dazzling cool*. . ." (II, 608-9). The visual and tactual sensations of "dazzling" and "cool" are simultaneous, but they do not fuse, since they are to be referred not to each other but to Endymion who experiences them. Compression is once more the principal synaesthetic agent. Yet another example occurs in *Isabella:*

> Soon she turn'd up a soiled glove, whereon
> Her silk had play'd in *purple* phantasies . . .
>
> (ll. 369-70)

Common sense may be easily satisfied by the reflection that "purple" is doubtless the color of the silk. But "purple" is also the sensuous contact of the lovers' gloved hands, and the emotion aroused by this contact. It is a sensuous-imaginative symbol of the warm, instinctive young love of Isabella and Lorenzo,[15] and epitomizes the whole generous, sensual, sentimental tone of a poem which Keats stigmatized as "too smokeable," "weak-sided," and afflicted with "an amusing sober-sadness."[16]

15. Purple synaesthetically used as an emblem of youthful, passionate love occurs also in *The Eve of St. Agnes:*
> Sudden a thought came like a full-blown rose,
> Flushing his cheek, and in his pained heart
> Made *purple* riot . . . (ll. 136-38).

Here "purple" has emotional associations with "thought—full-blown rose," and physical suggestions of the idea of "heart's blood."

16. *The Letters of John Keats,* p. 391.

Of a like complexity is this startling synaesthetic image from *Endymion:*

> . . . lost in pleasure at her feet he sinks,
> Touching with *dazzled* lips her starlight hand.
>
> (*Endymion*, IV, 418-19)

The interplay of sight and touch is very swift. [17] There is a trace of "wit," of conscious ingenuity, which lends to the image a certain flavour of modernity. The lips of Endymion are "dazzled," of course, because the hand which they touch is "starlight." But there is more to the image than its sensory content. Endymion is dazzled because he is dreaming that he is among the Gods on Olympus, kneeling before Hebe: a situation in which some bedazzlement seems excusable. The Immortals may reasonably be presumed to be possessed of "brightness," traditionally an attribute of Godhead. Even as Endymion dreams, he is floating high above the earth on the back of a supernatural steed, amid a dusk sky in which the first stars of evening and the moon are about to appear. Endymion is in love with the Moon-Goddess, and he is the hero of a poem saturated with references to moonlight. The image in question is on the surface a witty conceit, with undertones of meaning and tendrils of association attaching it on every side to its context, adding contrapuntal emotional and romantic strains which soften its initial hardness.

Much of Keats's most characteristic synaesthetic imagery reinforces sound or odor with strong tactual, organic, or kinesthetic sensations. In *Endymion*,

17. Miss June E. Downey has cited this image as a probable case of "true" synaesthesia, reflecting a genuine sense-idiosyncrasy in Keats.—"Literary Synesthesia," *op. cit.*, p. 497. I am inclined to doubt this; the peculiarities of the figure can be adequately accounted for in terms of purely literary considerations.

> . . . we might
> Be *incense-pillowed* every summer night
>
> (II, 998-99)

gives body, weight, and softness to an olfactory image. As is so frequently the case in Keats, the expression is complex and compressive. One may read the lines as "we might lie every summer night on clouds of incense so thick that they seem to have weight, and can even support our bodies"; and more matter-of-factly, "we might lie on pillows impregnated with incense." The overripe lusciousness which this image shares with so much of *Endymion* causes it to suffer by comparison with the very similar image "what soft incense hangs upon the boughs," in the *Ode to a Nightingale*, in which the implications of "soft" and "hangs" become plain only on careful scrutiny. These images of touch and weight function quietly and organically as single threads in the rich, heavy fabric of the verse. Likewise quiet and unobtrusive is the synaesthetic mingling of touch, temperature, odor, and sight in the description of Hyperion's palace-door, which is

> . . . like a rose in vermeil tint and shape,
> In fragrance *soft*, and *coolness* to the eye.
>
> (*Hyperion*, I, 209-10)

"Fragrance" is more vividly realized by virtue of the image of touch which accompanies it. "Coolness to the eye," although instantaneous in effect, proposes a sense-relationship familiar to most of us, and generally accepted as normal.

On one occasion Keats speaks of the coolness of light itself:

He turned—there was a whelming sound—he stept,
There was a *cooler* light . . .

(Endymion, II, 1018-19)

This close-knit combination of tactual and visual is fusional and intense. The poet is trying to describe in a single adjective the essential differentiating quality of the light, and he has found it necessary to resort to a different order of sensation. The image can also be explained naturalistically. The "whelming sound" and altered light is of the sea, which has but now swept over Endymion's head. "Cooler" can in part be referred to the feel of the water on his body, and to the fact that the sun's rays must obviously have less force when they are filtered through the sea above him. As in other instances, the image merges within itself a complex set of associations latent in its context.

There is a striking mixture of visual pleasure and tactual feeling at the beginning of *Hyperion*, Bk. III, as Keats invokes the delights of earth to welcome Apollo to his yet unconquered realm:

Let the rose *glow* intense and *warm* in the air.

(l. 15)

The image seems primarily verbal in origin, however. The notion of a *glowing* rose is not surprising. Keats appears to have used "glow" metaphorically, without considering its sensory properties, and to have been led by the tactual quality inherent in it to the more forthright and daring "warm."

Keats comes closest to the individuality of feeling and suddenness of effect which characterizes modern synaesthesia in an image which attributes color to organic feeling:

> The colours all inflamed throughout her train,
> She writh'd about, convuls'd with *scarlet pain*.
>
> (*Lamia*, I, 153-54)

"Scarlet" in undoubtedly an attribute of "pain," in a surprising and instantaneous sense-transference. As usual, however, the context provides a further explanation. The snake Lamia has herself turned scarlet in the process of her transformation into a woman, and the change naturally involves a good deal of suffering. Consequently there remains an ambiguity of meaning, resulting from the intense condensation of Keats's expression. "Scarlet" and "pain" on the one hand fuse with each other; on the other they are merely parallel and co-temporal.

Keats describes sound even more sensuously than light and odor, by the same device of reinforcing the weaker sense with a stronger: most frequently tactual, sometimes organic or kinesthetic, sometimes two or more different senses in conjunction. In his poetry sound and music are often tangible and material, with weight, texture and form.[18] In the banquet-room passage in *Lamia* music is possessed of architectural solidity and strength:

> A haunting music, sole perhaps and lone
> Supportress of the faery roof, made moan
> Throughout, as fearful the whole charm might fade.
>
> (II, 122-24)

Sound is sometimes silver or golden. The image

> . . . other harmonies, stopped short
> Leave the dinn'd air vibrating *silverly*,
>
> (*Hyperion*, II, 127-28)

18. Cf. Downey, "Literary Synesthesia," *op. cit.*, p. 495.

is the most definitely synaesthetic among Keats's figures of this sort, because it is most compact and unequivocal. The poet somehow manages to convey the impression that the unusual "silverly" is the only possible word for the occasion; there is, as it were, a matter-of-factness and calm certainty in his use of it. The music of the Bacchic revellers in *Endymion*—

> The earnest trumpet spake, and *silver* thrills
> From kissing cymbals made a merry din
>
> (IV, 197-98)

is closely analogous, but one cannot take "silver" so seriously and literally as the "silverly" of the previous passage. It is more closely connected with the idea of sound-vibration, and less nearly autonomous. "Golden," in

> And scarce three steps, ere Music's golden tongue
> Flattered to tears this aged man and poor
>
> (*The Eve of St. Agnes*, ll. 20-21)

has a significance almost entirely emotional; it is not visible or material. "Silver, snarling trumpets" (*Eve of St. Agnes*, l. 31) is ambiguous. Silver is naturalistically and prosaically the substance of the trumpets, and it is also the quality of their tone.

Sound in Keats's poetry often has texture. Whether it is the music of man or nature, it is generally soft and smooth, seldom harsh. The wind, for example,

> . . . that now did stir
> About the crisped oaks full drearily,
> Yet with as sweet a softness as might be
> Remembered from its *velvet summer song*
>
> (*Endymion*, IV, 294-97)

s heavy, tangible, and soft. There is much the same effect in

> . . . his palace-door flew ope
> In *smoothest silence*, save what solemn tubes,
>
> (*Hyperion*, I, 205-6)

but "smoothest" is fusional and complex. It is an attribute of "silence," of the movement of the doors, and by a transfer associational in origin, of "solemn tubes."

Taste-images occur with relative infrequency in Keats's synaesthetic imagery, but such as appear are powerful and vivid. On one occasion he combines taste with smell to produce one of the strongest of all his sensory images:

> Also, when he would taste the spicy wreaths
> Of incense, breath'd aloft from sacred hills,
> Instead of sweets, his ample palate took
> Savour of poisonous brass and metal sick . . .
>
> (*Hyperion*, I, 186-89)

The gustatory and the olfactory are thoroughly mingled, the stronger taste reinforcing the less immediate olfactory sensation. The whole has a massive solidity, from the concentration of effects in *taste, spicy, incense, breath'd, sweets, palate, savour,* and *poisonous;* to which are added suggestions of weight and solidity in *ample, brass,* and *metal. Sick* rounds off the passage with an organic image.

A complex but perfect and as it were unconscious fusion binds together taste, sound, and sight in the lines from *Isabella*

> . . . O turn thee to the very tale,
> And *taste* the *music* of that *vision* pale.
>
> (*Isabella*, ll. 391-92)

As was suggested in the previous chapter,[19] it sometimes appears that the primary source of Keats's inspiration lies in his senses. He begins with the feel, or in this particular instance with the taste, of the poem.[20] Three orders of sensation are here welded together with such ease and apparent inevitability that there is little feeling of jar or paradox. Keats is talking of his original in Boccaccio, and to his perceptions the "music" of the prose, the "taste" of it, and the visual images aroused by it are identical. Another example of the poet's ability to *feel* himself into a situation is "In *pale* and *silver* silence they remain'd. . ." (*Hyperion*, II, 356). The Titans, at sombre council in a rocky valley, are aroused by the first faint gleam of the rising sun as their brother Hyperion comes slowly into view over a distant peak. "Pale" and "silver" characterize "silence"; they describe the light now filtering down; they symbolize the mood of the fallen deities; and they cast a solemnity over the whole scene, harmonizing nature with the quiet despair of its late rulers. These images are highly functional, fusional, and compressive. They epitomize much in little space.

The easy naturalness and functional quality characteristic of the synaesthetic imagery of Keats is especially notable in his later poetry, more particularly in the six great odes. In the odes divergent sensations and notions are fused into complex but indivisible wholes by the intense concentration of his mature technique. His sense-analogies work quietly, in the main almost

19. See above, pp. 65-67.

20. A remark of Professor Finney's is appropriate: "A controlling principle in Keats's composition of a metrical romance was the particular sensuous atmosphere which he wished to produce."—*Op. cit.*, II, 549.

unnoticed, but they are effectual in aiding to produce the rich and sensuous atmosphere of his most finished poetry. The *Ode to Psyche* presents a remarkable instance of fusion and transference of multiple sensations, so quietly managed that the variety and diversity of the materials is likely to be overlooked:

> Mid *hush'd*, cool-rooted flowers, *fragrant-eyed*,
> Blue, silver-white, and budded Tyrian . . .
>
> (ll. 13-14)

Auditory, tactual, olfactory, and visual suggestions join together in one line in perfect amity, to be transformed by a synthesizing and compressive process into a unity different from any of these and yet comprising all.[21]

In the *Ode to a Nightingale* two single images and the

21. M. R. Ridley has traced the steps of this "distillation," as he calls it, through Keats's poetry in a passage well worth reproducing:

"At the very beginning of his [Keats's] career there is a picture of May flowers:

> And let long grass grow round the roots to keep them
> Moist, cool, and green (*I Stood . . . 32*)

Then there is a passage in *Endymion* in which he thinks of white flowers scattered on a dark-blue background as being like eyes:

> 'Tis *blue*, and over-spangled with a million
> Of little *eyes*, as though thou wert to shed,
> Over the darkest, lushest blue-bell bed,
> Handfuls of daisies. (l. 629)

Then there are two lines in *Hyperion*, which connect fragrance, the one with coolness, and the other with quietness:

> And like a rose in vermeil tint and shape,
> In *fragrance* soft, and *coolness* to the eye (l. 209)

> Where a sweet clime was breathed from a land
> Of fragrance, quietness, and trees, and flowers (ii. 263)

Let us just add to these one line from the Epistle to George Keats:

> Crowned with flowers purple, white, and red (l. 88)

And then ask whether there is anything essential in those pictures which is not given in the two perfect lines of the *Ode to Psycho*. . . ."—*Op. cit.*, pp. 193-94.

famous "blushful Hippocrene" passage exemplify the typical qualities of Keatsian synaesthesia.

> In some *melodious* plot
> Of beechen green . . .
>
> (ll. 8-9)

and

> . . . here there is no light
> Save what from heaven is with the breezes *blown*
>
> (ll. 38-39)

are "inevitable"; they are fully and immediately acceptable in their quiet rightness. In the first the idea of the bird is transferred to, and fuses with the locale. The song of the nightingale merges with the foliage of the soft spring night in a single impression. In the second image one overlooks the unusual sense-transference of light blown with the breezes because it is at once obvious that Keats has consummately described the effect of glancing light filtering down through leaves stirred gently by the wind.

The synaesthetic imagery of Keats reaches its highest level, however, in the complex fusion of sense, emotion, and concept of the second stanza of the Nightingale:

> O, for a draught of vintage! that hath been
> Cool'd a long age in the deep-delved earth,
> *Tasting* of Flora and the country green,
> Dance, and Provençal song, and *sunburnt* mirth!
> O for a *beaker* full of the *warm South*,
> Full of the true, the blushful Hippocrene,
> With beaded bubbles winking at the brim,
> And purple-stained mouth . . .

Keats has attained to the utmost degree of synthesizing

compression in this passage, packing into a few lines what prose could not have expressed in many times the number of words he has employed. As in the figure from *Isabella*, "*taste* the music of that vision pale," he begins sensuously with the *taste* of his experience. The imagined contact of the wine with his palate evokes through a complex associational process a series of pictures and feelings, very much as in Proust's *Swann's Way* the savour of a cup of tea draws up the emotional and pictorial drama of the past from the depths of the subconscious, where it has long lain buried.[22] The associations of the wine at first seem somewhat arbitrary. The relation between *Flora* and the *country green* is obvious enough: the thought of the Goddess of Flowers naturally calls up ideas of the fertile, peaceful greenness of a rural scene. Yet "Dance, and Provençal song, and sunburnt mirth" are further to seek. Each new image joins harmoniously with its predecessor, but if we stop to examine we observe that this is an imaginative, not a logical unity; to discern the agents of this synthesis one must put forth effort. *Country green* easily shifts into *country dance, dance* suggests its accompanying *song*, and *country, dance,* and *song* combine to produce the compressed synaesthetic fusion of *sunburnt mirth*, which when unfolded for examination discloses a merry festival of country folk, bronzed by their labors beneath the summer sun. *Dance* we may likewise relate to Flora through the flower-bedecked dance of goddesses in Botticelli's "Primavera." *Provençal* is generally associated, aside

22. *Swann's Way*, in *Remembrance of Things Past*, tr. C. K. Scott Moncrieff, I, 54-241. Proust, of course, recalls his own past experience, while Keats's images are complex products of his imagination.

from the fame of Provence in song, with ideas of gaiety.
It looks backward also to "Cool'd a long age in the
deep-delved earth," for the associations of the wine
are with the Romantic past, at one moment with some
dim mythological Golden Age of Flora,[23] the next with
the days of troubadours and the *gai science* of Provençal
poetry.

The image *tasting* is thus synaesthetically fused not
only with other sensations, but with concept and emotion as well in a single imaginative whole. The surprising figures,

> With beaded bubbles winking at the brim,
> And purple-stained mouth,

are synaesthetic through quick shifts of sensation, tactual, visual, and gustatory; but the effect of synaesthesia
comes principally from half-hidden but powerful personifications. As in earlier instances, the elements of
these analogies are referable not to each other, but to
an underlying agent of organization. Here, the beaker
is a bleary Silenus, with *winking*, drunken eyes, and
purple-stained mouth.

III   The synaesthetic imagery of Shelley is less
complex, less sensuous, and less spontaneous than that of Keats. It lacks the multiplicity of
association which in Keats so often forms a rich and
various background for the image. It is comparatively

23. Cf. *Sleep and Poetry:*
         "First the realm I'll pass
         Of Flora, and old Pan," etc. (ll. 101 ff.)
The description of the dancing nymph immediately following (ll. 113-16) is very
suggestive of Botticelli's painting.

poor in tactual quality, it makes little use of organic sensation, and no use whatever of the powerfully physical kinesthetic. Visual, auditory, olfactory, and motor impressions are its customary materials. The complex ambiguity of import frequently evident in Keats is absent in the synaesthesia of Shelley. His sense-analogies do not arise naturally and spontaneously from intensely concentrated expression, like those of Keats, but have a clearly defined purpose.

Shelley, indeed, merges and interfuses different orders of sensation in response to his yearning, both philosophic and temperamental, for Unity. Beyond and above the Many, the perplexing variety of things, lies the One, simple, perfect, and complete, "an elemental subtlety, like light."

> Life, like a dome of many-coloured glass,
> Stains the white radiance of eternity,

and Shelley strives to rise above this dome of shifting, transient, accidental color and merge himself with the ultimate purity of the Absolute. His synaesthetic images are likely to culminate in abstraction, just as the colors of the spectrum are fused into white light, imperceptible to the eye. They are to some extent intellectual and philosophical, symbols of Shelley's thought rather than portraits of the world of sensation; or better, perhaps, they image a world which has been refined and shaped anew by the powerful plastic influence of his mysticism.

Shelley's monism, however, is tempered and qualified by his keen sense of the infinite variety to be found in the world of phenomena. He is thoroughly aware of the "dome of many-coloured glass"; if he were not he

would have no need to make such vigorous efforts to transcend it. In his verse he passes swiftly and restlessly from object to object, seeing always change, flux, kaleidoscopic shiftings in the aspect of things. He seeks to pierce the finite veil;[24] but there is a veil beyond veil, and his aspiration remains unsatisfied even when he has penetrated as far as

> The loftiest star of unascended Heaven
> Pinnacled dim in the intense inane.

Strive as he will, the Ultimate eludes him. Demogorgon, the image of eternity, is a shapeless darkness, and his speech is beyond the comprehension of mortal ears.[25]

The stresses and strains occasioned by this tug of war between the One and the Many produce as by violent friction the characteristic emotional tone and imagery of Shelley's poetry. Since the contradiction remains unresolved, the struggle is real. Its outcome is in doubt, unlike that most shadowy of battles, the War of the Angels in *Paradise Lost*, in which we can have little interest since we know that victory has been predestined to all-conquering Messiah. This irreducible antinomy of thought would be a fault in a systematic philosopher, but in a poet it is a decided virtue. For by its agency Shelley is endowed with a vivid power of realizing the actual. His tendency toward rarefied intellectual abstraction is counteracted by his strong sense of the inescapable solidity of things, which resist his every effort to remould them closer to the heart's desire.

24. The veil-image recurs significantly in many of Shelley's longer poems.
25. See *Prometheus Unbound*, II, iv.

The single element most prominent in Shelley's synaesthesia is motion, just as a firm tactility is most
prominent in Keats. Shelley is not, however, entirely
devoid of sensations of touch, pressure, solidity, and
resistance in his synaesthetic imagery. The difference
of tactual quality and technique lies in this: that while
Keats uses the tactual to reinforce and solidify images
already strong in sensuous content, Shelley uses it to
objectify a sense-impression otherwise ungraspable by
ordinary perceptions. This objectification is with him
habitual, and when it is accomplished with more than
usual directness and concision it becomes synaesthesia.
In such fashion a single example from one of his many
"woven" images[26] so closely mingles sound, motion,
color, and texture that they become interchangeable:

> . . . its music long,
> Like *woven* sounds of streams and breezes, held
> His inmost sense suspended in its *web*
> Of many-coloured *woof* and shifting hues.
>
> (*Alastor*, ll. 154-57)

In this connection it should be noticed that Shelley
is far from the intensity and compression of Keats.
Although the present example is for Shelley unusually
close-knit and compact, yet it unrolls itself slowly, part
by part. By the simile, "like woven sounds," etc., the
poet tells us exactly what he is doing. We are rarely so
certain of the precise direction in which Keats's more
complex and instantaneous sense-analogies are moving.

Other examples of synaesthetic "objectification" in
Shelley are

26. See above, p. 49n.

> . . . Whither have fled
> The *hues* of heaven that *canopied* his bower . . .
> *(Alastor*, ll. 196-97)

in which "canopied" lends to the airy and generalized "hues" firmness, weight, and tangibility; and

> The emerald light of *leaf-entangled* beams,
> *(Prometheus Unbound*, IV, 258)

where rays of light both offer and receive a paradoxical resistance.

Light, odor, sound, and motion are the most characteristic materials of Shelley's synaesthetic imagery. These are combined, transfused, and dissolved into a variety of relationships, simple and complex: light-odor, sound-odor, sound-odor-light (color), sound-light (color), sound-motion, and sound-color-motion (with odor sometimes added).

In several instances starlight intermingles with fragrance. In

> The leprous corpse, touched by this spirit tender,
> Exhales itself in flowers of gentle breath;
> Like incarnations of the stars, when *splendor*
> Is changed to *fragrance*, they *illumine* death
> *(Adonais*, ll. 172-76)

the synaesthetic analogy is obviously more intellectual than sensuous. It unfolds itself slowly and systematically, setting forth in plain terms the two poles of comparison and indicating in "when splendor / Is changed to fragrance" the precise moment of their meeting. This slowness of development, however, sharply emphasizes the striking "illumine," which produces a

strange effect of bursting open. Part of this effect is owing to a sudden reversal of the logical movement, which passing from *light* to *odor* now suddenly reverts to *light*.

A more forthright light-odor analogy occurs in *Lines Written Among the Euganean Hills*, when Shelley speaks of

> . . . an air-dissolvéd *star*
> Mingling *light* and *fragrance* . . .
>
> (ll. 289-90)

There is in the same poem an interfusion of sensations more complex than this, but less sensuous:

> . . . living things each one
> And my spirit, which so long
> Darkened this swift *stream* of song,—
> *Interpenetrated* lie,—
> By the glory of the sky:
> Be it *love, light, harmony,*
> *Odor*, or the soul of all
> Which from heaven like *dew* doth fall
> Or the mind which *feeds* this verse . . .
>
> (ll. 310-18)

The absolute interchangeability of the sensuous and the abstract in this astounding *mélange* of orders indicates that the passage is symbolic, not naturalistic. *Light, harmony*, and *odor* possess no more appeal to sensation than does *love*, of the *soul of all*. A comparison more sensuously concrete and imaginative is

> . . . that star's smile whose *light* is like the *scent*
> Of a jonquil when evening breezes fan it,
>
> (*The Triumph of Life*, ll. 419-20)

an image whose definiteness and certainty of touch im-

poses upon the reader, so that he accepts the light-odor analogy as true and inevitable.

An example of simple sound-odor comparison furnishes perhaps Shelley's most striking synaesthetic image:

> . . . the hyacinth purple, and white, and blue,
> . . . flung from its *bells* a sweet *peal* anew
> Of *music* so delicate, soft, and intense
> It was felt like an *odor* within the sense.
>
> (*The Sensitive Plant*, I, 25-28)

Wit, a phenomenon not usually noticeable in Shelley's verse, is present here. The fulcrum of the image is the pun in *bells*, a word which develops and unrolls until Shelley suddenly and paradoxically returns to the original notion of the flower's scent. There is also a hint of color as music, suggested but not pressed.

Shelley sometimes combines images of sound, odor, and light or color to form a single, general impression. This interweaving of the senses appears in a brief passage of *Alastor*,

> *Bright* flowers departed, and the *beautiful* shade
> Of the *green* groves, with all their *odorous* winds
> And *musical motions* . . .
>
> (ll. 537-39)

The synthesis is vague, but lulling and pleasant. A figure in *The Sensitive Plant* transforms air into water and intermingles in this sea of air light, sound, and odor:

> The quivering vapors of dim noontide,
> Which like a sea o'er the warm earth glide,
> In which every sound, and odor, and beam
> Move, as reeds in a single stream.
>
> (I, 90-93)

The metaphor develops in leisurely fashion, exposing, as frequently with Shelley, each part in turn for examination. The sense-transference of air to water, which lends the image added visual and tactual strength, is natural and unobtrusive; fusion is here more important than analogy.

"Tonal vision," or sound portrayed as light or color, is not unusual in Shelley's poetry. A rather ambiguous example of it from *Prometheus Unbound* appears to be the result of a syntactical peculiarity rather than a genuine equating of music and color:

> . . . hear I not
> The *Aeolian music* of her *sea-green plumes*
> *Winnowing* the crimson dawn?
>
> (II, i, 25-27)

Both *Aeolian music* and *sea-green plumes winnow* the dawn; there is no reason to suppose that the music is sea-green. Rather the winnowing of the air by beating wings quite naturally produces a wind-like sound.[27] Three other passages from *Prometheus Unbound* are less open to doubt. In

> . . . this is the mystic shell.
> See the pale azure fading into silver,
> Lining it with a soft yet glowing light.
> Looks it not like lulled music sleeping there?
>
> (III, iii, 70-73)

there is a subtlety of shading and an imaginative exactitude typical of Shelley at his best. Much less vividly sensuous, but impressive because of its sudden impact, is

> See where the Spirits of the human mind,
> *Wrapped* in *sweet sounds*, as in bright veils, approach.
>
> (IV, 80-81)

27. Cf. Downey, *contra*, *Creative Imagination*, p. 99.

The third instance,

> Ye happy dead, whom *beams* of *brightest verse*
> Are clouds to hide, not colours to portray
>
> (IV, 534-35)

is almost unnoticeable, but significant of Shelley's synaesthetic turn of mind in its matter-of-fact linking of
meaning, sound, and color. A final example of tonal
vision,

> And the invisible rain did ever sing
> A *silver music* on the mossy lawn
> (*The Triumph of Life*, ll. 354-55)

seems almost to have more of Keats than of Shelley in it.
It is naturalistic, complex in its associations, and highly
compressed.

Whereas we have seen that to Keats music was often
material, massy, and tangible, to Shelley it is most often
associated with movement; a difference which epitomizes much of the characteristic quality of the two
poets, since the grave, slow stateliness of Keats is in
direct and continuous contrast to Shelley's fiery speed.
In two images from *Prometheus Unbound* music is concretely portrayed as the movement and sound of foot-
steps:

> The *music-stirring motion* of its soft and busy feet
>
> (I, 777)

.   .   .   .

> Like *footsteps* of weak *melody* . . .
>
> (II, i, 89)

In a vaguer fashion the same music-motion transference
is exhibited in

> As the song *floats* thou pursue . . .
>
> (II, i, 179)

The notion of *floating song* is not at all uncommon, and this image is worthy of notice only as a single representative of a large number of similar analogies in Shelley.

More elaborate complexes of music-water-color-motion are also frequent. Perhaps the best known of these images is from *Prometheus Unbound*,

> My soul is an enchanted boat,
> Which, like a sleeping swan, doth float
> Upon the *silver waves* of thy sweet *singing* . . .
>
> (II, v, 72-74)

The metaphors of the boat, the swan, and the "silver waves" are definite and strongly concrete. They react upon each other so as to heighten the general effect; the climactic "silver waves" is more vividly realized by virtue of the preparatory figures. Since, however, the boat is a symbol of the soul, we do not strongly feel the sense-transference in "waves-singing," for the image has committed itself to a subjectivity in which one moves at will from plane to plane.

The image of the World-Sphere in *Prometheus* is a particularly significant example of this type of synaesthesia, since it may be presumed to represent Shelley's most serious thought. It is undoubtedly an effort to portray imaginatively the pure idea of Earth. In this ideal sphere the notions of light, sound, and movement are fused into a unity:

> . . . through all its mass
> *Flow*, as through empty space, *music* and *light*.
>
> (IV, 239-40)

A few lines later Shelley gives specific expression to his intellectual and emotional urge toward Oneness:

> . . . the wild odor of the forest flowers,
> The music of the living grass and air,
> The emerald light of leaf-entangled beams,
> Round its intense yet self-conflicting speed
> *Seem kneaded into one aërial mass*
> Which drowns the sense.
>
> (IV, 256-60)

This appears to be a definite statement of the consummation toward which the Shelleyan synaesthesia continually strives: a blending of all sensation into one mystical, ineffable, supersensuous harmony; a dissolution which involves the spirit itself in willing self-surrender.

This doctrine of the essential Oneness of sensation is rather implied than stated in such images as

> I rise as from a bath of sparkling water,
> A bath of azure *light*, among dark rocks,
> Out of the stream of *sound*,
>
> (IV, 503-5)

with its swift complexities of experiencing; and the hazier, less realized

> . . . around them the *soft stream* did glide and dance
> With a *motion* of *sweet sound* and *radiance*.
>
> (*The Sensitive Plant*, I, 47-48)

Shelley's compulsive urge toward unity of experiencing is expressed also in a rather numerous group of images in which music and motion fuse in the medium of water. Of these I cite three:

> . . . two runnels of a rivulet
>
> . . . .
>
> Have made their *path of melody* . . .
>> (*Prometheus Unbound*, IV, 196-98)
>
> . . . .
>
> . . . Poesy's unfailing river
> Which through Albion winds forever
> Lashing with *melodious wave*
> Many a sacred poet's grave . . .
>> (*Euganean Hills*, ll. 184-87)
>
> . . . .
>
> . . . the fountains whose *melodious dew*
> Out of their mossy cells forever burst.
>> (*Triumph of Life*, ll. 67-68)

The last two of these are only mildly synaesthetic. *Poesy's river* has little sensuous force, derivative as it is from the overworked and familiar time-river symbol; while *melodious* strikes one as referring primarily to *poesy* and only secondarily to *wave*. In the last of the three the *melodious dew* of the fountains is little more than a variation of the commonplace "music of fountains," or "musical murmur of waters."

Another instance in which sheer lack of sensuous realization produces the effect of synaesthesia is

> . . . as each are mirrors of
> The *fire* for which all *thirst*.
>> (*Adonais*, ll. 485-86)

In Shelley's poetry "thirst" is rarely more than a symbolic counter; in this case the figure is entirely abstract. Yet so calm a toleration of incongruity is symptomatic of an imaginative breaking-down of the bars between the senses which is essentially synaesthetic in mode.

Shelley employs synaesthetic imagery most consistently, perhaps, in *To a Skylark*. The song of the bird is a

> . . . shrill delight
> *Keen* as are the *arrows*
> Of that *silver sphere*
> Whose intense *lamp* narrows
> In the white dawn clear
> Until we hardly *see*—we *feel* that it is there.
>
> (ll. 20-25)

Auditory, organic, tactual, and visual perceptions are fused here as one sensation.

> All the earth and air
> With thy voice is loud,
> As when Night is bare
> From one lonely cloud
> The moon *rains* out her beams, and Heaven is *overflowed*.
>
> (ll. 26-30)

The lark's song is so copiously, so generously bestowed upon the listener that it suggests a kind of *outpouring*, an *overflowing* bounteousness. It seems to me proof of an innate synaesthetic tendency in Shelley that he should think first of the less-obvious comparison with moonlight, and only afterwards of the more natural analogy with water. But the sound-water relationship is maintained once it is perceived:

> From *rainbow* clouds there *flow* not
> Drops so *bright* to *see*
> As from thy presence *showers* a *rain* of melody.
>
> (ll. 33-35)

The melody is now not only a simple shower, but by some obscure process of association it has taken on the

property of color. It is rainbow-tinted. Possibly the associational links run thus: rain > cloud > rainbow > rainbow-colored drops > rain > melody.

The poet now recurs to the image of the *overflowing* of the lark's song—the bird is

> Like a high-born maiden
> In a palace tower,
> Soothing her love-laden
> Soul in secret hour
> With *music* sweet as love—which *overflows* her bower.
>
> (ll. 41-45)

This bounteousness of the lark momentarily takes on a different form in another synaesthetic image—the bird is also

> Like a glowworm golden
> In a dell of dew
> *Scattering* unbeholden
> Its *aërial* hue . . .—
>
> (ll. 46-49)

an example of what I have termed "objectification," in which the intangible is endowed with a subtle tactility. Then there is a peculiar shift:

> *Sound* of vernal showers
> On the *twinkling* grass,
> *Rain-awakened flowers*
> All that ever was
> Joyous and clear and fresh, thy music doth surpass.
>
> (ll. 56-60)

The music, "Joyous and clear and fresh," is associated not merely with "sound of vernal showers," but also with the *twinkling* of grass, and the aspect of "rain-

awakened flowers.'' Shelley then returns to the music-stream analogy in

> I have never heard
> Praise of love or wine
> That panted forth a *flood* of *rapture* so divine
>
> (ll. 63-65)

and

> . . . how could thy notes *flow* in such a *crystal stream*,
>
> (l. 85)

which contains a hint of visual quality in *crystal*. The poem concludes with an image typically expressive of the goal toward which the Shelleyan synaesthesia moves:

> Such *harmonious madness*
> From my lips would *flow* . . .
>
> (ll. 103-4)

Sense is translated into a mystical and ecstatic plane of experience in which sense is as it were drowned, merged with emotion until it no longer has a separate and unique identity.

IV   The synaesthetic imagery of Shelley shows on the one hand a tendency toward vagueness. Sense-impressions are often generalized, described as ''music,'' ''sound,'' ''odor,'' ''fragrance,'' ''light,'' ''splendor,'' ''hues.''[28] They seem to be elements of a universe of simpler, more easily discernible design than is the actual world of our perceptions. Yet on the other hand Shelley's sense-analogies evince an exquisite feel-

28. In Shelley's poetry *fragrance* occurs 22 times; *music* 133; *hues* 80; *light* 553; *odor* 67; *sound* 225; *splendor* 58.—F. S. Ellis, *A Lexical Concordance to the Poetical Works of Percy Bysshe Shelley.*

ing for subtle gradations of coloring, changes of sensuous tone, degrees of relationship in sensation. He has an unerring sense of the inner harmonies between sound, odor, motion, and color; his images are never discordant. They establish connections which are instantly felt as true and really existing, although not previously perceived; a striking example of the creative imagination harmoniously functioning through imagery.

The materials from which the Shelleyan synaesthesia is woven are on the whole less powerfully sensuous than the characteristic stuff of Keats's images, although Shelley's intellectual and sensational perceptions of the variety of things are sufficiently strong to counteract his tendencies toward over-simplification. His typical synaesthetic imagery is built from auditory, olfactory, visual, and motor sensations, without the more substantial organic and kinesthetic impressions of Keats.

This comparative lack of sensuous force is, I believe, of set purpose. Shelley has chosen materials malleable to his shaping hand, in pursuit of unities rather than of diversities. His synaesthetic imagery is less concerned with sense-transference than with sense-fusion. He selects for description phenomena in which common properties can be discerned without unusual straining of the bounds of normal perception, as, for example, music and water possess in common the property of motion. He generalizes sufficiently so that the boundaries between the senses are vaguely defined, and one sensation passes easily and imperceptibly into another.

Synaesthesia in Shelley is the poetical expression of a conscious, intellectual quest after a cosmic and psychic unity, in which the merging into Oneness of disparate physical phenomena symbolizes the ideal unity toward

which the spirit strives. In the final stage of this process sense and spirit are themselves one, fused by intellect, sensation and emotion into an imaginative whole. Act IV of *Prometheus Unbound*, the summit of Shelley's poetical thought, is a rapturous hymn to this supersensuous unity, achieved in the hour of the fall of Jupiter. Chorus upon chorus exhorts to unity:

> But now, oh, weave the mystic measure
> Of music and dance, and shapes of light
> Let the Hours, and the Spirits of night and pleasure,
> Like the clouds and sunbeams, unite—
>
> (IV, 77-80)

When the grasp of accident and evil is at last relaxed, distinctions and separations will disappear. Sound, motion, shape, light, time, and spirit—all will be one, in a single harmony, profound and perfect.

Keats, with no intellectual or temperamental compulsion to impose upon the world a philosophic unity, employs harder and more resistant metals. His sense-images are stronger, more particularized, and more difficult to reconcile with each other. Yet his intuitive sense of the relationships between separate and dissimilar phenomena, his ability to sympathize with and humanize natural objects, are manifestations of a powerful, instinctive feeling of the Oneness of all things, and by his matchless sensory equipment he is enabled to pass easily from sensation to sensation without incongruity or discordance. By means of a natural compressive and associational power greater than Shelley's, he welds his more complex and refractory materials into wholes more organic and poetically satisfying, perhaps, than Shelley's psycho-cosmic syntheses, subtle and imaginative as these are.

·❧| CHAPTER |❧·
FOUR

EMPATHIC IMAGERY

I   Empathy, the involuntary projection of oneself into an object,[1] received its first extended formulation in the *Mikrokosmos* of Hermann Lotze, 1858.[2] To Lotze, *Einfühlung*, or empathy as it has been termed in English,[3] was a phenomenon which accounts for our knowledge of the external world. "The world [he said] becomes alive to us through this power to see in forms the joy and sorrow of existence that they hide: there is no shape so coy that our fancy cannot sympathetically enter into it." In this knowledge our consciousness of our own bodily sensations is a factor: "Unquestionably the vividness of these perceptions is added to by our abiding remembrance of the activity of our own body . . . every movement which we execute,

    1. Vernon Lee calls it "attributing what goes on in us when we look at a shape to the shape itself."—*The Beautiful*, p. 65.

    2. Empathy was noticed by Aristotle.—*Rhetoric*, III, 2, 1411b. The psychological phenomena which it accounts for were observed and recorded in the eighteenth century by an impressive number of critics and philosophers in isolated passages: by Dennis, Addison, John Baillie, Hume, Gerard, Kames, Reynolds, Herder, and Kant. Coleridge anticipated the observations of later aesthetic psychologists with remarkable exactness. See C. D. Thorpe, "Some Notices of 'Empathy' before Lipps," *Papers of the Michigan Academy of Science, Arts, and Letters*, XXIII, 525-26; "Empathy," *Dictionary of World Literature*, ed. Joseph T. Shipley, pp. 186-88.

    3. The term "empathy" was coined by Edward B. Titchener, in *Lectures on the Experimental Psychology of the Thought-Process*.

every attitude in which we repose, has its meaning rendered plain to us by the feeling of exertion or of enjoyment." Entering thus into our own sensations, by means of them we are also enabled to know the feelings of creatures and objects beyond their immediate range:

> . . . we, thus aided by our sentience, assuredly can comprehend also the alien silent form. Nor is it only into the peculiar vital feelings of that which in nature is near to us that we enter—into the joyous flight of the singing bird or the graceful fleetness of the gazelle; we not only contract our mental feelers to the most minute creatures, to enter in reverie into the narrow round of existence of a mussel-fish and the monotonous bliss of its openings and shuttings, we not only expand into the slender proportions of the tree whose twigs are animated by the pleasure of graceful bending and waving; nay, even to the inanimate do we transfer these interpretative feelings, transforming through them the dead weights and supports of buildings into so many limbs of a living body whose inner tensions pass over into our selves.[4]

Empathy, then, is in Lotze's view nothing less than our only means of knowing the external world, the non-Ego. The breadth of the conception is immense. Although he declares that the origins of this knowing lie in our awareness of our own sensations, the manner in which we attribute these sensations to "alien, silent forms" is by no means clear. Our conscious relationship with the external world is predominantly on the mental, not the physical, plane. Empathy is therefore fundamentally unobservable, an hypothesis impossible to verify. Its physical components are undefined. A certain mysticism pervades the terms of Lotze's definition, evident in his implicit assumption that our sentience is of

4. *Microcosmus*, tr. E. Hamilton and E. E. C. Jones, I, 584-86.

the same order as the sentience of the objects we observe, so that we not merely suppose ourselves to enter sympathetically into the forms of the external world, but do so in fact. Actually, however, we do not *know* that the openings and shuttings of the mussel constitute "monotonous bliss"; it would be equally reasonable to presume that they are manifestations of intense boredom. Lotze's *Einfühlung* is sympathetic and emotional, enabling us to "see in forms the joy and sorrow of existence that they hide." He does not, on the whole, distinguish clearly between sympathy and empathy.

The theory of empathy was notably developed and altered by Karl Groos (1899, 1902) and by Vernon Lee (1912, 1913).[5] Groos emphasized the physical element of incipient muscular activity, or "inner mimicry" of the object of perception. The earlier exponents of empathy had not ignored its physical and sensational foundations, as we have seen in the case of Lotze. They had, however, placed most weight upon its mental and spiritual aspects, prompted to do so in part because of an ambiguity in the word *Einfühlung* which led to a logical difficulty in definition.[6] Vernon Lee, along with her collaborator,

5. The work of Robert Vischer (1873) and Lipps's classic *Raumesthetik* (1893-1897) emphasize the mental and conceptual aspects of *Einfühlung*. See Thorpe, "Empathy," *op. cit.*

6. "Sich einfühlen" might mean either "to feel into" or "to feel *within* or *inside* of" the object of contemplation. Thus *Einfühlung* could be either a projection of the ego *into* the object or a merging of the ego *with* the object. In the first case the percipient could observe his own physical reactions during the act of contemplation; but if the ego is merged with the object it must be unconscious of its own existence and thus incapable of introspection. Empathy in this alternative would be an entirely hypothetical explanation for certain facts otherwise unexplainable. Thus, as Ogden, Richards, and Wood have noted, ". . . Lipps contended that if Empathy was in progress we could not be aware of the inner imitation or muscular movements which (in the similar view of Groos) accompany the process."—*The Foundations of Aesthetics*

C. Anstruther-Thomson, brought out the aesthetic implications of empathy more completely than had previous scholars, described specifically its physical elements, and added the factor of memory.

According to her account, through empathy we
attribute our own feelings and experience to the object
of our perception: not only our present feelings and
experience, but the memory of such of our past experience as is appropriate to the occasion. When we look
at a mountain we transfer to it from ourselves the notion
of rising, but what we are transferring "is not merely
the thought of the rising which is really being done by
us at that moment, but the thought and emotion, the
idea of rising as such which had been accumulating in
our mind long before we ever came into the presence
of that particular rising."[7]

Our contemplation of the object gives rise to an
adjustment of motor and kinesthetic sensations. The
nature of this adjustment depends upon the aesthetic
qualities inherent in the object. If the lines of its shape
are in such relation to each other and in themselves of
such quality as to arouse harmonious and beneficent
reactions in us, we are experiencing beauty. "When this
attribution of our modes of life to visible shapes and
this revival of past experience is such as to be favourable
to our existence and in so far pleasurable we welcome the
form thus animated by ourselves as 'beautiful'. . ."[8]
Beauty, then, in the view of Miss Lee, is that which is

[London, 1925], p. 70. But if this is so, how can we be sure that "inner imitation"
actually occurs?

7. *Op. cit.*, p. 67.
8. Vernon Lee and C. Anstruther-Thomson, *Beauty and Ugliness*, p. 21.

favorable to our existence, and we perceive Beauty through the dynamic and kinesthetic processes of empathy.[9]

Miss Lee is interested in empathy chiefly as it helps to explain our aesthetic appreciation of the visual and representational arts—sculpture and painting. Although more searching in her analysis of the sensational bases of empathy than were her predecessors, she falls into the same difficulty as they: a dilemma which she herself points out. For she is unwilling to define empathy as a projection of the ego; rather it is "another of those various mergings of the activities of the perceiving subject with the qualities of the perceived object," and "depends upon a comparative or momentary abeyance of all thought of an ego."[10] "Abeyance of all thought of an ego," however, even if we qualify the phrase with "comparative" or "momentary," involves also abeyance of the power to introspect. The characteristic processes of empathy consequently go unobserved, and the theory of empathy is an hypothesis impossible to substantiate. This difficulty persists in Miss Lee's distinction between empathy and sympathy, in which empathy is simply an unknown quantity which covers the space unaccounted for by sympathy, the more familiar and definable element.[11]

9. This definition of Beauty is obviously extremely broad. Surely there are objects "favourable to our existence" which we would hesitate to call beautiful. One may enjoy a football game, for example, without feeling that he has undergone an aesthetic experience.

10. *The Beautiful*, p. 67.

11. "Empathy exists or tends to exist throughout our mental life. It is, indeed, one of our simpler, though far from absolutely elementary, psychological processes, entering into what is called imagination, sympathy, and also into that inference from our own inner experience which has shaped all our conceptions of an outer world. . . ." —*Ibid.*, pp. 68-69.

Professor Herbert S. Langfeld lays even more stress than does Vernon Lee upon the physiological aspects of empathy. All of our perceptions, he contends, are dependent upon motor attitudes.[12] The observed object arouses memory of former movements, which establishes a nervous pattern within the body capable on further stimulation of producing actual movement. This pattern of nerve-paths is sufficient to give perception of "space, weight, form, smoothness, delicacy, and many of our other experiences." In Professor Langfeld's opinion, this explanation is adequate to account for empathy, without resorting to psychology.[13] Agreeing with earlier writers that empathy is a fusing or merging with the object, he brushes aside the difficulty of observing empathic responses.[14] His account of the rôle of empathy in aesthetic experience is specific: sensations of movement or tendencies to movement fuse with the object as perception, lending to it character and meaning. These motor sensations are also responsible for enjoyment, for objects cannot please unless they give rise to unified motor responses, which the nervous system requires. This physiological demand is "the ultimate reason why unity in the object is essential to beauty."[15]

Langfeld's most notable contribution to the theory of empathy is his distinction between the empathic and the sympathetic. Empathy is "feeling in the object. One's own personality is merged and fused in that of some external thing." Sympathy, on the other hand, is "feeling with; instead of being merged in the object,

12. *The Aesthetic Attitude*, p. 109.
13. *Ibid.*, p. 111.
14. *Ibid.*, p. 117.
15. *Ibid.*, p. 122.

our feelings run, so to speak, parallel with the object."
The sympathetic response is somewhat self-conscious
and self-satisfied, so that it is lacking in aesthetic
quality.[16] Sympathy is intellectual, and without the
sensational elements which play so important a rôle
in empathy.

II   Those attempts which have been made to
apply the theory of empathy to poetry
have in the main been distinguished by breadth and
vagueness of definition. Vernon Lee, in the small space
she allotted to empathy in verbal expression, speculated
upon the possibility that it might be used to explain all
metaphor.[17] Professor Langfeld's sole example of literary empathy is Charles Kingsley's "cruel, *crawling*,
foam,"[18] an image accepted since Ruskin as a pronounced
case of "pathetic fallacy." He makes no distinction between empathy and the emotional humanization of
the inanimate which typifies the "pathetic fallacy."
Among still more recent writers, Professors Gilbert and
Kuhn apparently identify empathy, as did Langfeld,
with personification.[19] Joseph T. Shipley describes it in
The Quest for Literature as a kind of emotional sympathy,
into which the factors of memory and sensation need
not enter.[20] To him empathy is emotional response to

16. *Ibid.*, pp. 137-38.
17. ". . . Empathy is what explains why we employ figures of speech at all,
and occasionally employ them . . . when we know perfectly well that the figure we
have chosen expresses the exact reverse of the objective truth."—*The Beautiful*, p. 62.
18. *The Aesthetic Attitude*, p. 135. The motor-content of "crawling" may be the
grounds of Langfeld's identification of this figure with empathy.
19. *A History of Esthetics*, pp. 537-38.
20. Pp. 373 ff.

art, more especially the emotional response of a spectator to a dramatic performance. It is the sort of thing we feel when we identify ourselves with our favorite actor, or it may also be the response of the actor himself to his rôle.

Louis Peter de Vries has given the most complete account of poetic empathy of which I am aware in *The Nature of Poetic Literature*.[21] His view of the problem, however, is too spacious to be entirely helpful. "Empathy," he declares, "is a significant feature of all artistic and poetic reactions. No true appreciation of art and poetic literature is conceivable without this process."[22] Yet he does not adequately distinguish between empathy and sympathy,[23] so that poetic empathy is to him identical either with personification ("symbolic empathy") or humanitarian sympathy ("human empathy").[24]

The objection to these theories of poetic empathy is that they are too generalized to be serviceable for practical application. If empathy is equivalent to emotion, sympathy, personification, or motor imagery, there is obviously no need for it as a distinct conception. This failure to "place" poetic empathy comes, I think, of the basic subject-object confusion present in empathic doctrine from the time of Lotze. Empathy is a merging of the percipient with the perceived; it is therefore by definition undiscernible. Students of poetry, recognizing

21. Seattle, Washington, 1930.

22. *The Nature of Poetic Literature*, p. 32.

23. "Empathy is closely allied with sympathy. As a matter of fact it is difficult to draw a sharp line of demarcation. Evidently sympathy presupposes our projecting ourselves into the situation of the other person."—*Ibid.*, p. 34.

24. *Ibid.*, pp. 35-38.

this, tend to regard it as an element in more complex modes of thinking and knowing, present but neutral, colorless, and invisible. Wordsworth in writing, "The moon doth with delight / Look round her when the heavens are bare," has allied his own humanity with "the alien silent form," says the critic;[25] therefore Wordsworth has felt empathy. The difficulty is, however, that this is mere hypothesis. There may be other equally plausible explanations of the poet's mode of expressing himself.

The critic makes the fundamental error of trying to point out indications of empathic response in passages which occasion no such response in himself. But surely such a response should be the touchstone and divining rod by which the presence of empathy is perceived. Otherwise the pursuit of empathy in poetry is a chase after shadows, vast, formless, and intangible.

In applying the theory of empathy to the poetry of Keats and Shelley I commence from the definition of Professor Clarence DeWitt Thorpe, as by far the most suitable for my purpose:

> The theory of empathy essays to explain imaginative experience in which there is an involuntary projection of ourselves into the object. More specifically, empathy is response to imagery that is produced by shapes, bodies, and movements, and in which, though more purely intellectual elements are present, dynamic or motor content is prominent; it owes its quality and force to accumulated and integrated experience brought into focus by an appropriate stimulus, with an instant and unconscious attribution of this experience to the thing perceived. Thus one's sense of firmness and weight, of solidity and strength and durability in observing a Norman arch is the result not only of the mind's comprehension of

25. See Gilbert and Kuhn, *op. cit.*, pp. 537-38.

facts about materials and structure, but even more of the tactile and muscular impressions, of tensions and other organic sensations, gained through experience with strongly poised, substantial objects throughout our lives. Likewise the easy flight of a sea gull sets off a complex of remembered motions and unconscious recognitions, all the store of hidden connotations that have centered in our being, through real or imagined experience, in connection with our idea of effortlessly soaring in space. And presently we soar with the gull, attribute to him the well-being and pleasure we ourselves experience.[26]

Professor Thorpe's account of empathy avoids the subject-object confusion which renders description of empathic experience logically impossible. If empathy is a merging of oneself with an object, then one's proper identity is lost, and with it the possibility of introspective analysis. Furthermore, *merging*, as we have seen in the case of Lotze, implies a mystical union between oneself and other orders of being and consciousness which is on the surface unlikely and in any event wholly unverifiable. The definition of empathy as *projection*, however, is not subject to these disadvantages. It permits the closest contact of self and the object without the loss of identity, so that the experience of empathy can be examined in retrospect; and it confines itself to what can be empirically proven: that we *attribute* our own feelings to beings which we cannot *know*.

Likewise, it establishes the respective rôles of the intellect and the senses in empathy, which is a matter "not only of the mind's comprehension . . . but even more of the tactile and muscular impressions, of tensions and other muscular sensations." The emphasis upon the sensational serves to distinguish empathy, which is bas-

26. "Empathy," *op. cit.*, p. 186.

ically physical and instinctive, from sympathy, which is intellectual and self-conscious. Finally, the definition of empathy as "response to imagery that is produced by shapes, bodies, and movements" provides a focus and convenient *locus standi* for the examination of empathy in poetry, confining it within a definite and limited scope.

Utilizing the work of Professor Thorpe as a basis, we may then conclude that the hall mark by which poetic empathy is to be identified is the presence of motor, kinesthetic, or organic imagery, so powerful in effect as to evoke kindred impulses in the reader. Such images as

> . . . mid-May's eldest child,
> The coming musk-rose, full of dewy wine
>
> (Keats)

and

> Thou, linnet! in thy green array,
> Presiding Spirit here to-day . . .
>
> (Wordsworth)

are not to be considered empathic, for they lack the characteristic sensational content of empathy.[27] They are examples of sympathy, which, as Langfeld has said, feels parallel with the object, not in it. Keats and Wordsworth have not projected themselves into the musk-rose and the linnet. They are viewing them sympathetically, but from without. One thinks within the object only after *physically* placing oneself within it. On the other hand, motor, kinesthetic and organic imagery are not necessarily and in themselves empathic; they are merely

27. These passages are cited as illustrations of empathy in de Vries, *op. cit.*, p. 41.

agents of the imaginative projection which is the end
of empathy. Shelley's lines,

> With mighty *whirl* the multitudinous orb
> *Grinds* the bright brook into an azure mist . . .

contain strong suggestions of motion and muscular
effort, but we do not identify ourselves imaginatively
with the orb, which is remote to us.

A. E. Housman's "Eight O'Clock" provides a notable example of true empathy, in which sensuous and
imaginative elements combine to produce the identification of self with the object:

> He stood, and heard the steeple
> Sprinkle the quarters on the morning town.
> One, two, three, four, to market-place and people
> It tossed them down.
> Strapped, noosed, nighing his hour,
> He stood, and counted them and cursed his luck;
> And then the clock *collected* in the tower
> Its *strength*, and *struck*.[28]

The empathic process is here rather complex, a product
of metre as well as meaning. It commences with the
motor-image "sprinkle," and is carried on in the movement of "One, two, three, four" with gradually increasing speed and force. With "tossed them down"
kinesthetic is added to the motor imagery. The final
effect is anticipated in the weighty stress and slowness
of "Strapped, noosed," which suggests a kind of gather-
ing-together. All these subtly prepare for the savage,
spasmodic effort portrayed in "collected . . . Its strength,
and struck," in which the extremely heavy alliteration

28. *Last Poems*, p. 24.

"Strapped," "strength," "struck" plays an important part. Aided by cumulative suggestion, one projects oneself through physical sensation into the object itself.

Poetic empathy is an imaginative process which begins with the physiological and culminates in the psychological. In empathy at its best strong motor, kinesthetic, or organic impulses are fused with poetic emotion. It is concerned, in poetry as in the representational arts, with lines, shapes, forms, and bodies, which it endows with human life and feeling. The physical sensations upon which it is founded aid in the imaginative perception of forms, through which the percipient gains the fullest insight possible to him of the world of things in its completeness. A sense of *body* must be present in empathy; but since poetry is not at bottom a pictorial or plastic medium this "body" will probably be suggested rather than described.

Empathy is aesthetically significant in that it provides the best and most complete means of contemplation. It is a fusion of the physical and spiritual, focussed and concentrated upon a single object. If this fusion is perfect the total effect is not merely of physical and emotional self-projection, but of imaginative projection balanced and tempered by an objective self-possession born of intense contemplation, which sees things as wholes, not partially. Seen in this light, poetic empathy is a kind of sensuous imagination, which bases perception firmly upon our muscular, nervous, and organic processes.

III   Through empathy the poet projects him-
             self into the object of his contemplation
by *feeling* as well as *thinking* himself inside it, so that
through sensation and intuition as well as thought he
comprehends it as fully as is possible within the limitations of his nature. Keats is, I believe, a poet typically
empathic. His sensory equipment is extensive and exquisitely delicate: we have earlier seen that with him
poetic inspiration often had its origin in sensation.[29]
Furthermore, he conceives of the poet as a neutral being
who takes on the characteristics of the object he contemplates—an idea which plainly suggests empathic
projection. He possesses an unparalleled ability to humanize nature, and in his concentrative and compressive
technique he wields a weapon peculiarly apt for achieving the sustained and focussed effects which the portrayal of empathy demands.

A familiar and unchallengeable instance of empathic
response in Keats is his reaction to Spenser's phrase,
"sea-shouldering whales." " 'He hoisted himself up,
and looked burly and dominant, as he said, "What an
image that is—sea-shouldering whales!" ' "[30] The importance of kinesthetic and organic sensation in this
example need not be enlarged upon. Another description
of Keats affords less clear-cut evidence of observable
empathic feeling, but is nonetheless significant:

Certain things affected him extremely, particularly when 'a

29. See above, pp. 65-67, 118.
30. Charles Cowden Clarke, quoted by Sir Sidney Colvin, *John Keats*, p. 20. A
comment by Hoxie N. Fairchild is apt: "The surest sign of poetic promise in this
anecdote is not so much the singling out of epithets as the organic response to them,
the being made to feel like a whale by words about whales."—*The Romantic Quest*,
p. 310.

wave was billowing through a tree,' as he described the uplifting surge of air among swaying masses of chestnuts or oak foliage, or when, afar off, he heard the wind coming across woodlands. 'The tide! the tide!' he would cry delightedly, and spring on to some stile, or upon the bough of a wayside tree, and watch the passage of the wind upon the meadow grasses or young corn, not stirring till the flow of air was all around him, while an expression of rapture made his eyes gleam and his face glow. . . .

The only thing that would bring Keats out of one of his fits of seeming gloomful reverie—the only thing, during those country rambles, that would bring the poet 'to himself again' was the notion 'of the inland sea' he loved so well, particularly the violent passage of wind across a great field of barley . . . he would stand, leaning forward, listening intently, watching with a bright serene look in his eyes and sometimes with a slight smile, the tumultuous passage of the wind above the grain.[31]

In this there are strong indications of motor response to the sweep of the wind, the waving of the grain. Apparrent also is the intuitional, spontaneous, emotional quality of the young Keats's relations with nature, which may well have originated in powerful empathic sensory impulses.

Keats's *Letters* evince a keenness of sympathy with the external world, whether human or natural, animate or inanimate, which frequently becomes empathy, and at all times has empathic tendencies. He conceives of the poet as a being who merges his identity with his perceptions; who becomes "a part of all he sees." "Men of genius," he declares, "are great as certain ethereal Chemicals operating on the Mass of neutral intellect— by [for *but*] they have not any individuality, any deter-

31. William Sharp, *The Life and Letters of Joseph Severn*, quoted by Colvin, *op. cit.*, p. 80.

mined Character."[32] Later he gives fuller expression
to the same idea:

As to the poetical Character itself (I mean of that sort of which,
if I am anything, I am a member; that sort distinguished from the
wordsworthian or egotistical sublime; which is a thing per se and
stands alone) it is not itself—it has no self—it is everything and
nothing—It has no character—it enjoys light and shade; it lives
in gusto, be it foul or fair, high or low, rich or poor, mean or
elevated—It has as much delight in conceiving an Iago as an Imogen.
What shocks the virtuous philosopher, delights the camelion poet.
. . .[33] A Poet is the most unpoetical thing in existence; because he
has no identity—he is continually . . . filling some other body—
The Sun, the Moon, the Sea and Men and Women who are creatures
of impulse are poetical and have about them an unchangeable
attribute—the poet has none; no identity—he is certainly the most
unpoetical of all God's Creatures.[34]

Applying this conception of the poet still more
closely to himself, he remarks, "When I am in a room
with People if I ever am free from speculating on crea-
tions of my own brain, then *not myself goes home to myself*
[italics mine]; but the identity of every one in the room
begins to press upon me that I am in a very little time
an[n]ihilated. . . ."[35] "Not myself goes home to myself"; it seems an exact and wonderfully concise description of empathic projection. He concludes by reflecting,
". . . even now I am perhaps not speaking from myself:

32. *The Letters of John Keats*, p. 67. Hereafter to be referred to as *Letters*.

33. Cf. Shelley: "Incest is, like many other incorrect things, a very poetical
circumstance." *The Works of Percy Bysshe Shelley*, ed. H. B. Forman, VIII, 143. Hereafter
to be referred to as *Works*.

34. *Letters*, pp. 227-28.

35. *Loc. cit.* Cf. p. 216, on his brother Tom in his last illness: "His identity presses
upon me so all day that I am obliged to go out . . . I am obliged to write, and plunge
into abstract images to ease myself of his countenance his voice and feebleness."

but from some character in whose soul I now live."[36]

This identification of himself with what he perceived extended also to lower orders of existence: ". . . if a Sparrow come before my Window I take part in its existince [sic] and pick about the Gravel."[37] Since Keats imagines himself to be actually participating in the movements of the sparrow, his response is empathic. Elsewhere he declares that he can share the being even of a billiard ball.[38] He perceives human qualities in landscapes, discerning in a flash of insight a profound relationship between man and nature.[39] Overwhelmed by the grandeur of mountainous scenery, he grows oblivious of himself in intense contemplation.[40]

Keats's reaction to "sea-shouldering whales" indicates that his imagination responded empathically to literature. On his own showing, his appreciation of art was of a similar nature. In a letter to the painter Benjamin Robert Haydon he employs poetical analogies to express his feeling for pictures in a fashion which significantly links his perceptions of these different mediums:

. . . when a Schoolboy the abstract Idea I had of an heroic painting—was what I cannot describe I saw it somewhat sideways large prominent round and colour'd with magnificence—somewhat

36. *Ibid.*, p. 229.
37. *Op. cit.*, p. 69.
38. On the authority of Richard Woodhouse, quoted by Amy Lowell, *John Keats*, II, 103.
39. "What astonishes me more than anything is the tone, the coloring, the slate, the stone, the moss, the rock-weed; or, if I may so say, the intellect, the countenance of such places. . . ."—*Letters*, p. 156.
40. "I cannot think with Hazlitt that these scenes make man appear little. I never forgot my stature so completely—I live in the eye; and my imagination, surpassed, is at rest—."—*Ibid.*, p. 157.

like the feel I have of Anthony and Cleopatra. Or of Alcibiades, leaning on his Crimson Couch in his Galley, his broad shoulders imperceptibly heaving with the Sea. . . .[41]

This masterly word-portrait of Alcibiades both expresses and evokes empathy. One feels mass, body, motion, organic response. In a manoeuvre too swift to follow Keats becomes Alcibiades himself, in all his pride of power and physical well-being. I hazard the suggestion that this process commences at the very beginning of Keats's imagined contemplation of "an heroic painting." The "abstract Idea" focusses and assumes concreteness and reality in "Anthony and Cleopatra," seated, no doubt, in their gorgeous Shakesperian barge. A dynamic sense of line emerges, already suggested in "sideways large prominent round." The focussing process continues, as if a kaleidoscope were being adjusted to bring into sharp relief its colored forms and shapes; and these fall into their culminating and most vivid pattern in the magnificent figure of Alcibiades. The empathic sense of an actual living body originates with the perception of line, dynamically composed to elicit this effect not on a material, objective canvas, but in Keats's imagination.

A self-projection more purely literary, emotional, and sympathetic, yet with some traces of empathy, occurs in an introspective discussion of Beauty and Imagination:

No sooner am I alone than shapes of epic greatness are stationed about me, and serve my Spirit the office which is equivalent to a King's body guard—then 'tragedy with scepter'd pall comes sweeping by.' According to my state of mind I am with Achilles shouting in the Trenches, or with Theocritus in the Vales of Sicily.[42]

41. *Ibid.*, p. 129.
42. *Letters*, p. 241. Mario Praz has interpreted this passage as a typical example

The dynamic force of "sweeping," and the concreteness with which the shouting Achilles is realized, arouse an empathic response.

The empathy of Keats is not mere self-abandonment. The instinctive, sensuous, and intuitional qualities of his perception are balanced and steadied by an intellectual self-awareness which restrains him from indulging in emotional sympathy for its own sake.[43] This nice equilibrium of self-projection and self-restraint is most fully indicated in a long journal letter to George and Georgiana Keats:

The greater part of Men make their way with the same instinctiveness, the same unwandering eye from their purposes, the same animal eagerness as the Hawk. The hawk wants a Mate, so does the Man—look at them both they set about it and procure on[e] in the same manner. They want both a nest and they both set about one in the same manner—they get their food in the same manner— The noble animal Man for his amusement smokes his pipe—the Hawk balances about the Clouds—that is the only difference of their leisures. This it is that makes the Amusement of Life—to a speculative Mind. I go among the Fields and catch a glimpse of a Stoat or a fieldmouse peeping out of the withered grass—the creature hath a purpose and its eyes are bright with it. I go amongst the buildings of a city and I see a Man hurrying along—to what? the Creature has a purpose and his eyes are bright with it. . . . May there not be superior beings amused with any graceful, though instinctive attitude my mind m[a]y fall into, as I am entertained with the

---

of the Romantic love for far-off times and distant places, analogous to Flaubert's heavily picturesque *Salammbo.—La Carne, la Morte e il Diavolo,* p. 200. It illustrates, in his opinion, an escapist decadence. I disagree; the tone is not languidly aesthetic, but healthy and exuberantly imaginative.

43. ". . . supplementary to his demand for a detached state of spirit for poetic experience was his conception of the poetic nature as a free entity with capacity to penetrate wherever it may choose, able to project itself into and merge itself in complete identification with the objects of its contemplation."—C. D. Thorpe, *The Mind of John Keats,* pp. 105-6.

alertness of a Stoat or the anxiety of a Deer? Though a quarrel in
the Streets is a thing to be hated, the energies displayed in it are fine;
the commonest Man shows a grace in his quarrel. . . .[44]

Keats combines in these observations the attitude of
the spectator and of the participant.[45] The spectator
predominates here, perhaps; one is struck first of all by
his detachment. He looks down as from a great height.
The affairs of man and beast alike are to him trivial,
capable of arousing in him only a calm, speculative
amusement. Yet this Olympian calm stems from a complete and selfless participation in the emotions and sensations of the Man, the Hawk, the Stoat. How he hits
off each one: the alertness of the stoat, the anxiety of
the deer, the timidity of the fieldmouse peeping out
of the withered grass. Of all these the most meaningful,
I think, is the hawk empathically *balancing* about the
clouds—an image effortless and casual, but inevitable
and unique in its fusion of the human and the natural.

IV   Although Keats shows empathic tenden-
            cies in sensory equipment, in theory, in
quality of emotion, and in technique, yet clear and unmistakable examples of empathy in his verse are comparatively few. This is because of the nature of empathy,
which is like an iceberg, with the greater part of it
hidden beneath the surface. Every instance of it represents a concentration of sensation, emotion, and expression which it would be neither possible nor desirable
to maintain. Even poetry cannot (and should not) be

44. *Letters*, pp. 316-17.
45. See Shipley, *op. cit.*, p. 219.

perpetually at white-heat. Furthermore, empathy becomes perceptible only within the object upon which it is focussed, and since poetry is not basically a pictorial or plastic medium empathy at an observable level occurs in it infrequently. These reservations made, however, it is still possible to affirm the high importance of empathic imagery as a factor in Keats's poetry.

Critics have noted and praised in Keats the "potential" force of his static images. These convey a sense or power held momentarily in restraint; of massive repose, which yet gives promise of decisive action.[46] This "potential" quality, I believe, derives for the most part from empathy. An early and slight example is

> Here are sweet peas, *on tiptoe* for a flight.
> (*I Stood Tiptoe*, l. 57)

On the plane of sensation the image works through implied motor and kinesthetic impulses, by means of which Keats endows the sweet peas with human form and sentience. The shapes and attitudes of the flowers suggest to him an anticipatory stretching and flexing of muscles.

A potential empathic image richer in shape and body is the picture of young Adonis in sleep, the coverlet not hiding

> . . . an Apollonian curve
> Of neck and shoulder, nor the *tenting swerve*,
> Of knee from knee, nor ankles *pointing light* . . .
> (*Endymion*, II, 399-401)

46. ". . . the secret of Keats's imagery, the excellence which sets him above his contemporaries in mastery of phrase, is a highly dynamic power momentarily caught at rest and concentrated and imprisoned within an otherwise static image . . . this concentration in Keats is effected with no loss, but indeed with a startling gain, in strength, life, and intensity."—W. J. Bate, *Negative Capability*, p. 61.

The figure of Adonis takes on life from the purposeful movement of the lines of his body, from the kinesthetic implications of *tenting* and *pointing*. The total effect is sculptural yet animated. Keats's ability to endow static figures with organic life is also demonstrated in this description of Endymion:

> His youth was fully blown,
> Showing like Ganymede to manhood grown;
> And, for those simple times, his garments were
> A chieftain king's; beneath his breast, half bare,
> Was hung a silver bugle, and between
> His *nervy* knees there lay a boar-spear keen.
>
> (*Endymion*, I, 169-74)

The image is built around *nervy*, which projects the detail which precedes it into life. By virtue of its organic and kinesthetic force Endymion is a sturdy young man, capable of physical action; without it he would have been a mere lay-figure. In the fine lines,

> At this with madden'd stare,
> And lifted hands, and trembling lips he stood;
> Like old Deucalion *mountain'd* o'er the flood,
> Or blind Orion hungry for the morn,
>
> (*Endymion*, II, 195-98)

depth of concept and poignancy of emotion is heightened and vivified by the weighty organic image *mountain'd*.

These passages, save for the last one, have chiefly exemplified the physical, sensuous aspect of empathy. In the famous opening of *Hyperion* sensation is given a far-reaching symbolic meaning. The essence of the mighty idea which underlies Keats's epic is compressed into a few lines of objective description. One might say

that all the thought and motion of *Hyperion* lies packed
together in one small object: the hand of Saturn.

> Upon the sodden ground
> His old right hand lay nerveless, listless, dead,
> Unsceptred . . .
>
> (I, 17-19)

This is empathic by paradox. Organic, kinesthetic, and
motor feelings are conjured up by Keats's insistence upon
their absence. By a technique of repetition and compression one is forced to participate in the seeming
independent being of this hand, to attribute to it ideas
and emotions which go far beyond what Keats is to all
appearances saying. For all his adjectives are more or
less literal and objective; the hand is *old, nerveless, listless,
dead, unsceptred.* Of course it is *unsceptred;* why should
it be otherwise? And yet the word is crowded with
implications.

> . . . and his realmless eyes were closed;
> While his bow'd head seem'd list'ning to the Earth,
> His ancient mother, for some comfort yet.
>
> (I, 19-21)

On the surface the predominating impression is visual
and sculptural. By the weighty quietness of Saturn's
attitude we are hypnotically drawn into the picture.
"Realmless," however, is a bridge between the subjective and objective modes. Great Saturn, Lord of Titans
and Father of the Gods, is realmless: and this is of enormous, cosmic consequence. But these immensities of
meaning are contracted to a physical point. They reside
not merely within the corporeal body of Saturn, but
actually in his eyes. "Realmless" is an "intense" word,

the ultimate result of great pressures, which contains within itself both subject and object epitomized. Through the processes of empathy, set in motion by almost imperceptible motor, organic, and kinesthetic responses, we step gradually to higher levels of perception, the levels on which "realmless" moves, and to which it introduces us. The whole passage illustrates the use of empathy to give solid, finite substantiality to conceptions formless of themselves because of their very size. In it Keats symbolizes in sculptural forms the entire story of the Titans: their greatness, the magnitude of their fall, and its inevitability.

Hyperion contains several other examples of static, "potential" empathy, although no others so complex. The den in which the defeated Titans hold their council is surrounded by

> Crag jutting forth to crag, and rocks that seem'd
> Ever as if *just rising from a sleep*,
> Forehead to forehead held their monstrous horns . . .
>
> (II, 10-12)

This image recalls Vernon Lee's "rising mountain." It is empathic because fully realized. The "rising" is visible through strong personification, reinforced by kinesthetic and tactual sensations. It is a motionless tableau of two bucks, straining against each other horn to horn, static but intense with fierce life.

A sense of still more violent effort in motionlessness pervades the description of the Titans imprisoned below Tartarus:

> . . . the *brawniest* in assault
> Were *pent* in regions of *laborious breath;*

> *Dungeon'd* in *opaque* element, to keep
> Their *clenched* teeth still *clench'd*, and all their limbs
> *Lock'd up* like veins of metal, *crampt* and *screw'd;*
> Without a motion, save of their *big* hearts
> *Heaving* in *pain*, and horribly *convuls'd*
> With *sanguine feverous boiling gurge* of *pulse*.

> (II, 21-28)

Keats is applying all his powers of expression to a single purpose, returning again and again to the attack. The verses surge with kinesthetic and organic impressions, enforced upon the reader by unusually weighty stresses, which give each suggestion its full value. In the final line each accent strikes like a hammer blow, in part because of the repeated parallelism of the syntax. There is nothing subtle about the method. Keats begins with a clear notion of the effect he desires and brings his strongest weapons to bear in order to achieve it. The empathic quality of the passage is not, however, simply a matter of kinesthetic and organic suggestions, which do not initiate self-projection unless they are localized in forms. Human bodies are implicitly indicated in "brawniest" and "big."

The savage emotions and the immense physical force of the more warlike Titans are less directly but just as forcefully portrayed in

> Creüs was one; his ponderous iron mace
> Lay by him, and a shatter'd rib of rock
> Told of his rage, ere he thus sank and pined.
> Iäpetus another; in his grasp,
> A serpent's plashy neck; its barbed tongue
> Squeez'd from the gorge, and all its uncurl'd length
> Dead; and because the creature could not spit
> Its poison in the eyes of conquering Jove.

> (II, 41-48)

The strength and despair of Creüs and Iäpetus are not in their proper forms, but reside in the "ponderous iron mace," the "shatter'd rib of rock," and the dead serpent. As in the preceding passage, single words are enunciated with peculiar force and emphasis. The personifying significance of "rib" should be noticed; the word is unremarkable in its context, but indispensable to the empathic effect.

A final example of empathy in motionlessness may be pointed out in a sculptural image of Cupid and Psyche:

> They lay calm-breathing on the bedded grass;
> Their arms embraced, and their pinions too;
> Their lips touch'd not, but had not bade adieu,
> As if disjoined by soft-handed slumber,
> And ready still past kisses to outnumber . . .
>
> (*Ode to Psyche*, ll. 15-19)

The organic "calm-breathing" determines empathy, sustained by tactual feelings in "bedded," "embraced," "lips touch'd not," "disjoined," and "soft-handed." Motor content is implicit; action is suspended only momentarily.

The characteristic quality and peculiar impact of these "potential" images comes in large part from the combination of compression with sustained concreteness of physical suggestion. Keats attains the maximum of condensation; at the same time, however, he as it were revolves the object he is describing slowly before his reader's eyes, so that each particular can be fully apprehended. This lingering, careful attention to significant detail is apparent also in his most typical empathic images of motion.

Motion as he empathically portrays it is generally

slow, smooth, and hypnotic, evocative of organic reactions through which one is insensibly drawn within its charmed circle. Most notable for mesmerizing power is this flower-wave metaphor from *Endymion:*

> . . . the floral pride
> In a *long whispering* birth *enchanted* grew
> Before his footsteps; as when *heav'd* anew
> Old ocean rolls a *lengthen'd* wave to the shore,
> Down whose green *back* the *short-liv'd foam*, all *hoar*,
> *Bursts gradual*, with a *wayward indolence*.
>
> (II, 345-50)

Slow, even movement joins in the first line with a hint of strangeness in "enchanted." In "heav'd" commences a rhythmical rising and falling. The repeated "o" sounds in "Old ocean rolls" unite with "lengthen'd" to heighten the feeling of motion, which becomes a curving, dizzying glide. All this prepares for the effect of the wave itself, within which there are two planes of movement. Within the motion of its green body is contained the steady, "gradual" bursting of the foam, which takes on a wavering, dancing swirl from "wayward." This harmonious diversity of movement focusses one's attention like the crystal ball of a fortune-teller. The undercurrent of personification in "short-liv'd," "back," and "hoar" completes and synthesizes the empathic content of the passage.

Less hypnotic but still strongly empathic is the description of Cybele later on in Book II of *Endymion:*

> Forth from a rugged arch in the dusk below,
> Came mother Cybele: alone—alone—
> In sombre chariot; dark foldings thrown
> About her majesty, and front death-pale,

> With turrets crown'd. Four maned lions *hale*
> The sluggish wheels; solemn their toothed maws,
> Their surly eyes *brow-hidden*, heavy paws
> *Uplifted drowsily*, and *nervy* tails
> Cowering their tawny brushes. Silent *sails*
> This shadowy queen athwart, and *faints away*
> In another gloomy arch.
>
> (ll. 639-49)

Empathy is observable chiefly in the lions. One responds
to Keats's suggestions of weight, form, effort, and movement. It is to be noted that this image is a picture in a
frame, appearing momentarily in the open space between
two rocky arches. The imagination is bounded within
a narrow compass. As in other empathic images, Keats
is at the top of his form; the description of Cybele is a
set-piece upon which he lavishes all of his powers. The
apparently irrelevant "alone—alone" is atmospheric in
its portentous repetition. The repeated "o" sounds—

> Forth from a rugged arch, in the dusk bel*ow*
> Came mother Cybele: al*o*ne—al*o*ne—
> In s*o*mbre chariot; dark f*o*ldings thrown . . .—

have a "dark" sound; their rounded tonalities lend
subtle aid to the general effect of ominous, trancelike
gloom. The "undersong" in "rugged," "dusk," and
"mother" harmonizes with the louder majors of the
"o" in achieving it.

In the strongly empathic picture of the lions a heavy
calm intermingles with threatening suggestions of restrained power. Sound once more plays a part: the as-
sonances "surly-nervy," "brow-hidden-drowsily-cower-
ing" serve to emphasize the antithetical balance of

> Their surly eyes brow-hidden, heavy paws
> Uplifted drowsily, and nervy tails
> Cowering their tawny brushes.

Finally the image disappears amid slighter physical sensations, but it remains "intense" to the last. The "shadowy queen" does not "fade away" as one would prosaically expect, but "faints away." The whole is insistently empathic by virtue of sustained artistic effort; Keats plays every card in his poetical hand to entrap the reader into yielding himself up.

This sustained, repetitive concentration is more obviously apparent in a vividly empathic description of the physical agonies of Hyperion:

> At this, through all his *bulk* an *agony*
> *Crept gradual*, from the *feet* unto the *crown*.
> Like a *lithe serpent vast* and *muscular*,
> Making *slow way*, with *head and neck convuls'd*
> From *over-strained might* . . .
>
> (*Hyperion*, I, 259-63)

Empathy emerges from concreteness of realization ("from the feet unto the crown," "head and neck convuls'd"), from the slowness of movement by which the idea of pain receives its full value and emphasis, and from the violence of organic and kinesthetic sensation in "agony," "lithe," "muscular," "convuls'd," and "over-strained."

A final example of Keats's characteristic slowness in empathic imagery is of a very different nature, filled as it is with a warm, luxurious languor:

> Dash'd by the wood-nymph's beauty, so he *burn'd*
> Then, *lighting* on the printless verdure, turned
> To the *swoon'd* serpent, and with *languid* arm,
> *Delicate*, put to proof the *lythe* Caducean charm.

One enters into the body of Apollo through warmth, "lighting," the idea of hovering, and "languid." More indirectly "swoon'd" and "lythe" are working closely with these to establish the desired effect. Through hints of physical sensation we are brought within the atmosphere of the calm, sensuous, heartless, pagan love of Apollo and the nymph.

Keats is seldom in dancing mood, but in two instances he evokes an irresistible intoxication of rhythmical, swift, excited motion, against a background of thrilling music. One is a puzzling image from *I Stood Tiptoe*, so concrete that commentators have felt that it must derive from some specific literary source, as yet undetermined: "Stepping like Homer at the trumpet's call" (l. 217), evocative in its admirable condensation of strong motor and organic imagery. The second of these two is from the song of the Indian Maiden, in *Endymion:*

> And as I sat, over the light blue hills
> There came a noise of revellers: the rills
> Into the wide stream came of purple hue—
> 'Twas Bacchus and his crew!
> The earnest trumpet spake, and silver thrills
> From kissing cymbals made a merry din—
> 'Twas Bacchus and his kin!
> Like to a moving vintage down they came,
> Crown'd with green leaves, and faces all on flame;
> All madly dancing through the pleasant valley,
> To scare thee, Melancholy!
>
>   (IV, 193-203)

Empathy makes itself felt in the closing verses, but only after intensive preparation. At the very beginning Keats imposes upon us with his "light blue hills," so certain

of touch, so definitive. Then there is the rich and heavy web of literary associations surrounding "Bacchus and his crew" to be taken into account. The powerful organic effects of the three lines commencing, "The earnest trumpet spake" set in motion a definitely physical reaction, which tends to become empathic feeling through delicate personification in "*kissing* cymbals" and the felicitous "earnest."[47] Engendered as it were by these complex causes, empathy bursts into life embodied by the remarkable "moving vintage," in which landscape and figures dissolve into delirious motion, so that animate and inanimate, sentient and insentient, are fused in a dance.

In all the examples which I have cited Keats produces empathy objectively; only twice, to my knowledge, does he describe its effects. The first instance occurs in *The Eve of St. Agnes*, in the oppression aroused in the beadsman by the stone effigies of dead knights and ladies.

> The sculptur'd dead, on each side, seem to freeze,
> Emprison'd in black, purgatorial rails:
> Knights, ladies, praying in dumb orat'ries
> He passeth by; and his weak spirit fails
> To think how they may ache in icy hoods and mails.
>
> (ll. 14-18)

Deluded momentarily by the apparent reality of these figures, he projects into them the cold and ache which he himself is experiencing. This passage both describes and exemplifies empathy. The baleful effect of the philosopher's eye upon Lamia may also be called an account of the empathic process, although it fails, in my opinion, to call forth empathic response:

47. For an even more notable use of the word see *Hyperion*, I, 74: "Tall oaks branch-charmed by the earnest stars."

> The bald-headed philosopher
> Had fix'd his eye, without a twinkle or stir
> Full on the alarmed beauty of the bride,
> Brow-beating her fair form, and troubling her sweet pride.
>
> (II, 245-48)

> . . . .
>
> Some hungry spell that loveliness absorbs;
> There was no recognition in those orbs.
>
> (259-60)

> . . . .
>
> . . . the sophist's eye
> Like a sharp spear, went through her utterly,
> Keen, cruel, perceant, stinging . . .
>
> (299-301)

One may interpret the deathly trance of Lamia as a physical response to a physical property of the eye, so powerful that all self-possession is quelled by it.[48]

Empathy is in part responsible for the effect of two of the great Odes, the *Ode to a Nightingale* and the *Ode on a Grecian Urn*. The *Nightingale*, however, is predominantly sympathetic, while the *Grecian Urn* is empathic. To distinguish between the two it will be necessary for once to stretch the definition of empathy a little, assuming the presence of the characteristic empathic motor, organic, and kinesthetic content where it cannot be fully shown.

48. Cf. Coleridge, *Christabel*, II, 601-9:
> "So deeply had she drunken in
> That look, those shrunken serpent eyes,
> That all her features were resigned
> To this sole image in her mind:
> And passively did imitate
> That look of dull and treacherous hate!
> And thus she stood, in dizzy trance,
> Still picturing that look askance
> With forced unconscious sympathy . . ."

Sympathy, it will be recalled, has been defined as a feeling parallel with. Empathy represents a more perfect fusion of subject and object, being a feeling within[The relations between Keats and the nightingale are in the main sympathetic, for he does not suppose himself to have merged his identity with it.[49] The bird is a convenient object into which to project poetic emotion, but Keats imposes upon it a type of being which it could not possibly possess.] More to the point, he deceives neither himself nor his reader into thinking so. Empathy is a process which enables one to know as much as is possible about the object of one's perceptions, within the limits inherent in the nature of the percipient. The *Ode*, however, is about Keats, not about a nightingale. The bird is a shadowy thing.

There are moments when the poet does indeed seem to be experiencing empathy: in the organic intensity of

> 'Tis not through envy of thy *happy* lot,
> But being too happy in thine happiness,
>
> (ll. 5-6)

in

> . . . thou, *light-winged Dryad* of the trees,
>
> (l. 7)

and in

> Singest of summer in *full-throated* ease.
>
> (l. 10)

There is also a hint of empathy in the sudden shift of scene between stanza three and stanza four, which indirectly suggests flight in Keats by way of the bird.

49. See for a contrary view L. P. de Vries, *op. cit.*, pp. 40-47.

Finally, "plaintive anthem" (l. 75) is a blend of empathy and sympathy. Keats is not warranted in attributing his sudden feeling of disenchantment to the nightingale. On the other hand, this "plaintiveness" is the effect of distancing on sound, and fuses his emotion with his perception. [The poet and the bird, however, are for the most part two, not one. Keats does not propose to enter into the nightingale, but "*with* thee fade away into the forest dim." (l. 20)]

The *Ode on a Grecian Urn* is Keats's consummate expression of empathic feeling and thought. In it empathy arises from prolonged and passionate contemplation of a beautiful object[50] and is refined into aesthetic emotion, which in turn is expanded and uplifted into more comprehensive perceptions culminating in the Platonic merging of Beauty and Truth at the end of the poem. This refining and sublimating process is the result of the action upon empathy of another element, the "spectator" attitude—the calm detachment with which we have seen Keats observing the affairs of the hawk, the stoat, the fieldmouse, and the man. The relations of these two elements in the poem present themselves as a steady movement of advance into the object and withdrawal from it.

The workings of empathy begin with perceptions of line and shape, by the motion of which Keats is drawn within the scenes of the vase. It is a concentrative

50. J. M. Murry seems to deny that the *Grecian Urn* is a poem about art. "The supremacy which he [Keats] asserts is the supremacy of the changeless, and in the strict metaphysical sense, eternal world of the Imagination. He is not asserting the supremacy of Art over Nature; but of the Imaginative vision of Nature over the immersion in Nature to which, in our total animal existence, we are 'condemned.' "—*Studies in Keats, New and Old*, p. 75n. Mr. Murry's distinction is over-ingenious, but his analysis of the *Ode* is brilliant.

process, in which rich and deep emotions and thought
are directed into and focussed upon a single, concrete,
finite form. It is sculptural and pictorial.

The commencement of the *Ode* is muted, chaste, and
cold:

> Thou still unravish'd bride of quietness,
> Thou foster-child of silence and slow time,
> Sylvan historian . . .
>
> (ll. 1-3)

The severe and simple harmonies of the vase do not
easily yield up their secret; its cold classicism is not
immediately evocative of emotion. But Keats begins to
respond to its slowly disclosed invitation in

> What leaf-fring'd legend haunts about thy shape,[51]
>
> (l. 5)

as the measured movement of line and pattern beckons
him inward.

> What men or gods are these? What maidens loth?
> What mad pursuit? What struggle to escape?
> What pipes and timbrels? What wild ecstasy?
>
> (ll. 8-10)

The flat figures take on dimension and life, a perspective
unrolls before him, the scene grows more spacious as he
steps inside it, staring about him like a sleeper newly
awakened. To his eyes all is at first generalized: men
and maidens, excited movement and sound, ecstasy. The
import of it all is not immediately clear.

Soon, however, the meaning of the figures reveals

51. "In calling the scene a 'leaf-fringed legend' Keats will have remembered that
the necks and shoulders of this kind of urn are regularly encircled by bands of leaf-
pattern ornament."—Colvin, *op. cit.*, p. 416.

itself more fully. Caught up by a dynamic sense of motion, he enters into the feelings of the lover. Yet he is
perfectly conscious of the difference between life and
art, and this very consciousness invokes a new, complex
emotion:

> Bold lover, never, never canst thou kiss,
> Though winning near the goal—yet, do not grieve;
> She cannot fade, though thou hast not thy bliss,
> For ever wilt thou love, and she be fair!
>
> (ll. 17-20)

The lover is betrayed by art; he is forever imprisoned
in a timeless frustration. Yet, paradoxically, he is not
to grieve. His love will be present always, and always
fair. Cold comfort, one would unthinkingly say; but
this eternity of aesthetic contemplation is the highest
glory of art.

> Ah, happy, happy boughs! that cannot shed
> Your leaves, nor ever bid the Spring adieu;
> And, happy melodist, unwearied,
> For ever piping songs for ever new;
> More happy love! more happy, happy love!
> For ever warm and still to be enjoy'd,
> For ever panting, and for ever young;
> All breathing human passion far above,
> That leaves a heart high-sorrowful and cloy'd,
> A burning forehead, and a parching tongue.
>
> (ll. 21-30)

This stanza extends and enlarges the suggestions of
stanza two. The tension between empathy and intellect,
participation and contemplation, life and art, becomes
explicit. Keats enters in turn into the boughs, the
melodist, and the lovers, joining fully in their feelings.

The colder intellect tells him, however, that this is not life but the artistic reflection of it, subject to other laws than those which govern mortals. And as in stanza two, this realization issues forth in new and complex ways; emotion, channeled in a new direction, takes on not less but more force from the strangeness and novelty of its course. The impact of empathy is strongest in these lines; Keats tries to fix its significance and intensity in the organic sensations aroused by the heavy, lingering repetitions of "happy." He identifies himself with the lover, feels impulses of movement and kinesthesia. He experiences warmth, he pants; he consummates his love, and goes on to the inevitable human aftermath of "A burning forehead, and a parching tongue." With this line the tide of empathy reaches its height in the poem: yet inseparable from it is the realization that these physical experiences are precisely what do not happen and could not happen. For the figures of the vase are contained forever in another medium than life.

The calmer tone of stanza four is indicative of a steady, progressive withdrawal.

> Who are these coming to the sacrifice?
> To what green altar, O mysterious priest,
> Lead'st thou that heifer, lowing at the skies,
> And all her silken flanks with garlands drest?
> What little town by river or sea shore,
> On mountain-built with peaceful citadel,
> Is emptied of this folk, this pious morn?
> And, little town, thy streets for ever more
> Will silent be; and not a soul to tell
> Why thou art desolate, can e'er return.

Keats is still within the picture, or more aptly, on the

actor's side of the proscenium arch. He is no longer, however, taking active part in the drama. In the exquisitely sympathetic "mysterious" he seals the essential quality of the play with his stamp. The priest is mysterious by simple association, for he partakes in religious mysteries, Eleusinian and Dionysian. He is mysterious because remote from us in time. He is mysterious because he embodies the secret of the greatness and the magic of old Greece. And he is mysterious with the mystery of art. But in all this Keats is not entering into the body and mind of the priest, but is seeing him objectively from without. With the paradox of the village, forever deserted because its inhabitants have been spirited away by the magic piping of art and are caught in the timeless urn, he steps outside the frame of the proscenium arch once more. In stanza five he is outside, reflecting upon what he has experienced.

This stanza is frequently with some justice considered the least satisfactory part of the *Ode*. Its commencement is generally deemed unpromising, a cold eighteenth-century apostrophe:

> O Attic shape! Fair attitude! with brede
> Of marble men and maidens overwrought . . .

These lines are empathically significant, however. The aesthetic and emotional experience which constitutes the *Ode* began with the perception of a shape, an attitude. The chill of stanza five is a reflection of the contemplative mood, as Keats tries to fix permanently what he has seen and felt. "Cold Pastoral" hits off exactly his new point of view. And in the famous final lines beginning, "Beauty is truth, truth beauty," he comes to a satisfying and inevitable conclusion, which could not

have been concretely felt and "proved upon the pulses"[52] without the powerful physical aid of empathy.

With the consideration of the *Ode* this discussion of the empathic qualities of Keats's poetry may well end. For the *Ode on a Grecian Urn* is a perfect and complete expression of its processes, which are rooted in strong and vivid physical sensations, and are capable of growing from this firm and fertile earth to the highest and most subtle reaches of emotion and thought.

V   Unlike that of Keats, Shelley's poetry contains few examples of empathy, although it has a number of empathic tendencies. He habitually personifies the inanimate and insentient, and he displays an intense sympathy with nature. In *Prometheus Unbound* he explicitly and philosophically links man with nature in his imaginative construction of the ideal world of the millennium.[53] Yet despite these apparent indications of empathic feeling and thinking, his verse yields up little evidence of empathy itself.

Shelley, indeed, is a poet of sympathy rather than of empathy. The sensory elements of the empathic process are lacking in him. He projects himself into the object intellectually and emotionally, but not physically; he has too little sense of the human body to be able to do so. When he describes the inanimate or the insentient the object is perfectly there, faithfully recorded, but the human subject is missing.

This lack of feeling for the body manifests itself in

52. ". . . axioms in philosophy are not axioms until they are proved upon our pulses."—Keats, *Letters*, p. 142.

53. See III, iii, 84f.; III, iv; IV, 206f.

his inability to describe complex, organic forms. He expresses kinesthetic, motor, and organic sensations with great vividness, but seldom localizes them in human beings. His figures are generally airy and incorporeal as wind.[54] The visioned maid in *Alastor*, for example, and Asia, Panthea, and Ione in *Prometheus Unbound*, are beautiful but evanescent apparitions. In the latter poem, where his opportunities for sculptural moulding of the "human form divine" are great, the contrast with the parallel *Hyperion* of Keats is very striking. The figures of Keats's Titans are vast, bulky, muscular, Michelangeloesque;[55] one participates with them in the strains and stresses of their immense physical effort against the conquering Gods. Prometheus, Jupiter, and Mercury in *Prometheus Unbound*, however, are almost bodiless. When was there ever so fine a subject for sculptural representation as Prometheus, bound to his rock? Yet Shelley does not utilize him.[56] And without concrete shape or form empathy will not work. The ideal union of man and nature through love with which *Prometheus Unbound* concludes is intellectual and philosophical, not physical and instinctive. The personifications of the Earth and Moon, which I have previously

54. "What was, in my opinion, deficient in his poetry, was . . . the want of reality in the characters with which he peopled his splendid scenes, and to which he addressed or imparted the utterance of his impassioned feelings."—T. L. Peacock, *Peacock's Memoirs of Shelley*, p. 83.

55. It is perhaps significant that Shelley heartily disliked Michelangelo for his "rude, external, mechanical quality."— *Works*, VIII, p. 121.

56. The organic reactions of Prometheus to the tortures of "Jove's winged hounds" are painfully vivid, but we have too little sense of his body to share them. Shelley describes, but fails to exemplify empathy in

"Whilst I behold such execrable shapes
Methinks I grow like what I contemplate,
And laugh and stare in loathsome sympathy." (I, 449-51)

discussed at some length, are ideally suited for empathic description, but in Shelley's hands they remain symbols without humanity, marvellous though they are.[57]

Shelley has ample sense of form and line, but it is simple, elemental, and geometrical. He is more at home with orbs and spheres than with the complex inter-reactions of the planes and surfaces of organic bodies. He is most completely in sympathy with objects and states of mind too remote from our experience for us to participate fully in his feeling for them.[58] He un-questionably identifies himself wholly with his object in *The Cloud*, an amazing feat of imaginative penetration. He unites himself with it in dizzying images of speed and height. But this is a purely private experience; he has gone where no man may pursue. We cannot think or feel ourselves into the cloud, for it has no body for us to get into; none, at least, which invites the ordinary imagination.[59] Thus in *To a Skylark* there is a momentary, abortive feeling of empathic rising in the soaring of the lark, but it is dissipated because of the bird's essential "disembodiedness."[60]

His closest approaches to empathy, as a matter of

57. See above, pp. 49-54. This statement is not intended as a qualitative judgment.

58. ". . . in this have I long believed that my power consists," Shelley wrote; "in sympathy and that part of the imagination which relates to sentiment and con-templation. I am formed, if for anything not in common with the herd of mankind, to apprehend minute and remote distinctions of feeling. . . ."—*Shelley's Literary and Philosophical Criticism*, pp. 160-61.

59. ". . . as to real flesh and blood, you know that I do not deal in those articles; you might as well go to a gin-shop for a leg of mutton, as expect anything human or earthly from me."—*Works*, VIII, 244.

60. See Mark Rampion's amusingly choleric comment in Aldous Huxley's *Point Counter Point*, p. 144. "The lark couldn't be allowed to be a mere bird, with blood and feathers and a nest and an appetite for caterpillars. Oh no! That wasn't nearly poetical enough, that was much too coarse. It had to be a disembodied spirit."

fact, are usually accompanied by images of dizzy speed,
swift rising, immense heights. His treatment of the sea
is sometimes close to empathy; he makes it live, although he does not enter into it himself or make it
accessible to human feelings.[61] Sometimes his swift motion, aided by a manipulation of metrical stresses unexampled before him, catches one up into itself.[62] In a
single instance an image of swift speed and power, aided
by environing ideas of rising and height, becomes truly
empathic:

> If I were a dead leaf thou mightest bear;
> If I were a swift cloud to fly with thee;
> *A wave to pant beneath thy power*, and share
> The impulse of thy strength . . .[63]
>
> (*Ode to the West Wind*, ll. 43-46)

Here, for once, the personification is of a nature to evoke
feelings of breathing, struggling humanity.

Into *The Cenci* alone, for Shelley the exception which
proves the rule,[64] does empathy enter prominently. Two
long speeches of Beatrice are plainly empathic. In the
first she attributes her own horror and confusion to the
scene before her:

> The pavement sinks under my feet! The walls
> Spin round! I see a woman weeping there,

61. See *Alastor*, ll. 323-25; *A Vision of the Sea*.
62. See *Prometheus Unbound*, II, iv, 163-74; v, 1-5.
63. Cf. l. 62: ". . . Be thou me, impetuous one!"
64. "His success was a double triumph; and often after he was earnestly entreated
to write again in a style that commanded popular favor, while it was not less instinct
with truth and genius. But the bent of his mind went the other way; and even when
employed on subjects whose interest depended on character and incident, he would
start off in another direction, and leave the delineations of human passion. . . ."—
Mary Shelley, Note to *The Cenci*.

And standing calm and motionless, whilst I
Slide giddily as the world reels.—My God!
The beautiful blue heaven is flecked with blood!
The sunshine on the floor is black! The air
Is changed to vapors and as the dead breathe
In charnel-pits! Pah! I am choked! There creeps
A clinging, black, contaminating mist
About me—'tis substantial, heavy, thick;
I cannot pluck it from me, for it glues
My fingers and my limbs to one another,
And eats into my sinews, and dissolves
My flesh to a pollution, poisoning
The subtle, pure, and inmost spirit of life!

(III, i, 9-23)

The mental struggle of Beatrice to throw off the sin
forced upon her by the diabolical Cenci is powerfully
projected into physical actuality: the stupor of despair,
the hovering on the verge of madness, and the brave
effort to conquer the ineluctable sense of contamination,
are symbolized in poignant tactual, organic, and kinesthetic imagery.

The second example is a remarkable projection of
human sensations and emotions into inanimate nature:

. . . I remember
Two miles on this side of the fort the road
Crosses a deep ravine; 'tis rough and narrow,
And winds with short turns down the precipice;
And in its depth there is a mighty rock,
Which has, from unimaginable years,
Sustained itself with terror and with toil
Over a gulf, and with the agony
With which it clings seems slowly coming down;
Even as a wretched soul hour after hour
Clings to the mass of life; yet, clinging, leans;

> And, leaning, makes more dark the dread abyss
> In which it fears to fall; beneath this crag
> Huge as despair, as if in weariness,
> The melancholy mountain yawns . . .
>
> (III, i, 243-57)

The ominous shadow of murder hangs over this scene, for it is here that old Cenci is to be done away with. The rock, sustaining itself "with terror and with toil," is Cenci, long ripe for the grave; it is also, however, Beatrice herself, whose life he has in effect destroyed, and who clings to an existence without hope. The kinesthetic force of the repeated *cling* emphasizes the emotional and conceptual implications, and the slow motor alternation of "yet, clinging, leans / And leaning, makes more dark" prepares for the climatic "despair." "Yawns," the final word, is a masterly empathic fusion of the objective and subjective modes. The spacious curve of the mountain yawns beneath the rock as Hell-mouth yawns for the laboring souls of Beatrice and Cenci.

These examples of empathic feeling are, however, exceptions to the habitual mode of Shelley's poetry, which seldom localizes sensation and emotion within the individual human body. Whereas Keats endeavors to bring home to us strong and intimate organic and kinesthetic impulses, drawing us to identify ourselves physically and spiritually with the object of his poetic contemplation, Shelley seeks "to apprehend minute and remote distinctions of feeling," too far from our ordinary sensations and associations for us to participate with him. Mrs. Shelley remarks that "More popular poets clothe the ideal with familiar and sensible imagery.

Shelley loved to idealize the real—to gift the mechanism of the material universe with a soul and a voice, and to bestow such also on the most delicate and abstract emotions and thoughts of the mind."[65] A human voice and soul, but not a human body endowed with sensation: and therefore he is usually incapable of eliciting the strong physical response essential to empathy.

65. Note to *Prometheus Unbound*.

CONCRETE AND ABSTRACT IMAGERY

I   Critics are generally agreed that the imagery of Keats is "concrete." Robert Bridges, for example, in comparing his *Sleep and Poetry* with Wordsworth's *Tintern Abbey*, points out "the extreme difference between Keats' objective treatment and Wordsworth's philosophising," citing to show the contrast the older poet's

> The coarser pleasures of my boyish days
> And their glad animal movements

over against Keats's

> A pigeon tumbling in clear summer air;
> A laughing schoolboy, without grief or care,
> Riding the springy branches of an elm.[1]

A. C. Bradley declares that Keats tends to "a concrete method of treatment; to the vivid presentment of scenes, individualities, actions, in preference to the expression of unembodied thoughts and feelings."[2] A. Clutton-Brock contrasts the "concreteness" of Keats with the "abstractness" of Shelley: to the former, he says, "excel-

1. Introduction, *Poems of John Keats*, ed. G. Thorn Drury, I, xxxv-xxxvi.
2. *Oxford Lectures on Poetry*, p. 238.

lence was in minute particularity," the aim of the poet
"to draw everything in its peculiarity."[3] Sir Sidney
Colvin remarks that "Keats could only think in images,
and almost invariably in images of life and action."[4]

Keats's bent toward the description of concrete objects is, in point of fact, evident even in his earliest
verse; in the midst of the artificiality of the *Imitation of
Spenser*, his earliest known poem:

> There saw the swan his neck of arched snow,
> And oar'd himself along with majesty;
> Sparkled his jetty eyes; his feet did show
> Beneath the waves like Afric's ebony . . .,

and in such a juvenile effusion as the *Specimen of an
Induction to a Poem*, which begins with

> Lo! I must tell a tale of chivalry,
> For large white plumes are dancing in mine eye,

and concludes

> . . . so will I rest in hope
> To see wide plains, fair trees and lawny slope:
> The morn, the eve, the light, the shade, the flowers;
> Clear streams, smooth lakes, and overlooking towers.

His friends have borne witness to this proclivity in
the young Keats. "He was fond of imagery," says Henry
Stephens, an acquaintance in medical school; "the most
trifling similes appeared to please him."[5] The sentimental George Felton Mathew observes somewhat re-
gretfully that "His eye admired more the external deco-

3. "Keats and Shelley—a Contrast," in *The John Keats Memorial Volume*, ed.
G. C. Williamson, p. 116.
4. *John Keats*, p. 63.
5. Quoted by Colvin, *op. cit.*, p. 31.

rations than felt the deep emotions of the Muse. He
delighted in leading you through the mazes of elaborate
description, but was less conscious of the sublime and
the pathetic."[6]

In his later, mature verse Keats also writes custom-
arily about objects. The *Ode on Indolence* is typical of
his method. Under his hand three abstractions, Love,
Ambition, and Poesy, are powerfully projected into the
world of life, form, and movement:

> One morn before me were three figures seen,
> With bowed necks, and joined hands, side-faced;
> And one behind the other stepp'd serene,
> In placid sandals, and in white robes graced . . .
>
> (ll. 1-4)

The *Ode on a Grecian Urn* originates, I think, in the
intense contemplation of a lovely shape.[7] The *Ode to
Psyche* centers about a static, sensuous image of lovers
locked in each other's arms. And the magnificent *To
Autumn* is composed of human figures on a background
of natural beauty.

In the *Letters* one sees how powerfully Keats is affected by shapes of physical beauty. A casual meeting
with a cousin of his friends, the Reynolds, lives in his
memory for weeks.

> She is not a Cleopatra, but she is at least a Charmian. She has
> a rich eastern look; she has fine eyes and fine manners. When she
> comes into a room she makes an impression the same as the Beauty
> of a Leopardess. . . . I always find myself more at ease with such a
> woman; the picture before me always gives me a life and animation
> which I cannot possibly feel with anything inferior—I am at such

6. *Ibid.*, p. 25.
7. See above, pp. 172-73.

times too much occupied in admiring to be awkward or on a tremble. I forget myself entirely because I live in her. You will by this time think I am in love with her; so before I go any further I will tell you I am not— she kept me awake one Night as a tune of Mozart's might do. . . .[8]

Of the same lady he says elsewhere, ". . .the voice and the shape of a Woman has haunted me these two days."[9] Later, in deeper vein, he tells Fanny Brawne that her beauty is a necessary condition of his love:

Why may I not speak of your Beauty, since without that I could never have lov'd you. I cannot conceive any beginning of such love as I have for you but Beauty. There may be a sort of love for which, without the least sneer at it, I have the highest respect and can admire it in others: but it has not the richness, the bloom, the full form, the enchantment of love after my own heart.[10]

The forms of Nature and of Art impress themselves upon him with equal force. Much of the early *I Stood Tiptoe* is a joyous catalogue of natural objects. The gorgeous but uneven *Endymion* is studded with descriptions of Nature unequalled in their kind. "Like poor Falstaff," says Keats, "though I do not babble, I think of green fields. I muse with the greatest affection of every flower I have known from my infancy—their shapes and coulours [sic] are as new to me as if I had just created them with a superhuman fancy."[11] The painter Haydon declared of him, "he was in his glory in the fields. The humming of a bee, the sight of a flower, the glitter of the sun, seemed to make his nature tremble; then his eyes flashed, his cheek glowed, his mouth quivered."[12]

8. *The Letters of John Keats*, pp. 232-33. Hereafter to be referred to as *Letters*.
9. *Ibid.*, p. 217.
10. *Ibid.*, p. 357.
11. *Ibid.*, p. 465.
12. *The Autobiography and Memoirs of Benjamin Robert Haydon*, I, 301.

His response to the forms of Art was no less powerful. *Sleep and Poetry* "originated in sleeping in a room adorned with busts and pictures."[13] His two sonnets on the Elgin Marbles evidence his feeling for plastic art: a feeling more notably exemplified in the sculptural *Hyperion* and the *Ode on a Grecian Urn*.[14] He was a lover and connoisseur of painting, and a frequenter of galleries.[15] To Haydon, on the latter's ambitious *Christ's Entry Into Jerusalem*, he wrote enthusiastically,

> I am nearer myself to hear your Christ is being tinted into immortality—Believe me Haydon your picture is a part of myself— I have ever been too sensible of the labyrinthian path to eminence in Art (judging from Poetry) ever to think I understood the emphasis of Painting. . . . I know not you[r] many havens of intenseness— nor ever can know them—but for this I hope no[u]ght you adchieve [sic] is lost upon me. . . .[16]

This preoccupation with human, natural, and artistic objects is, I think, intimately related with certain typical qualities of Keats's poetic technique. He has an unrivalled ability to focus his perceptions upon single things, and to extract from these the last drop of beauty and meaning. He lingers over them, examines them from different aspects, repeats with gradually increasing force, in an effort to achieve the final word, the ultimate completeness of expression. In these terms various peculiarities of Keats's style and imagery are in part explainable

13. Leigh Hunt, quoted in *John Keats: Complete Poems and Selected Letters*, ed. C. D. Thorpe, p. 70.

14. On this point see Colvin, *op. cit.*, especially pp. 414-17; C. D. Thorpe, *The Mind of John Keats*, pp. 127-37; S. A. Larrabee, *English Bards and Grecian Marbles*, pp. 204-32.

15. See his careful criticism of the work of Haydon's protégé Cripps, and his comment on Benjamin West's *Death on the Pale Horse.—Letters*, pp. 50-51, 71.

16. *Ibid.*, p. 129.

So apparently trivial a matter as his habitual use of the accented *-éd*, a practice not followed by any of the other great Romantics, has its significance in this connection.[17] The peculiar effect of this device is a kind of meditative lingering over the object described, an accentuation of the individual quality attributed to it, as in the instances of "globéd peonies" (*Ode on Melancholy*), "warméd jewels" (*The Eve of St. Agnes*), and "wild-ridgéd mountains" (*Ode to Psyche*).[18] This seems to be a result partly of the actual semantic value of the suffix thus accented, and partly of the slowing of pace consequent upon the extra syllable. [One might further cite such examples as the "light-wingéd Dryad," "deep-delvéd earth," "embalméd darkness," and "muséd rhyme" of the *Ode to a Nightingale*, in which the stress calls attention insistently to the essential quality with which Keats has endowed the object.]

This focussing intensity of contemplation is also responsible for his close-packed repetition of adjectives or nouns, the "Sanguine, feverous, boiling gurge of pulse" of *Hyperion*, or the "hush'd, cool-rooted flowers, fragrant-eyed"[19] of the *Ode to Psyche*. In the latter poem this concentrative repetition is present on a larger scale:

> . . . temple thou hast none,
> Nor altar heap'd with flowers;
> Nor virgin-choir to make delicious moan
> Upon the midnight hours;

17. Ernest de Sélincourt points out that Keats is not entirely consistent in his use of the stressed *-éd.*—Preface, *The Poems of John Keats*, p. v. In the great majority of cases, however, the *e* is either pronounced or else elided.

18. See W. J. Bate, *Negative Capability*, p. 62.

19. Note "fragrant-ey*ed*," an exception to the *-éd* rule which corroborates de Sélincourt.

No voice, no lute, no pipe, no incense sweet
From chain-swung censer teeming;
No shrine, no grave, no oracle, no heat
Of pale-mouth'd prophet dreaming.

(ll. 28-35)

A tendency in the same direction is Keats's use of compounds. Drawing again from the *Ode to Psyche* because it is close at hand, we find *soft-conched, cool-rooted, fragrant-eyed, silver-white, calm-breathing, soft-handed, pale-mouth'd, eye-dawn, chain-swung, sapphire-regioned, virgin-choir, dark-cluster'd, moss-lain*, and *wild-ridged*. Such an embarrassment of riches is unusual, but leafing casually through the *Odes* one comes upon *side-faced, deep-disguised, summer-indolence, fever-fit, new-leav'd*, and *cool-bedded* in Indolence, and *Lethe-wards, light-winged, full-throated, deep-delved, purple-stained, spectre-thin*, and *leaden-eyed*, in the *Ode to a Nightingale*.[20]

Again, innovations and eccentricities complained of by austere commentators generally represent attempts by Keats to get at the heart of an object, mood, or situation. Admittedly the attempt is not always successful, especially in the earlier poems. Robert Bridges is correct in his assertion that "the *melting, fainting, swimming, swooning*, and *panting* words are overfrequent" in these.[21] Keats is trying to achieve in their use the maximum of intensity and meaning through an expedient too easy, direct, and crude. At the same time, it should be noted

20. The compound is peculiarly a feature of Keats's mature style, more especially of the *Odes*. One finds them earlier, as for example in the impressive "their surly eyes *brow-hidden*" of *Endymion* (II, 645), in the "Tall oaks, branch-charmed" of *Hyperion* (I, 74), and in "sole-thoughted" in *The Eve of St. Agnes* (l. 42), but not in the same abundance. They are not, on the other hand, particularly prevalent in the late *Fall of Hyperion, Prince Otho*, or *The Cap and Bells*.

21. *Op. cit.*, p. lxxxiv.

how effective these "intense" words are when embedded in the denser fabric of his later work: in

> . . . on a sudden, *fainting* with surprise . . .
> > (*Ode to Psyche*)

> My heart *aches*, and a drowsy numbness *pains* . . .
> > (*Ode to a Nightingale*)

> Forever *panting*, and forever young . . .
> > (*Ode to a Grecian Urn*)

Keats's archaisms are often used with this purpose of intensifying and objectifying. Of Thea's plea to the fallen Saturn in *Hyperion*, "Open thine eyes eterne, and *sphere* them round," W. T. Arnold remarks that "A word could hardly be used in a more arbitrary and fantastical manner."[22] Nor, be it added, in a manner more effective and satisfying. Saturn is, or has been until now, the ruler of the universe; his eyes are accustomed to piercing immensities. "Sphere them round" has suggestions of enormous grasp and power, appropriate to deity. *Sphere* coöperates with *eterne* to evoke ideas of a cosmic system of world beyond world in harmony under the sway of a single hand, that of the now-vanquished Saturn. Arnold objects also to the use of verbs as nouns as "A singular license in Keats' diction." To cite but one example of this usage, however, the "voices of soft *proclaim*" of *Hyperion* seems to me to be singularly felicitous.[23] It has the soft, full tone and bursting plangency of a plucked

22. Introduction, *The Poetical Works of John Keats*, p. xliii.

23. *Loc. cit.* I do not assert that Keats's archaisms are invariably happy, but merely that they are concentrative and intensive in purpose and effect. See Arnold's examples, "When this planet's sphering time shall close" (*Endymion*); "Twelve sphered tables, by silk seats insphered" (*Lamia*); "no mad assail"; "with glad exclaim," etc.

harp string; and this effect is mainly attributable to the nervous terseness of the locution.

The static quality so often noted in Keats's imagery is evidence of this same desire to examine, to contemplate, to pierce to the heart of things. Keats is at once concentrated and leisurely; he will not leave an object until he has caught its essence. Thus the situation at the beginning of *Hyperion* epitomizes silence and motionlessness; nature and humanity are alike in the grip of a timeless and trancelike moment. This lack of movement is one of the reasons why *Hyperion* could never have been completed as an epic. Keats is too greatly interested in single objects, effects, and scenes to attend to the imperious demands of action. The massive quietude of the opening lines of the *Ode on a Grecian Urn* is another case in point. The urn is the "still unravished bride of quietness," the "foster-child of silence and slow time." The scenes of the sacrifice and the abandoned "little town" have the same movelessness as the urn itself. They live in a never-ending moment, and by this release from the demands of motion, which blurs outlines and hints at change and impermanence, they are preternaturally heightened and solidified.[24]

Linked closely with the prevailing slowness of Keats's imagery is the leisurely movement of his metres. It has been noted that whereas Shelley sings, Keats generally talks;[25] he is too measured of pace, too deep of tone, for the higher notes of lyricism.[26] And this

24. Cf. J. M. Murry, "Beauty is Truth," *Studies in Keats, New and Old*, pp. 71-92.
25. By A. Clutton-Brock, *op. cit.*, p. 63.
26. See above, pp. 97-99, on the prevalent slowness of Keats's metres. There are exceptions, of course, like the "Song of the Indian Maiden" in *Endymion*, *Fancy*, *Robin Hood*, and the *Lines on the Mermaid Tavern*. Even the shifting dance of his tetram-

slowness both contributes to and results from his power
of focussing on the single object in its particularity.

II   The poetic process in Keats generally be-
            gins, I think, with deep and intense con-
templation of concrete shapes and forms. This contemplation, as I have tried to establish in a previous chapter,
is enriched by Keats's exquisite and comprehensive sense-
perceptions. He is delicately receptive to impressions
from Art, Nature, and Humanity in almost equal measure; being more concerned, perhaps, with Nature at the
beginning of his career and with Man towards its end.
    The unique quality of his poetic experience arises
from his wholehearted love of the external world, at
first instinctive and spontaneous,[27] later conscious, complex, and philosophical. The rapturous enumeration of
natural beauties in *I Stood Tiptoe* represents the early
mode; the deeper and subtler perceptions of the *Ode to a
Nightingale*, the *Ode on a Grecian Urn*, and the *Ode on
Melancholy* reflect the later. The power and concentration
of the contemplative attitude in Keats are a result of
his conviction that appearances can be trusted to the
full; that Beauty and Truth reside in the phenomenal
world itself and may be found there if one will take the
trouble to seek them out. As A. C. Bradley remarks,
there is a tendency in Keats working "against any in-

---

eters, however, has more of the smooth and weighty roll of *L'Allegro* and *Il Penseroso*
than of the speed and lightness so often present in Shelley's verse.
    27. "The 'passiveness' of Keats is simply the passiveness of delight . . . his
characteristic attitude is that of the delighted watcher or listener."—John Bailey,
"The Poet of Stillness," in *The John Keats Memorial Volume*, p. 30.

clination to erect walls between ideal and real."[28] Nor need one seek the unusual, the *recherché*, for the secret lies as well close at hand as far off.[29] His natural landscapes are homely and English.

I have said that for Keats Beauty and Truth resided in the actual, the world of phenomena. This is true, however, only metaphorically. Human life and the world are not to him the be-all and end-all of existence, but the faithful mirror and reflection of the ideal. The finite is to him intimately related with the infinite.[30] The action of Imagination upon the evidence offered by the senses provides us with the only knowledge we can have of that which lies beyond the senses. This correspondence of the Actual and the Real is described in a notable passage from one of Keats's most famous letters:

It is 'a Vision in the form of Youth' a Shadow of reality to come—and this consideration has further convinced me for it has come as auxiliary to another favorite Speculation of mine, that we shall enjoy ourselves here after by having what we called happiness on Earth repeated in a finer tone and so repeated. . . . Adam's dream will do here and seems to be a conviction that Imagination and its empyreal reflection is the same as human Life and its Spiritual reflection. . . . The Prototype [sic] must be here after.[31]

28. *Op. cit.*, p. 237.

29. ". . . another of his chief characteristics . . . is his close relationship with common nature: he is forever drawing his imagery from common things, which are for the first time represented as beautiful. . . ."—Bridges, *op. cit.*, p. xcv.

30. Cf. the "Hymn to Pan," *Endymion*, I, 296-302:

> ". . . be still the leaven,
> That spreading in this dull and clouded earth
> Gives it a touch ethereal—a new birth:
> Be still a symbol of immensity;
> A firmament reflected in a sea;
> An element filling the space between;
> An unknown . . ."

31. *Letters*, p. 68.

Since "human Life and its Spiritual reflection" are thus closely related, two aspects of a single unity, then human life must be accepted in its entirety, with all its imperfections on its head. And since the relationship between Imagination and its reflection is the same, then it seems logical that imaginative expression, or Poetry, should be the most faithful representation possible to humanity of the spiritual reflection of life, the embodiment of that Imagination whose prototype we shall see only hereafter. What Bradley calls "the real and the ideal" are not identical, and yet are inseparable. The reflection cannot exist without the reality, and it is not clear which is reality and which reflection.

Keats's doctrines of "negative capability" and "passive receptivity" are, I think, akin to this earlier idea.

> . . . it is more noble to sit like Jove than to fly like Mercury—let us not therefore go hurrying about and collecting honey, bee-like buzzing here and there impatiently from a knowledge of what is to be aimed at; but let us open our leaves like a flower and be passive and receptive—budding patiently under the eye of Apollo and taking hints from every noble insect that favours us with a visit—sap will be given us for meat and dew for drink.[32]

If "real" and "ideal" are inseparable, then we need not search and struggle for the meaning of things, but submit ourselves quietly to their influence, "open our leaves" to them. The visible world is itself a symbol of a higher reality; then wherefore seek to burst its bounds, or rearrange according to our mind's desire an

---

32. *Ibid.*, p. 104. Cf. *What the Thrush Said*, ll. 9-12:
> "O fret not after knowledge—I have none,
> And yet my song comes native with the warmth.
> O fret not after knowledge—I have none,
> And yet the Evening listens."

order already profoundly significant? Keats's confidence in the deep meaning of the everyday commonplaces of life and the world appears in his casual comparison of Shakespeare and Byron:

> . . . they are very shallow people who take everything literally. A Man's life of any worth is a continual allegory—and very few eyes can see the Mystery of his life—a life like the scriptures, figurative—which such people can no more make out than they can the hebrew Bible. Lord Byron cuts a figure—but he is not figurative —Shakespeare led a life of Allegory: his works are the comments on it. . . .[33]

The poet's rôle is that of the self-abnegating observer, not of the self-conscious philosopher. He seeks, indeed, to fathom the beauty and meaning of appearances, but this beauty and meaning reside in the appearances themselves and not in the reasoning intellect. He must be *negatively capable,*

> capable of being in uncertainties, mysteries, doubts, without any irritable reaching after fact and reason—Coleridge, for instance, would let go by a fine isolated verisimilitude caught from the Penetralium of mystery, from being incapable of remaining content with half-knowledge.[34]

Feeling thus, that the poet should subordinate the "irritable reaching" of his ego to what he feels and sees, he was irritated by the elaborate reflectiveness of Wordsworth:

> . . . for the sake of a few fine imaginative or domestic passages, are we to be bullied into a certain Philosophy engendered in the in the whims of an Egotist—Every man has his speculations, but

33. *Ibid.*, p. 305.
34. *Ibid.*, p. 72.

every man does not brood and peacock over them till he makes a false coinage and deceives himself. . . . We hate poetry that has a palpable design upon us—and if we do not agree, seems to put its hand in its breeches pocket. Poetry should be great and unobtrusive, a thing which enters into one's soul, and does not startle it or amaze it with itself, but with its subject.[35]

Believing in the profound significance of man and nature as they are, Keats is a naturalistic poet, as Matthew Arnold and after him J. M. Murry have said. He expresses both his peculiar view of nature and his notion of the deliberate forbearance which the poet must exercise in *When I Have Fears:*

> When I behold, upon the night's starr'd face,
> *Huge, cloudy symbols* of a high romance,
> And think that I may never live to trace
> Their shadows, *with the magic hand of chance* . . .[36]

35. *Ibid.*, p. 96.
36. Cf. *To Homer:*
> "Standing aloof in giant ignorance,
> Of thee I hear and of the Cyclades,
> As one who sits ashore and longs perchance
> To visit dolphin-coral in deep seas.
> So thou wast blind!—but then the veil was rent;
> For Jove uncurtain'd Heaven to let thee live,
> And Neptune made for thee a spumy tent,
> And Pan made sing for thee his forest-hive;
> Aye, on the shores of darkness there is light,
> And precipices show untrodden green;
> There is a budding morrow in midnight,—
> There is a triple sight in blindness keen;
> Such seeing hadst thou, as it once befell
> To Dian, Queen of Earth, and Heaven, and Hell."

See also *The Poet,* to whose sight
> "The hush of natural objects opens quite
> To the core: and every secret essence there
> Reveals the elements of good and fair;
> Making him see, where Learning hath no light." (ll. 4-7)

Since he has a deep conviction of the importance of human life and visible nature, Keats has also a profound need of acceptance. Nothing is irrelevant, nothing inharmonious, if properly understood. In a sense the history of his life and poetry is the chronicle of his efforts to absorb and assimilate the fullness of experience, under conditions of increasing difficulty, until the waters of adversity finally closed over his head. He sought not only "to see life steadily and see it whole," but also to discern the relations between its parts:

> Now comes the pain of truth, to whom 'tis pain;
> O folly! for to bear all naked truths,
> And to envisage circumstance, all calm,
> This is the top of sovereignty.
>
> (*Hyperion*, II, 202-5)

His belief in the necessity of accepting the fullness of experience has its counterpart in what Professor Finney has called "the principles of excess, intensity, and spontaneity"[37] in his imagery:

I think Poetry should surprise by a fine excess and not by Singularity—it should strike the Reader as a wording of his own highest thoughts, and appear almost a remembrance. Its touches of Beauty should never be half way ther[e] by making the reader breathless instead of content: the rise, the progress, the setting of imagery should like the Sun come natural too [sic] him—shine over him and set soberly although in magnificence leaving him in the Luxury of twilight—but it is easier to think what Poetry should be than to write it—and this leads me on to another axiom. That if Poetry comes not as naturally as the Leaves to a tree it had better not come at all.[38]

37. C. L. Finney, *The Evolution of Keats's Poetry*, I, 245.
38. *Letters*, p. 108.

All should be complete, whole, rounded, and natural.
In the reconciliation of elements towards which Keats's
poetry tends there are no rough edges. In an early letter
to his brothers this reconciliation is stated as the function of art: "The excellence of every art is its intensity,
capable of making all disagreeables evaporate, from their
being in close relationship with Beauty and Truth."[39]

This is not to deny the reality of evil and pain, but
to conquer them by establishing their place in the harmony of life, through imaginative insight. Keats early
recognized beneath the smiling face of Nature a savage
and fratricidal struggle:

> . . . I saw
> Too far into the sea, where every maw
> The greater on the less feeds evermore.—
> But I saw too distinct into the core
> Of an eternal fierce destruction . . .
>
> . . . .
>
> The Shark at savage prey,—the Hawk at pounce,—
> The gentle Robin, like a Pard or Ounce,
> Ravening a worm . . .
>
> (*Epistle to John Hamilton Reynolds*, ll. 93ff.)

The society of men, furthermore, was in no way different
from the society of beasts. There was the same fierce
competition, the same selfishness. Yet this was inherent
in the nature of things, and had therefore to be accepted.
Disinterestedness pushed too far would overturn the
system by which we live. "For in wild nature the Hawk
would loose [sic] his Breakfast of Robins and the Robin
his of worms—the Lion must starve as well as the
swallow. The greater part of men make their way with

39. *Ibid.*, p. 71.

the same instinctiveness, the same unwandering eye from their purposes, the same animal eagerness as the Hawk.[40]

Acceptance is all the more necessary since man and nature are indissolubly connected. Since unalloyed happiness does not exist in nature, it cannot exist in man. Perfectibilitarians and "Godwin-Methodists" like Shelley and Charles Dilke hope in vain for the millennium:

The point at which Man may arrive is as far as the paral[l]el state in inanimate nature and no further—For instance suppose a rose to have sensation, it blooms on a beautiful morning it enjoys itself—but there comes a cold wind, a hot sun—it cannot escape it, it cannot destroy its annoyances—they are as native to the world as itself: no more can man be happy in spite, the worldly elements will prey upon his nature.[41]

Yet this conclusion is not a gloomy one. The inevitable ills of human existence are to Keats the teachers, not the scourges, of mankind. The world, with all its tribulations, is not a "vale of tears,"[42] but the "vale of Soul-making." Without its shaping influence man has neither soul nor identity. Says Keats,

I will call the *world* a School instituted for the purpose of teaching little children to read—I will call the *human heart* the *horn book* used in that School—and I will call *the Child able to read, the Soul* made from that School and its *horn-book*. Do you not see how necessary a World of Pains and troubles is to school an Intelligence and make it a Soul? A place where the heart must feel and suffer in a thousand diverse ways! Not merely is the Heart a Hornbook,

40. *Ibid.*, p. 316.
41. *Ibid.*, p. 335.
42. Cf. Shelley, *Hymn to Intellectual Beauty*, ll. 17-18:
      "Why dost thou pass away, and leave our state,
        This dim vast vale of tears, vacant and desolate?"

It is the Minds Bible, it is the Minds experience, it is the teat from which the Mind or intelligence sucks its identity. As various as the Lives of Men are—so various become their Souls, and thus does God make individual beings, Souls, identical Souls of the Sparks of his own essence.[43]

Thus does he sweeten an acceptance which he has already considered to be not merely desirable but inevitable. This passage marks the high tide of his thought upon the relation of man to his environment, and constitutes his fullest explanation of the existence of evil.

This reconciliation was not easily won, nor was it evenly maintained. Keats's strong political opinions,[44] the humanitarian feelings[45] which were in him concomitant with his contemplative and empathic powers, and finally his personal misfortunes at times disturbed the harmonious balance of his hard-bought serenity. In the "ledger-men" passage of *Isabella*, for example,[46] his fiery indignation at the spectacle of social injustice breaks strangely, "like sweet bells jangled, out of tune and harsh," into the delicate romance. Significantly, he falls in the midst of his tirade into a type of verse more Byronic than Keatsian, but without Byron's lucidity and force:

> The hawks of ship-mast forests—the untired
> And pannier'd mules for ducats and old lies—
> Quick cat's-paws on the generous stray-away,—
> Great wits in Spanish, Tuscan, and Malay.
>
> (ll. 133-36)

43. *Letters*, p. 336.
44. See C. D. Thorpe, "Keats's Interest in Politics and World Affairs," *PMLA*, XLVI, 1228-45.
45. See C. D. Thorpe, *The Mind of John Keats*, pp. 74-78ff.
46. See G. B. Shaw, "Keats," in *The John Keats Memorial Volume*, p. 175.

Realizing the incongruity of this interlude, the poet asks pardon of his original, "eloquent and famed Boccaccio,"

> For venturing syllables that ill beseem
> The quiet glooms of such a piteous theme.

He is right to do so; in this instance "disagreeables" are not evaporated by intensity of imagination.

The Fall of Hyperion portrays most searchingly the conflict between the poet and life, the demands of art and of humanitarianism, without being able entirely to resolve it. The resolution must be made:

> "None can usurp this height," returned that shade,
> "But those to whom the miseries of the world
> Are misery, and will not let them rest . . ."
>
> (ll. 147-49)

Yet it is not to be found in the tortured complexities of the Induction, nor in Moneta's recounting of the melancholy fate of the dynasty of Saturn. *The Fall* is deeply and unrelievedly sad: Hyperion's fall is all too clearly foreshadowed, but in this poem, unlike the earlier *Hyperion*, we hear nothing of the rise of Apollo. Keats broke off before that point was reached.

The Fall of Hyperion was written within the limits of August-December, 1819,[47] by which time the burden of unhappy love, financial misfortunes, and ill-health had grown too great for equable endurance. The flawless *To Autumn*, composed in September, presents the last example of his ability to reconcile the conflicting elements of life.[48] But in *The Eve of St. Agnes* and in the

47. See J. M. Murry, "The Date of Hyperion," *Keats and Shakespeare;* C. D. Thorpe, *John Keats: Complete Poems and Selected Letters*, p. 381n.
48. ". . . for the last time in this world his own free master, he found all his

great *Odes*, covering a period from January to May, 1819, are to be found the consummate expression of the Keatsian synthesis.

III   In the imagery of these poems Keats's acceptance of and delight in the world of phenomena; his perception of the relationship between this world and its reflection, the imaginative world of Art; the humor and irony[49] generated by this perception and necessary to it; the close union of thought and sensation typical of him—all are expressed in a peculiarly spontaneous and concrete symbolism, which comes as naturally "as the Leaves to a tree," and as unobtrusively.

The Eve of St. Agnes is too often thought of as sheer faery romance, deliberately remote from actuality. It is indeed in the highest degree romantic, but it is erected four-square and solid upon a foundation of materials from the actual world. I would dissent from the verdict of those modern critics who, admitting the perfection of its technique, complain of its slightness.[50] *St. Agnes* has a rounded fullness, a complexity and seriousness, and a balance which remove it from the realm of mere magnificent tour-de-force.

---

disciplined powers, of observation, of imagination, of craftsmanship, combining in one moment of power to produce the most serenely flawless poem in our language. . . ." —M. R. Ridley, *Keats' Craftsmanship*, p. 289.

49. ". . . earnestness . . . may certainly account for his want of humour."— Bridges, *op. cit.*, p. ci. "He had an exquisite sense of humour. . . ."—Haydon, *op. cit.*, I, 301. I prefer the word of Haydon, who knew Keats, and I find strong corroborative evidence for my preference in the *Letters*.

50. ". . . in its kind, even though that kind be slight, it is not far short of perfection."— Ridley, *op. cit.*, p. 96.

The poem is built upon a carefully arranged series of contrasts.[51] The young lovers, Porphyro and Madeline, are precisely balanced by the Beadsman and Angela, who typify the inexorable demands of time, accident, and death. They are a pair of *memento mori's*, like the slave in the chariot of the victorious general at a Roman triumph. The poem begins and ends in images of cold and of physical suffering. The Beadsman, "meagre, barefoot, wan," walking slowly along the chapel aisle with his lamp casting pale beams toward the castle, is a strange symbolic curtainraiser to the romantic drama. As the curtain falls the wheel of life comes full circle; the lovers flee to their happiness, but

> Angela the old
> Died palsy-twitched, with meagre face deform;
> The Beadsman, after thousand aves told,
> For aye unsought for slept among his ashes cold.[52]

It is important that Keats in one draft of the poem would have emphasized the irony of this conclusion savagely:

> . . . with face deform
> The beadsman stiffen'd, twixt a sigh and laugh
> Ta'en sudden from his beads by one weak little cough.[53]

To return to the beginning, the drama may be said to commence with

> At length burst in the argent revelry,
> With plume, tiara, and all rich array,

51. This element of contrast has of course been recognized. See E. de Sélincourt; "The Warton Lecture on Keats," in *The John Keats Memorial Volume*, pp. 14-15, Finney, *op. cit.*, II, 549, 559; Amy Lowell, *John Keats*, II, 170-71.

52. "It is the old story of the cruelty of nature. For two who are happy, life demands the insatiable toll of death."—Lowell, *op. cit.*, II, 171.

53. Quoted from Ridley, *op. cit.*, p. 190.

Numerous as shadows haunting fairily
The brain, new stuff'd, in youth, with triumphs gay,
Of old romance.

(ll. 37-41)

This passage is highly self-conscious, ironic, and intro-spective. On the one hand, there is deliberate emphasis on fairy unreality. Keats is demanding directly of his reader the "willing suspension of disbelief" necessary for the success of his play: this is the poet in his rôle of enchanter. Yet the enchanter frankly does not believe in his own magic, as is clearly evident from the overtones of "Numerous as shadows haunting fairily / The brain, new stuff'd, in youth. . . ." Perhaps "does not believe" is too strong; let us say rather that Keats warns us that these are creatures of imagination, who never were on land or sea. The imagery is deliberately vague; it evokes rather than pictures. "Argent" has almost no denotative force. Obviously it does not mean "silver," but has a value exclusively of emotion and association. Signifi-cantly the poet uses an abstract noun, "revelry," to describe the train, so that the individuality of the figures is lost in a dimly realized sense of the whole.

These verses work in a complex and even self-con-tradictory manner. They are a bridge between reality and romance, furnishing a kind of aesthetic distancing for the story. They impart to the loves of Madeline and Porphyro an ethereal and idealized quality, for the lovers belong to this atmosphere of vague glamour. They are also, however, a contrasting background for the main action, since the lovers are far more human and solid than these shadowy figures. In contrary manner, these figures are menacing, "barbarian hordes" and "hyena

foemen" who threaten the happiness and even the existence of the hero and heroine. The passage, indeed, is
richly ironic, exhibiting the poet both as spectator and
participant, his characters as figures at once of fancy and
reality. This is not the poetry of a simple romancer.

   The Eve of St. Agnes is remarkable for spontaneous and
unobtrusive but subtle symbolism, involving constant
contrast, yet always resolving at the end into harmony.
As the Beadsman and Angela set off Porphyro and
Madeline, the cold of the winter night heightens the
warmth of young love. The castle is a bulwark of romance against actuality; the lovers flee "into the storm,"
which is at the same time

> . . . an elfin-storm from faery land,
> Of haggard seeming, but a boon indeed . . .

The "little moonlight room" in which Angela inter-
views Porphyro is an ironic shadow of Madeline's chamber. "Pale, lattic'd, chill, and silent as a tomb," it
contrasts with the warm colors amid which the meeting
of the lovers takes place, while it serves also to introduce
the "hush'd and chaste" quality of Madeline's surroundings.

   Keats's natural and unforced symbolism is at its best
in the going-out of the taper as Madeline enters her
room:

> Out went the taper as she hurried in;
> Its little smoke, in pallid moonshine, died . . .
>
> (ll. 199-200)

It is a gesture of finality; by the act of entering she has
sealed her fate. Yet as always in Keats this dying of the

taper is inseparably part of the naturalistic description of what takes place, and if we press the meaning too hard we lose the effect of the whole. Thus the "casement high and triple-arch'd" and the feast "Of candied apple, quince, and plum, and gourd" are symbols of sensuous love, but should be touched upon lightly. The very linen in which Madeline sleeps suggests at once sensuousness and chastity:

> And still she slept an azure-lidded sleep,
> In blanched linen, smooth, and lavender'd,

while her sleep has a twofold meaning. It is the sleep of unawakened maidenhood, "Impossible to melt as iced stream." Yet Madeline is dreaming ardently of her lover and the joys which the future holds for her.

These motifs conflict yet harmonize. By images of cold and pallor the love of Madeline and Porphyro is restrained from becoming an affair of mere sensuality; the lovers are after all innocent. To be chaste is not to be bloodless, however, or to lack passion. This delicate balance is preserved in the color scheme of *The Eve of St. Agnes*, which is for the most part silver and rose. The thread of silver commences faintly with the "argent revellers" and continues in the pale moonshine with which the whole poem is bathed, until its spell is symbolically broken and the lovers must depart from the enchanted castle:

> . . . the frost-wind blows
> Like Love's alarum patterning the sharp sleet
> Against the window-panes; St. Agnes' moon hath set.

The image of the rose is the counterpart of the silver

image. Porphyro's first concrete hope of obtaining Madeline is "like a full-blown rose, Flushing his brow." In the description of the casement the two motifs merge. Most striking among the features of this window is "A shielded scutcheon blush'd with blood of queens and kings." This scutcheon throws "warm gules" and "Rose-bloom" upon Madeline. Yet this warm light originates with "the wintry moon," so that chastity and sensuousness are in this image wedded. Furthermore, she is enveloped not only in rose-bloom, but

> . . . on her silver cross soft amethyst,
> And on her hair a glory, like a saint:
> She seem'd a splendid angel, newly drest,
> Save wings, for heaven.

The rose image is repeated in the description of Madeline's sleep, which holds her as it were suspended, momentarily apart from life,

> Blinded alike from sunshine and from rain,
> As though a rose should shut, and be a bud again.

In this are mingled implications of virginity and fulfillment. A more definite but still delicate and subtle hint of sexuality is given in

> Into her dream he melted, as the rose
> Blendeth its odour with the violet,—
> Solution sweet . . .

Finally, the two elements of sensuousness and restraint are once more mingled in

> Say, may I be for aye thy vassal blest?
> Thy beauty's shield, heart-shap'd and *vermeil* dyed?

> Ah, *silver shrine*, here will I take my rest
> After so many hours of toil and quest . . .

As Keats offers the reader a door into the castle and the poem at the same time, he also clearly indicates the point of exit in

> And they are gone: aye, ages long ago
> These lovers fled away into the storm,

which once more draws a line of demarcation between art and life in its raw and unselective actuality. The story belongs to the remote past, the lovers are long dead: but this imaginative projection of the essential values of young love is immortal. And these values are arrived at not by forgetting what everyday existence is like, but by using the mean, sordid, and commonplace as a foundation upon which to build a high romance.

Keats's sense of the fullness and complexity of human modes of experience, the irony begotten of this sense, and his acceptance of experience, are most notably present in the great *Odes*. Since I have in other connections discussed *To Autumn* and the *Ode on a Grecian Urn* at some length, and since the *Ode to Psyche* and the *Ode on Indolence* are in my opinion inferior to the others, I take the *Ode to a Nightingale* as my text, omitting the *Ode on Melancholy* for reasons of space.

Douglas Bush remarks of Keats's poetry in general, "From first to last Keats's important poems are related to, or grow directly out of . . . inner conflicts," and of the *Odes* he says

> At first sight Keats's theme in the *Ode to a Nightingale* and the *Ode on a Grecian Urn* . . . is the belief that whereas the momentary experience of beauty is fleeting, the ideal embodiment of that

moment in art, in song, or in marble, is an imperishable source of joy. If that were all, these odes should be hymns of triumph, and they are not. It is the very acme of melancholy that the joy he celebrates is joy in beauty that must die.[54]

This is valuable, but misleading in emphasis. There are indeed conflicts in Keats's poetry, but in the *Odes* cited by Professor Bush these conflicts are reconciled. The *Odes* do not express "the very acme of melancholy" any more than they express the very acme of joy. They express an exquisite awareness of the existence of joy and melancholy, pleasure and pain, and art and life. They express a feeling that these are inseparable, although not identical, and they express acceptance of this inseparability of the elements of human experience. In the *Ode to a Nightingale* Keats portrays a state of intense aesthetic and imaginative feeling, too poignant for long duration, which arises with the song of a bird and vanishes when the song is done. The poet records his emotion and its passing without comment.

The impossibility of maintaining this mood of exaltation is the condition of its existence, for it is relative, and describable only by comparing it with more commonplace states of mind. Also, no mood is simple and unalloyed by other feelings. Keats begins,

> My heart aches, and a drowsy numbness pains
> My sense, as though of hemlock I had drunk . . .

This is not from grief, or envy of the nightingale, but from "being too happy in thine happiness." As in the *Ode on Melancholy*,[55] he declares that intense pleasure is almost indistinguishable from numbing pain.

54. *Mythology and the Romantic Tradition in English Poetry*, pp. 82, 107.
55.   "Ay, in the very temple of Delight
             Veil'd Melancholy has her sovran shrine . . ." (ll. 25-26)

The *Nightingale* moves with the same steady advance and withdrawal as does the *Ode on a Grecian Urn*. Its motion is circular.[56] Stanzas II and III represent as it were a false start, after the mood has been established in I. The "draught of vintage" by whose magic power Keats would escape "The weariness, the fever, and the fret" of life is rejected. If the last five lines of stanza III are drawn from Keats's own suffering, that suffering is here sublimated.

> Where Beauty cannot keep her lustrous eyes, ·
> Or new Love pine at them beyond to-morrow

has a serenity and ironic undertone not to be found in the poet's relations with Fanny Brawne.

The true beginning comes in stanza IV. Keats flies to the nightingale

> Not charioted by Bacchus and his pards,
> But on the viewless wings of Poesy.

The poem reaches its full intensity in this stanza and the three following. This outpouring of imaginative exaltation is contrasted with the melancholy of the low-pitched stanza III, by itself unremarkable but functioning as an integral part of the poetic whole. As in the

---

In the *Ode on Melancholy* Keats emphasizes the close relationships between different modes of experience even more thoroughly than in the *Nightingale:*

> "Make not your rosary of yew-berries
> Nor let the beetle, nor the death-moth be
> Your mournful Psyche, nor the downy owl
> A partner in your sorrow's mysteries;
> For shade to shade will come too drowsily,
> And drown the wakeful anguish of the soul." (ll. 5-10)

Melancholy in its simple state is invisible; it is beheld only by him "whose strenuous tongue / Can burst Joy's grape against his palate fine."

56. Olwen Ward Campbell, *Shelley and the Unromantics*, p. 230.

Eve of St. Agnes Keats uses life at its most unpromising as a point of departure. Only by being aware of sorrow can the poet devote himself wholeheartedly to joy, conscious the while that his respite will be brief. The soft and heavy texture of the imagery in IV and V reflects a spontaneous luxuriance of feeling and perception, a self-abandonment which is merely another aspect of his previous depression.

Stanza VI commences,

> Darkling I listen; and for many a time
> I have been half in love with easeful Death.

The vivid sensuousness of the two preceding stanzas has been leading toward this. Death itself may offer the fullest sense of Life: "Now more than ever seems it *rich* to die." If the *Nightingale* is a lament for the brevity of life and joy, as Professor Bush has said, these are sentiments difficult to explain; but if the poem is simply an imaginative reflection of the complexity and intensity of human experience, Death may quite reasonably be viewed as its culmination.[57] highest point

The spell is deepest in stanza VII, of which M. R. Ridley has said that it "would, I suppose, by common consent be taken along with 'Kubla Khan,' as offering us the distilled sorceries of Romanticism."[58] In these lines the apparent contrast between the immortality of the Bird and the fugitive temporality of its hearers is strongly insisted upon.[59]

57. Cf. *Why Did I Laugh*, with its conclusion,
> "Verse, Fame, and Beauty are intense indeed,
>   But Death intenser—Death is Life's high meed."
58. *Op. Cit.*, p. 227.
59. One must agree here with Amy Lowell that to object that the nightingale

> No hungry generations tread thee down;
> The voice I hear this passing night was heard
> In ancient days by emperor and clown:
> Perhaps the self-same song that found a path
> Through the sad heart of Ruth, when, sick for home
> She stood in tears amid the alien corn . . .

Yet this opposition is not real. The "sad heart of Ruth" is as enduring as the nightingale, and after the same fashion. The temporal Ruth died long ago, the eternal Ruth lives on in poetry. Nor can one separate the temporal from the eternal, for it is by virtue of her grief, her exposure to accidental circumstance long since passed away, that she remains alive. So with the "magic casements" which follow, but with a difference. Paradoxically, these are immortal because they have long since vanished, or alternatively because they never in cold fact existed. This paradox is the essence of their charm and their reality; viewed faintly across long vistas of time, or created consciously by imagination from diverse materials seized from the actual world, they have a unique being of their own. They exist as fully as the stubbornest, most intractable actuality, but they arise from actuality and cannot live apart from it. In this stanza the notions of temporality and timelessness do not conflict, but are brought together in harmonious relationship.

It is not mere accident that Keats breaks off here, at the peak of imaginative intensity, on the word

---

is obviously not immortal (see Bridges, *op. cit.*, p. lxiv) is to miss the point, although her manners in this argument are enough to provoke a saint (*John Keats*, II, 252). She has certainly provoked H. W. Garrod (*Keats*, pp. 113-14), whose saintliness as regards Miss Lowell is non-existent.

"forlorn," which has its feet in two worlds. For the value and identity of the imaginative experience depends upon its transience; it is only one mode, albeit the highest, among many. With consummate irony and psychological truth "forlorn" breaks in like the tolling of a bell to signal the end of his emotional exaltation. The "faery lands" were "forlorn" because remote and strange; the word itself is enchanted. The second "forlorn" is homely and familiar, with a half-humerous ruefulness; it dwells upon the common earth, to which the poet now returns.[60]

The final stanza fills out the perfect rondure of the poem in a slow withdrawal, symbolized by the retreat of the bird itself so that objective description and subjective emotion are fused. The fading-away is slow and regular,

> Past the near meadows, over the still stream,
> Up the hill-side; and now 'tis buried deep
> In the next valley-glades . . .

and in the last two verses the process of withdrawal, now solely within the poet, comes to a smooth and quiet end:

> Was it a vision, or a waking dream?
> Fled is that music:—Do I wake or sleep?

Keats does not moralize after the event, nor utter lyric cries of pain, as he might be expected to if he were writing, for example, about the sadness of mutability. He has been writing about a full and rich experience, and having described that experience he stops.

60. Cf. Cleanth Brooks, *Modern Poetry and the Tradition*, p. 31.

IV   Critical opinion has been unanimous about
the "abstractness" of Shelley, as it has
been on Keats's "concreteness." In a previous chapter
I have attempted to show that Shelley's poetry is not
lacking in solidity of technique or in sensory grasp of
the natural world; it remains, therefore, to demonstrate
of what this abstractness of his consists.

Shelley's poetic world is not a literal transcription
of his perceptions of the natural world, but a conscious
arrangement and composition of these perceptions. Keats,
who believes fully in the deep truth of appearances,
seldom feels called upon to alter them or go beyond
them. Shelley, however, has less confidence in appearances, although he is fascinated by them.[61] To put this
difference in another way, Shelley does not believe so
thoroughly as Keats in the correspondence of the human
mind to what it perceives. While Keats permits things
to rest in their complexity, Shelley consciously imposes
upon them the order of his intellect, reshaping them
according to his restless and masterful will.

He is sometimes concerned less with the world as it
is than with the world as he would have it.[62] In *Prome-*

61. "The natural scenery of Shelley has a quality very different from Wordsworth's. It is less realistic, less familiar. It is an imaginative composite of features
taken from nature and put together in a pattern suitable to the poet's thought and
mood. . . . The sensory appeal is as rich and constant in Shelley as in Wordsworth;
but it is on a different level of experience, less familiar. . . ."—J. W. Beach, *The Concept
of Nature in Nineteenth Century English Poetry*, p. 210.

62. The relationship of Shelley's reforming instincts to his poetry is perhaps
most wisely to be left to himself to define: "Let this opportunity be conceded to me of
acknowledging that I have what a Scotch philosopher characteristically terms 'a
passion for reforming the world'. . . . But it is a mistake to suppose that I dedicate
my poetical compositions solely to the direct enforcement of reform. . . . Didactic
poetry is my abhorrence. . . . My purpose has hitherto been simply to familiarize the
highly refined imagination of the more select classes of poetical readers with beautiful

theus Unbound, for example, he is the architect of a universe idealized by Love, in which accident disappears, incongruous and conflicting elements vanish, and all is harmony. Man is not, indeed, exempt from "chance, and death, and mutability," but he rules them like slaves (III, iv, 200-1). They are subjugated to the pattern of e whole. His conception of the relationship between man and nature, between subject and object, is not fixed, however, but varies and shifts. If one cares to describe this relationship in philosophic terms, one may declare Shelley to be at varying periods idealistic and materialistic, Platonic and neo-Platonic, Naturalistic and Necessitarian. To apply any of these terms too rigidly to his poetry, however, is unfortunate. Obviously there is a slow and steady motion away from the bald mechanism and necessitarianism of the juvenile *Queen Mab*, with its recurring image of "the chain of being,"[63] its emphasis on cold geometrical symmetry; but Shelley does not lend himself to labelling. He escapes from under the hand of the philosophic critic.

The elusiveness of his poetic thought is reflected in the disagreement which obtains among many of his commentators. Professor Gingerich considers Shelley a deep-dyed and unredeemed Necessitarian, who covers his traces with a thin layer of superficial Platonism.[64] To A. T. Strong and Miss Winstanley he is a Platonist of

---

idealisms of moral excellence; aware that, until the mind can love, and admire, and trust, and hope, and endure, reasoned principles of moral conduct are seeds cast upon the highway of life which the unconscious passenger tramples into dust, although they would bear the harvest of his happiness."—Preface to *Prometheus Unbound*.

63. Cf. Pope, *Essay on Man;* A. O. Lovejoy, *The Great Chain of Being.*

64. S. F. Gingerich, *Essays in the Romantic Poets*, p. 217 *passim.*

the inner circle.[65] Joseph Warren Beach discerns in his poetry an unresolved conflict between Platonism and Naturalism.[66] A. E. Powell expounds the doctrine of the Platonic forms to account for his imagery,[67] a view of the question which Professor Solve appears to share.[68] Carl Grabo emphasizes the neo-Platonic elements of Shelley's poetry, while admitting an appreciable amount of Platonism as well.[69] A. A. Jack in an essay written in 1904 declared that Shelley's Nature is the cold mechanistic world of science, suggesting also a touch of Platonism in Shelley by remarking that "the secret of things is what has charm for him, not the things themselves."[70]

This brief chronicle of divergence in criticism might easily be extended. The moral is, I believe, that as a poet Shelley is not to be confined to any single set of beliefs. His deep interest in philosophy is undeniable; but his poetry is a refractory creature which takes the bit between its teeth and seeks its ends after its own fashion. This is as much as to say that Shelley is a philosophic poet, not a poetic philosopher. His imagery is intellectual and consciously symbolic to an unusual degree, but it should not be regarded as a set of fixed counters used to objectify and visualize a philosophic system. Neither is his verse a rhymed manual of natural

65. A. T. Strong, *Three Studies in Shelley;* Lilian Winstanley, "Platonism in Shelley," *Essays and Studies by Members of the English Association*, IV, 72-100.

66. *Op. cit.*, pp. 242ff.

67. *The Romantic Theory of Poetry*, pp. 206-16.

68. ". . . to the mature Shelley, art was not copying mundane forms, but imitation of the infinite and archetypal forms, so far as imagination was able to apprehend them."—M. T. Solve, *Shelley: His Theory of Poetry*, p. 115.

69. *The Magic Plant*, pp. 412-38.

70. *Shelley: an Essay*, pp. 33-34, 38ff., 127.

science. Professor Grabo is guilty of this form of didactic fallacy in his comment upon *The Cloud:*

> Shelley elaborates the theme with much ingenuity, with beautiful color effects and varied imagery, but the essential facts under the fanciful dress are sound. It is good meteorology. Therefore it is an excellent brief instance of Shelley's poetic processes, his ability to raise a beautiful and imaginative superstructure upon a basis of fact.[71]

He appears to believe that by justifying Shelley as a scientific observer he is establishing his value as a poet. This method of defence, however, is essentially irrelevant.

Shelley, indeed, seeks Truth in poetry. But it is a poetic Truth which he pursues, by means of the creative imagination, synthetic and intuitional, which is embodied in "vitally metaphoric" poetic language, in itself creative insofar as it "marks the before unapprehended relations of things." Shelley's distinction between reason and imagination[72] should be sufficient warning for those who insist upon making his poetry a hanger-on of philosophy and science, unless they believe that he misrepresented his own creative processes.

The Truth toward which Shelley's poetry from first to last aspires is a shifting, tantalizing, elusive thing which he is always striving to catch and clothe in words. It seems to him so close that he grasps for it as for a mirage, yet it is at the same time evident to him that through words he can never attain it, the means being

---

71. *The Magic Plant*, pp. 282-83. Grabo is saying what had previously been said by Stopford Brooke: "Strip off the imaginative clothing from 'The Cloud' and Science will support every word of it."—Introduction, *Selections from Shelley*, pp. xli-xlii. To this A. A. Jack very properly retorted, "Yes, but what then?"—*Op. cit.*, p. 42.

72. *A Defence of Poetry.*

inadequate to the end. For although at one point in the *Defence of Poetry* he declares that "language is arbitrarily produced by the imagination, and has relation to thoughts alone," that it is "as a mirror which reflects" the light of which it is the medium, the quality and substance of his own poetry is better represented by his statement in the same essay of the relationship between inspiration and expression:

. . . the mind in creation is as a fading coal, which some invisible influence, like an inconstant wind, awakens to transitory brightness; this power arises from within, like the colour of a flower which fades and changes as it is developed, and the conscious portions of our natures are unprophetic either of its approach or its departure. Could this influence be durable in its original purity and force, it is impossible to predict the greatness of the results; but when composition begins, inspiration is already on the decline, and the most glorious poetry that has ever been communicated to the world is probably a feeble shadow of the original conceptions of the poet.

The characteristic imagery of Shelley seeks through "vitally metaphorical" and creative language to grasp and express an unseen and unattainable truth. To this restless energy of aspiration is to be attributed both his virtue and defect: fierce power and a wearing lack of repose. Feeling the inadequacy of language to produce the precise effect at which he is aiming (and little wonder, for he seeks absolute Truth), he nevertheless indomitably goes on trying. He cannot tell, as he would wish, exactly what manner of creature the skylark is:

> What thou art we know not;
> What is most like thee?

But by creative imagery he can roughly approximate

his archetypal conception of it, as far as the resources of language will aid. The bird is like a Poet hidden in the light of thought, a high-born maiden in a palace tower, a glowworm golden, and so on. The skylark itself, a symbol of Perfection and Truth, is significantly unseen and remote.

This passage combines the abstract and the concrete in a fashion very typical of Shelley. For while the figures are concrete, each one is emblematic of the remoteness and the invisibility of the lark. The poet is *hidden* in the light of thought; the maiden is secluded in a tower, symbol of withdrawal from actuality; the glowworm scatters *unbeholden* its aërial hue; the rose is concealed within its own green leaves. This concrete-abstract dualism is notably present elsewhere. One may not pierce to the secret being of the west wind, for it is an "unseen presence." In the visible world it is objictified by the leaves, the seeds, the clouds, the waters upon which it acts. In the *Hymn to Intellectual Beauty* the subject of the poem is at two removes from our perceptions:

> The awful shadow of some unseen Power
> Floats though unseen among us . . .

As in *The Skylark*, the images through which Shelley attempts to come at the quality of Beauty themselves embody the unseen; Beauty is

> As summer winds that creep from flower to flower;
> Like moonbeams that *behind* some piny mountain shower.

This Beauty becomes visible only through its effects upon perceptible objects:

> It visits with inconstant glance
> Each human heart and countenance . . .
>
> . . . .
>
> Like hues and harmonies of evening,
> Like clouds in starlight widely spread.

In the *Ode to Heaven* Shelley is frankly hopeless of doing justice to his immense subject. He throws out a variety of imaginal suggestions almost at random. These suggestions are voiced by three Spirits of decidedly diverse opinions. To the First Spirit Heaven is the boundless space above us, a "palace-roof of cloudless nights," a "paradise of golden lights," a

> Presence-chamber, temple, home,
> Every-canopying dome
> Of acts and ages yet to come . . .

It is the physical void, but more than physical in that it is eternal, transcending actuality. The Second Spirit holds that Heaven is

> But a dim and noonday gleam
> From the shadow of a dream

of reality to come; it is "the mind's first chamber," giving only a faint notion of the "world of new delights" stretching out to the infinite capacity of the human mind. This confidence in human potentialities is abruptly rejected by the Third Spirit:

> Peace! the abyss is wreathed with scorn
> At your presumption, atom-born![73]

73. According to Mrs. Shelley, in these lines Shelley "expresses his despair of being able to conceive, far less express, all of variety, majesty, and beauty, which is veiled from our senses in the unknown realm, the mystery of which his poetic vision sought in vain to penetrate."—Quoted in *The Complete Poetical Works of Percy Bysshe Shelley*, p. 366.

Heaven is embodied and symbolized in "a globe of dew," a flower, insofar as it can be grasped by the human intellect. Essentially, however, it cannot be known at all.

Shelley's poetry strives continually to express by images an absolute truth or beauty beyond the scope of imagery. Face to face with this ultimate reality, he is unable to summon the words which will fix its identity; he falls back in defeat. Demogorgon, the symbol of the Absolute, is a "mighty darkness," without limb, form, or outline, and his answers to the questions of Asia and Panthea are shadowy, ambiguous, and inclusive (*Prometheus Unbound*, II, iv). The answer of Demogorgon to Asia's query, "Whom called'st thou God?" reflects most exactly Shelley's dilemma:

> If the abyss
> Could vomit forth its secrets—but a voice
> Is wanting, *the deep truth is imageless.*

(ll. 113-15)

Shelley, then, is abstract in that his poetry continually climbs toward abstraction on steps of concrete imagery. He is abstract also in that mind is as real to him as matter.[74] He is abstract, too, because in his poetry mind and matter are not fused as they are, for example, in Keats, who is able to speak with perfect and instinc-

---

74. Cf. "Speculations on Metaphysics": "It has commonly been supposed that those distinct thoughts which affect a number of persons, at regular intervals, during the passage of a multitude of other thoughts, which are called *real* or *external objects*, are totally different in kind from those which affect only a few persons, and which recur at irregular intervals, and are usually more obscure and distinct, such as hallucinations, dreams, and the ideas of madness. No essential distinction between any one of these ideas, or any class of them, is founded on a correct observation of the nature of things. . . ."

tive spontaneity of the soul as a web upon which Man
should "weave a tapestry empyrean full of symbols for
his spiritual eye, of softness for his spiritual touch, of
space for his wandering, of distinctness for his luxury."[75]
Instead of finding the subject within the object, as does
Keats, Shelley often goes directly to the subject itself
as a separate and distinct entity. Quite frequently he
terminates a rising succession of concrete images with
an abstraction, to which he apparently assigns a poetical
value identical with them.

I cite two closely adjoining passages from *Prometheus
Unbound* to demonstrate this tendency, which could be
pointed out in almost any poem of Shelley's. The Earth,
exulting over the fallen tyrant Jupiter, anathematizes
him as a

> Sceptred *curse*
> Who all our green and azure *universe*
> Threatenedst to muffle round with black *destruction* . . .
>
> (IV, 338-40)

She cries to him,

> How thou art sunk, withdrawn, covered, drunk up
> By thirsty nothing, as the brackish cup
> Drained by a desert troop, a little drop for all;
> And from beneath, around, within, above,
> Filling thy void annihilation, love
> Bursts in like light on caves cloven by the thunder-ball![76]
>
> (IV, 350-55)

75. *Letters*, p. 103.
76. Cf. William Empson's unfavorable interpretation of this Shelleyan usage:
". . . not being able to think of a comparison fast enough he compares the thing to
a vaguer or more abstract notion of itself . . . he was too helplessly excited by one
thing at a time, and that one thing was too often a mere notion not conceived in action
or environment."—*Seven Types of Ambiguity*, p. 203.

Since Shelley believes that the mind is as real as the external world, and of the same order of reality, he often begins with subjective ideas and states and clothes them with natural and concrete imagery. This is the converse of what I believe to be the typical procedure of Keats, who begins with sensuous perception and goes on to build upon it. In the Preface to *Prometheus Unbound* Shelley declares that

> The imagery which I have employed will be found, in many instances, to have been drawn from the operations of the human mind, or from those external actions by which they are expressed. This is unusual in modern poetry, although Dante and Shakespeare are full of instances of the same kind; Dante indeed more than any other poet, and with greater success. But the Greek poets, as writers to whom no resource of awakening the sympathy of their contemporaries was unknown, were in the habitual use of this power; and it is the study of their works (since a higher merit would probably be denied me) to which I am willing that my readers should impute this singularity.

To pass over the problem of Shelley's antecedents in Dante, Shakespeare, and the Greek dramatists, I believe that the difference he mentions between his procedure and that of his contemporaries arises from a greater than usual consciousness of mind as a separate entity. To him mind is coequal with the phenomenal world and of the same order, but the two are not identical, nor are they fused. There is always a gap between them. To bridge this gap Shelley is forced to make greater and more conscious adjustments than are necessary to other poets, notably Keats. *Prometheus Unbound* is a drama of the mind in a sense in which Keats's *Hyperion*, for example, is not. Its characters are a step closer to the abstractions

of allegory; they have less reality independent of the mind of their creator.

Prometheus Unbound is "expressionistic."[77] Prometheus on his rock is mentally tortured by Furies[78] "From the all-miscreative brain of Jove," who is himself simply that quality of the mind of Prometheus which inhibits the free play of his spirit until by conquering himself he shall win release. The Furies have form and reality only in the minds of their victims:

> So from our victim's destined agony
> The shade which is our form invests us round;
> Else we are shapeless as our mother Night.
>
> (I, 470-72)

The spiritual sufferings inflicted by them upon Prometheus are transposed into vivid organic imagery: they will rend him bone from bone and nerve from nerve, working like fire within. The ambiguous relationship which here obtains between the physical and mental is best displayed in a speech of the Third Fury:

> Thou think'st we will live through thee, one by one,
> Like animal life, and though we can obscure not
> The soul which burns within, that we will dwell
> Beside it, like a vain loud multitude,
> Vexing the self-content of wisest men;
> That we will be dread thought beneath thy brain,
> And foul desire round thine astonished heart,

77. In the modern theatrical sense, as Eugene O'Neill's *Emperor Jones* is expressionistic. Subjective moods, concepts, and mental states are projected into dramatic visibility. As Jones is done to death by Little Formless Fears, scenes from his past, and so on, Prometheus is tortured by his own mind.

78. These Furies are one indication of Shelley's indebtedness to Greek drama in his imagery. The Furies who hounded Orestes are their obvious parents, and are employed in precisely the same fashion.

And blood within thy labyrinthine veins
Crawling like agony?

(I, 483-91)

The poet tells us plainly what he is doing in his initial simile, "*like* animal life." The agonies are purely subjective. Yet so nice a balance is maintained that one never quite decides to relegate them entirely to the realm of mere abstraction. The powerful sensuous realization of the last four lines sees to that.

Shelley is also abstract in his conscious and consistent use of symbolism. Of all the elements of his poetic style this is perhaps the most essential. By his recurring use of the veil, the lyre, the stream, the boat, the cloud, and like images, his poetry is most easily and confidently to be identified. Henry Salt was the first, to my knowledge, to mark this fact:

> The repetition of certain images and words is one of Shelley's most marked characteristics. Among metaphors frequently used are those drawn from the instruments of weaving, the warp, woof, and web; from a lyre or Aeolian harp hung up to the wind; an eagle and serpent locked together in fight. The references to serpents are very numerous. Perhaps the strangest instance of Shelley's recurrence to a favourite idea is in his references to Ahasuerus, the Wandering Jew.[79]

A. T. Strong repeated this observation in 1921, mentioning as of special significance the veil image, which he interprets as an emblem of the thinness of the barrier separating the finite and the infinite; the eagle and the serpent; the meteor; poison and the scorpion as images of evil; the boat, the stream, and the guardian spirit;

79. *A Shelley Primer*, pp. 42-43.

and the moon, as a symbol of loveliness.[80] A. C. Bradley pointed out in his essay, "Shelley's View of Poetry,"[81] that "the light of hidden power" was one of Shelley's favorite metaphors. In *The Magic Plant* Carl Grabo devoted considerable attention to Shelley's symbolism, with particular reference to their sources in the neo-Platonists. The value of his comment is, in my opinion, damaged by his insistence upon regarding Shelley's images as inflexible and inert scientific and philosophic counters:[82] a type of emphasis which implicitly denies the independent validity of poetry as a mode of meaning.

G. Wilson Knight offers a more productive and less rigidly bounded interpretation of Shelley's symbolism, paying particular heed to Shelley's domes, his image of the chariot, his treatment of sleep, and his sea-river-cave journeys.[83] Bennett Weaver interprets the Shelleyan cave anew, and calls attention to Shelley's symbolic use of kings, priests, and judges.[84] Newman Ivey White, like Professor Grabo, is interested primarily in the intellectual content and sources of Shelley's imagery, while admitting that poetry is more than logic.[85]

---

80. "Shelley's Symbolism," *op. cit.*, pp. 68-106.

81. *Op. cit.*, p. 152.

82. Note the emphasis in such statements as the following: "Shelley's fondness for certain images and symbols and his repeated use of them in a form increasingly adequate to his thought is one of his marked characteristics as a poet."—P. 104.

". . . Shelley was, unconsciously perhaps, preparing for his use a medium of peculiar efficacy in the expression of philosophic ideas in the form needful for poetry." —P. 169.

". . . in later poems, he employs these symbols and others kin to them, and with a growing sense of their suitability as poetic counters, expressing both physical facts and metaphysical theories."—P. 176.

83. "The Naked Seraph—an Essay on Shelley," *The Starlit Dome*.

84. *Toward the Understanding of Shelley*, pp. 69, 189.

85. "Words in their logical meaning being by nature often inadequate to the uses

W. B. Yeats, aided by the insight of his poetic genius, has given the most fully satisfying account of Shelley's symbols, although his view is perhaps colored overmuch by mysticism. To him a symbol is an image "that has transcended particular time and place," and "passes beyond death, as it were, and becomes a living soul." By this transcendence of time and place the poet, who is a mystic striving always to be absorbed into the surrounding universe, through reverie places himself in contact with the vast reservoir of world-memory, from which his symbols are drawn.[86] These symbols are valuable because of their depth and universality. By means of them the poet passes beyond the limitations of his own personality,[87] and is linked to all the human heritage of past and present. By virtue of this deep-rooted kinship with all that is, the poet's imagery grows infinitely rich, flexible, and meaningful, drawing upon the connotations with which his symbols have been invested by a thousand poets before him. It is not merely fantastic or capricious, but is based upon enduring verities.[88] Such

of great poetry, images and symbols may sometimes be employed to speak more directly to the imagination and intuition."—*Shelley*, I, 425.

86. "The Philosophy of Shelley's Poetry," *Ideas of Good and Evil*, pp. 80-81. Cf. Shelley, "On Life": "Those who are subject to the state called reverie, feel as if their nature were dissolved into the surrounding universe, or as if the surrounding universe were absorbed into their being. They are conscious of no distinction."

87. Cf. *Prometheus Unbound*, IV, 394ff :

"Man, oh, not men! a chain of linked thought,
Of love and might to be divided not,
Compelling the elements with adamantine stress;

. . . .

Man, one harmonius soul of many a soul,
Whose nature is its own divine control,
Where all things flow to all, as rivers to the sea . . ."

88. "It is only by ancient symbols, by symbols that have numberless meanings beside the one or two the writer lays an emphasis upon, or the half-score he knows of,

symbolism as this, then, is essentially private and unique,[89] but nevertheless universal in its significance.

The worth of Yeats's interpretation of Shelley's symbols is primarily that he conceives them to be poetic, not in the narrow sense philosophical: fluid, not fixed: emotional and sensuous as well as intellectual. Shelley's symbols are expressive of his search for Truth, but a poetic Truth imaginatively pursued. It is this pursuit which evokes the deepest feelings of Shelley's spirit. His most characteristic imagery embodies an attempt to establish the relationship between the finite and the infinite. This relationship is variable according to his mood; it is not exclusively Platonic, nor neo-Platonic, nor Naturalistic, but is all by turns, or partakes of all simultaneously. Shelley's philosophic studies furnish an important part of the subject matter of his verse, but a part not more important than does his love of and response to natural beauty; and the result, when Shelley is writing well, is always poetry.

It is not too daring, I think, to assert that this finite-infinite relationship is the focal point of Shelley's imagery. Shelley is intellectually a Monist, emotionally and instinctively a Dualist. He is always attempting to reconcile these two poles of his nature and never quite succeeding. He is continually putting together Time and

---

that any highly subjective art can escape from the barrenness and shallowness of a too conscious arrangement, into the abundance and depth of nature. . . .

". . . his [Shelley's] poetry becomes the richer, the more emotional . . . when I remember that these are ancient symbols, and still come to visionaries in their dreams." —"The Philosophy of Shelley's Poetry," pp. 90, 92.

89. ". . . voices would have told him how there is for every man some one scene, some one adventure, some one picture that is the image of his secret life, for wisdom speaks first in images. . . ."—*Ibid.*, p. 98.

Eternity, Relative and Absolute, Fluctuating and Fixed, Seen and Unseen, to determine how they will relate and interact. The stress thus set up is the essential condition of his poetry, the climate in which it exists.

This relationship appears perhaps most frequently in the image of the veil, and in this form is plainly evident as early as *Queen Mab*. The "glowing limbs" (I, 32) of the sleeping Ianthe are an envelope covering a secret light, perceptible only through this fleshly mask. The Fairy Queen, herself supernatural, has it in her power "to rend / The veil of mortal frailty" and set free the spirit, "Clothed in its changeless purity" (I, 180-82). The ocean acts as a mirror to reflect the "pale and waning stars," the fiery wake of the Fairy's chariot, and the light of morn; this foreshadows other, more conscious images of reflection (I, 225-30). In this case fleeting appearances are caught and held fast in a changeless medium, but there are other images in which eternity is mirrored in shifting waters emblematic of time. Time and Eternity are contrasted in the figure of the Spirit of Ianthe peering down from above at the earth:

> The Spirit seemed to stand
> High on an isolated pinnacle;
> The flood of ages combating below . . .
>
> (II, 253-55)

Images of curtaining, canopies, and robes, not infrequent in Shelley, are probably merely descriptive in *Queen Mab*, innocent of an ulterior meaning. Yet as variations of the veil image they have their interest. "Heaven's ebon vault" is like a canopy "which love had spread / To curtain her sleeping world" (IV, 4-8); the hills are

"Robed in a garment of untrodden snow" (IV, 9). It should be noted that in these instances the covering itself is beneficent and significant, not something to be torn away.

The Time-Eternity contrast is explicit in

> . . . the storm of change, that ceaselessly
> Rolls round the eternal universe and shakes
> Its undecaying battlement . . .
>
> (VI, 160-62)

It is somewhat confusedly presented in

> Soul of the Universe! eternal spring
> Of life and death, of happiness and woe,
> Of all that chequers the phantasmal scene
> That floats before our eyes in wavering light,
> Which gleams but on the darkness of our prison
> Whose chains and massy walls
> We feel but cannot see.
>
> (VI, 190-96)

This image seems to be derivative from Plato's image of the cave, without reference to which it is barely intelligible.

The image of the veil as a delusive covering hiding reality occurs in Ahasuerus' bitter description of the Christ:

> . . . humbly he came,
> Veiling his horrible Godhead in the shape
> Of man, scorned by the world . . .
>
> (VII, 163-65)

It may be remarked in passing that the figure of Ahasuerus himself, the wandering Jew, which had a singular fascination for Shelley, is an ironic symbol of the Time-

Eternity relationship. This relationship, faintly adumbrated in an image of a giant oak braving a wintry storm (VII, 259-63), is direct in

> . . . the cradles of eternity
> Where millions lie lulled to their portioned sleep
> By the deep murmuring stream of passing things,
>
> (VIII, 6-8)

is pictured in a shroud ("Tear thou that gloomy shroud" [VIII, 9]), in a veil ("Through the wide rent in Time's eternal veil" [VIII, 12]), and in a lighthouse:

> And, 'midst the ebb and flow of human things,
> Show somewhat stable, somewhat certain still,
> A light-house o'er the wild of dreary waves.
>
> (VIII, 55-57)

To trace the course and ramifications of this basic image in its various forms throughout the body of Shelley's poetry would be work for a book rather than part of a chapter. I shall therefore confine myself to citing a few instances of it in significant poems. In *Alastor*, the visioned maid who appears to the poet in dreams is *veiled* (l. 151). Her body, like the body of Ianthe in *Queen Mab*, is a covering concealing yet permeated by an inner fire:

> Soon the solemn mood
> Of her pure mind kindled through all her frame
> A permeating fire . . .
>
> (ll. 161-63)

In like fashion her "eloquent blood" tells "an ineffable tale" in "the branching veins" of her fair hands (ll. 166-69). The poet, viewing the maid, sees

> . . . by the warm light of their own life
> Her glowing limbs beneath the sinuous veil
> Of woven wind . . .

(ll. 174-76)

I have previously cited the statement of A. T. Strong that the veil is emblematic of the thinness of the barrier between the finite and the infinite. That is doubtless in some cases true, but the matter is not quite so simple, as the present passage shows. It is equally true that this image betrays Shelley's hopelessness of piercing the barrier, or even forming a clear notion of what lies beyond it, for there is here not one veil but many. One grasps at seeming reality only to find it merely the covering of a still deeper truth. The maid is the object of attainment, "beneath the sinuous veil," yet her "glowing limbs" are themselves merely the veil for a purer essence, in itself composed of complex elements, as is indicated by the "self-inwoven" image[90] "the warm light of their own life." Something of this complexity is present also in the lament for the poet with which *Alastor* ends:

> But thou art fled,
> Like some frail exhalation, which the dawn
> Robes in its golden beams . . .

(ll. 687-89)

Which is the essence, the exhalation or that which robes it? The relationship between covering and the thing covered is ambiguous.

Prometheus Unbound is rich in images of the finite-infinite relationship. The sea is "Heaven's ever-changing shadow" (I, 27-28). The Earth tells Prometheus of a world which is the shadow of our world,

90. I am indebted for this term to William Empson's *Seven Types of Ambiguity*.

> . . . where do inhabit
> The shadows of all forms that think and live,
> Till death unite them and they part no more.
>
> (I, 197-99)

One is not quite sure which is the shadow, which the reality; and the last line hints that both "shadows" and "forms" are but shadows of a truth still more remote. Prometheus calls before him not Jupiter but the Phantasm of Jupiter from the world of shades, while in the world of appearances Pain and Ruin are the shadows of Love (I, 779-80).

The dizzying elusiveness of an essence or absolute concealed from perception beneath many veils is powerfully suggested in such images as

> Those eyes which burn in smiles that fade in tears,
> Like stars half-quenched in mists of silver dew.
> Beloved and most beautiful, who wearest
> The shadow of that soul by which I live . . .
>
> (II, i, 28-31)

The whirling, overlapping syntax of the first line perfectly represents the bewildering involutions of the thought.

In some instances the veil itself is the essential element, notably in Panthea's dream of Prometheus:

> . . . the overpowering light
> Of that immortal shape was shadowed o'er
> By love; which from his soft and flowing limbs,
> And passion-parted lips, and keen, faint eyes,
> Steamed forth like vaporous fire . . .
>
> (II, i, 71-75)

The finite-infinite image lies at the heart of the daz-

zling "Life of Life" lyric, from which one may strip off layer after layer without arriving at any solid certainty:

> Life of Life, thy lips enkindle
> With their love the breath between them;
> And thy smiles before they dwindle
> Make the cold air fire; then screen them
> In those looks, where whoso gazes
> Faints, entangled in their mazes.
>
> Child of Light! thy limbs are burning
> Through the vest which seems to hide them;
> As the radiant lines of morning
> Through the clouds, ere they divide them;
> And this atmosphere divinest
> Shrouds thee whereso'er thou shinest.
>
> . . . .
>
> Lamp of Earth! where'er thou movest
> Its dim shapes are clad with brightness,
> And the souls of whom thou lovest
> Walk upon the winds with lightness,
> Till they fail, as I am failing,
> Dizzy, lost, yet unbewailing!

This song celebrates the quest and not the gaining of the quarry. "Life of Life" is itself a finite-infinite image, portraying an essence within outer coverings. Yet in what does this essence lie? "Thy lips enkindle / With their love the breath between them." It seems, however, equally likely that the breath may enkindle both. And why, if the smiles of the spirit "make the cold air fire," should they be screened

> In those looks, where whoso gazes
> Faints, entangled in their mazes?

For these "smiles" and "looks" are presumably identical, and both presumably derive from a deeper source.

Then, the limbs of the Child of Light are burning
"Through the vest which seems to hide them": obviously the container and its contents. But these limbs
themselves seem merely a veil for a further reality; and
this burning does not reveal the naked truth, but con-
ceals it: "this atmosphere divinest / Shrouds thee where-
so'er thou shinest." The "Lamp of Earth" indeed in-
fuses the merely human with divinity, but the divine
is known only as it manifests itself in the "dim shapes"
of humanity. The source of this secret fire remains hidden. The souls whom this spirit loves "walk upon the
winds with lightness," indeed, but whence their blessed-
ness comes is unknown to them.

In the later stages of *Prometheus Unbound* the image of
the veil becomes more simply an opposition of the accidental and imperfect to the perfect and permanent, as
Shelley depicts the world of his desire:

> And, veil by veil, evil and error fall.
>
> (III, iii, 62)

Even in this confident speech, however, evil and error
do not fall instantaneously; there is a suggestion of
layer upon layer to be stripped off. There is, of course,
the famous

> . . . painted veil, by those who were, called life,
> Which mimicked, as with colors idly spread,
> All men believed and hoped, is torn aside,
>
> (IV, 189-91)

in which reform and revelation are immediate.

In *Adonais* still another aspect of the finite-infinite relationship appears: dread of the consequences of success in the pursuit of the absolute. In his self-portrait he refers to himself as one who

> Had gazed on Nature's naked loveliness
> Actaeon-like, and now he fled astray . . .
>
> (ll. 275-76)

A few lines later he characterizes himself as "A love in desolation masked"—an unusual variation on the container-content theme, but reminiscent of the mingling of love with desolation and ruin in *Prometheus Unbound*.

The spirit of Keats is an essence hindered in life by its mortal covering:

> Dust to the dust! but the pure spirit shall flow
> Back to the burning fountain whence it came,
> A portion of the eternal . . .
>
> (ll. 338-40)

The relationship between life and death is not constant, however, for

> . . . death is a low mist which cannot blot
> The brightness it may veil.
>
> (ll. 391-92)

The temporal veil appears in a new guise in

> The One remains, the many change and pass;
> Heaven's light forever shines, Earth's shadows fly;
> Life, like a dome of many-colored glass,
> Stains the white radiance of Eternity,
> Until Death tramples it to fragments.
>
> (ll. 460-64)

It is to be noted that this veil has very decided attrac-

tions. Shelley, despite his brave words, is not wholly anxious to desert the beautiful world of appearances for the cold perfection of the One. There is a certain ambiguous emotion in "Until Death tramples it to fragments." This hesitation to take the final step, to tear the veil asunder once for all, pervades the last three stanzas of *Adonais*, striking an ominous note amid their joyous prophecy. "The soft sky smiles,—the low wind whispers near"—am I mistaken in imagining here a certain dread lest this invitation prove a betrayal? The The next stanza is unquestionably a hymn to the One, a Light and a Beauty, a Benediction and a Love,

> Which through the web of being blindly wove
> By man and beast and earth and air and sea,
> Burns bright or dim, as each are mirrors of
> The fire for which all thirst . . .

Yet the imagery betrays some mental conflict. The "web of being" is apparently at least in part opaque, and if it is "blindly wove" it is woven by creatures in some degree blind, who cannot in consequence be perfect mirrors of the fire. This fire, of course, "burns bright or dim" according to the stage of being in which it is reflected; nevertheless, the images of the web and the mirror do not entirely harmonize.

In the final stanza awe, exaltation, and repulsion are closely intertwined:

> The breath whose might I have invoked in song
> Descends on me; my spirit's bark is driven
> Far from the shore, far from the trembling throng
> Whose sails were never to the tempest given;
> The massy earth and spherèd skies are riven!

> I am borne darkly, fearfully afar;
> Whilst, burning through the inmost veil of Heaven,
> The soul of Adonais, like a star,
> Beacons from the abode where the Eternal are.

The soul of Adonais is at once a strong wind which blows the bark of the spirit into dark, fearful waters and a fixed star which guides the mariner, comfortably like the beacon of a lighthouse. Yet before this light can be reached the poet must pierce not one, but many veils. "The massy earth and spherèd skies are riven"; actuality disappears as at a thunderclap before the divining perception of the seeker. The light, however, is still far to seek. Heaven itself is composed of layer within layer of mystery, veil beyond veil.

Of the various symbols which move constantly through Shelley's pages I have offered only a brief glimpse at that key-symbol of his verse which is most typically represented by the image of the veil. This symbol, like his other symbols, is abstract insofar as it is, in the words of Yeats, an image "that has transcended particular time and place," and has a predetermined meaning not wholly dependent upon the sensuous and natural context in which it is framed. Like his other symbols, it is symptomatic of a fundamental dualism in Shelley's conception of the relationship between mind and nature—a dualism all the more evident because of his continuous efforts to resolve it into unity.

What I have chiefly attempted to show, however, is that Shelley's images are not lifeless pawns in a game of philosophic chess. They are living, flexible, various in the subtle shades of meaning which attach to them. Reflecting a consistent view of life, each image is never-

theless a response to a particular poetic stimulus and situation, dictated by a thousand considerations of mood, tone, and artistic necessity. Shelley's imagery is always dramatic, expressive of struggle and aspiration toward heights which he did not, as some would have it, conceive as easy of attainment, but which he felt to be inexpressibly enchanting through the very difficulty of scaling them.[91] The stress beneath which it labors is the condition of its unique identity and value, for it is indicative of an appreciation of complexity and a love of natural beauty for which Shelley is not always given credit. The "dome of many-coloured glass" was perhaps as dear to him as the "white radiance of eternity," although he did not find the two compatible.

91. Cf. the *Ode to Heaven* and Mrs. Shelley's comment, quoted above, p. 221.

ROMANTIC BARDS

AND METAPHYSICAL REVIEWERS

I   The reputations of all the English Romantic poets, and of Shelley in particular, have
suffered much within the last three decades at the hands
of a single influential group of critics: the "New"
Critics, as John Crowe Ransom has called them. They
are too powerful to be ignored. They command respect
because of their seriousness and their undoubted regard
for the honor of poetry. They have, I think, succeeded
in damaging Shelley seriously even with intelligent
readers of poetry.[1] Since their attack is directed very
largely against Romantic and especially Shelleyan metaphor, it is worth while to examine it in some detail.
In order, however, to discuss the objections of the New
Critics to Romantic Imagery, and more specifically to
the imagery of Shelley, it is necessary to give some
account of the development and nature of the central
tenets of their imaginal doctrines, so as to make clear
the issues at stake. For the purposes of this chapter the

1. "With the ascendancy of T. S. Eliot, the Elizabethan dramatists have come
back into fashion, and the nineteenth-century poets gone out. . . . It is as much as
one's life is worth nowadays, among young people, to say an approving word for
Shelley or a dubious one about Donne."—Edmund Wilson, *Axel's Castle*, pp. 116, 117.

men chiefly to be considered are T. S. Eliot, F. R. Leavis, John Crowe Ransom, Allen Tate, and Cleanth Brooks, with I. A. Richards indirectly figuring in the movement insofar as he furnishes the bases of its theory.[2]

Before commencing this examination a number of qualifications must be made. The critics under discussion, if seen in a different perspective, would appear very much less alike than I shall show them here. With reference to their attitudes upon English Romantic poetry they form a solid and cohesive body; a closer view of their interrelationships would reveal notable divergences, which however lie outside the scope of this essay. The point to be emphasized is that they present a common front against Romanticism, and condemn it from doctrines substantially though not identically the same.

The issues debated here must also be enlarged upon a little, even at the risk of explaining the self-evident. I am about to embark upon a [I trust] vigorous defense of Romantic poetry, and of Shelley especially, and this defense involves a counter attack. Upon what grounds, then, can an attack be justly based?

It is not to be expected that any critic should be able to present a complete and invulnerable theory, from the nature of critical terms and the immensity of the job he is trying to do. With the positive aspects of the New Criticism one cannot seriously quarrel—their formulation of new critical concepts and their reworking of old ones. Only by this process, of course, can criticism maintain its vitality, and critics truly creative should have

2. William Empson's *Seven Types of Ambiguity*, although an important New Critical document, has little applicability to this discussion. I omit also Robert Penn Warren, despite his honorable position in the New Criticism, since his stand upon the immediate problem has been relatively cautious and unpredictable.

due honor. But where these concepts seem inadequate for the job to be done, or where they are misapplied through insufficient sympathy with and consequently insufficient knowledge of the materials to be examined, we may justly complain.

To be more specific, the New Critics share an absolutism which in intention is worthy of praise, but open to many objections in practice. It is praiseworthy insofar as it endeavors to supply objective, permanent, and invariable standards for the evaluation of literature. It is objectionable when it leaps to conclusions without first examining the evidence; when it short-circuits due process of law and becomes judge, jury, prosecuting attorney —and finally executioner—all at once. The New Critical standards which are appropriate to this discussion are called Irony and Organic Unity. As applied to the Romantic poets they are used as weapons, or as yardsticks to demonstrate the failures of Romantic poetry. The intention of this essay is to maintain that they are misapplied, and consequently that the judgments based upon them are erroneous and unjust.[3]

II   The attitude of the New Critics toward the Romantics is foreshadowed in T. E. Hulme's tentative but important "Romanticism and Classicism,"[4] an opening shot against nineteenth-cen-

---

3. Here it must be pointed out that Mr. Allen Tate has never explicitly accepted the doctrines of Irony and Organic Unity, while Mr. Ransom explicitly repudiates them. Their practice, however, at any rate when dealing with Romantic poetry, is identical with the practice of critics who do accept these doctrines; and from the viewpoint of the present essay the basic theories are very closely akin.

4. *Speculations*, pp. 113-40.

tury poetry. Hulme takes the essence of Romanticism to be the Rousseauistic belief that man is good and a creature of infinite possibilities.[5] This belief obviates the necessity of formal religion, the faith in the existence of a Supernatural Being. Belief in God, however, is deeply ingrained in human nature. If it is abandoned there must be some kind of compensating substitution. What happens in Romanticism, then, is this:

> You don't believe in Heaven, so you begin to believe in a Heaven on earth. In other words, you get romanticism. The concepts that are right and proper in their own sphere are spread over, and so mess up, falsify and blur the clear outlines of human experience. It is like pouring a pot of treacle over the dinner table. Romanticism then . . . is spilt religion.[6]

The Romantic is always talking about the infinite, because he believes that man is infinite, and this leads to extravagance of speech and empty rhetoric. In contrast, the classic has his feet always on the ground; he is faithful to "the concept of a limit."[7] Romantic poetry, thinks Hulme, is for this reason at last on the point of death, and a very good thing, too. But while romantic verse has passed away, the attitude of mind which demands romantic qualities in verse lives on.

> I object [he says] even to the best of the romantics. I object still more to the receptive attitude. I object to the sloppiness which doesn't consider that a poem is a poem unless it is moaning or whining about something or other. I always think in this connection of the last line of a poem of John Webster's which ends with a request I cordially endorse:

5. *Ibid.*, p. 116.
6. *Ibid.*, p. 118.
7. *Ibid.*, p. 119.

'End your moan and come away.'[8]

The thing has got so bad now that a poem which is all dry and hard, a properly classical poem, would not be considered poetry at all.[9]

Luckily, however, Romanticism is dying, to be succeeded by "a period of dry, hard classical verse."[10] For this Hulme suggests a new aesthetic and theory of imagery. Aesthetic pleasure, in his opinion, lies in the communication of experience; and poetry, which is a "visual, concrete" language, "a compromise for a language of intuition which would hand over sensations bodily," is the ideal vehicle for this communication. In this fact is the sufficient justification for poetry.[11]

In this account there are several points of special significance. First to be noticed is the sweeping contemptuousness of Hulme's attitude toward Romanticism. He formulates a narrow and rigid definition, epigrammatic and denunciatory. Although at the outset he warns the reader that he is using the terms "Romanticism" and "Classicism" in a limited and special sense, he permits them throughout his essay to assume a general significance. He confesses that there are other things in the poetry of the Romantics besides the qualities which he condemns,[12] but the general effect of his remarks is implicitly damaging to it.[13]

Of interest, too, is his assertion that the justification

---

8. The line is slightly misquoted.

9. *Speculations*, p. 126.

10. *Ibid.*, p. 133.

11. *Ibid.*, pp. 134-36.

12. *Ibid.*, p. 124.

13. Elsewhere he speaks scornfully of "genteel poetry like Shelley's."—*Notes on Language and Style*, p. 12.

of poetry lies in its accurate delineation of things and experiences, almost a substitute for the intuition of the things and experiences themselves. Clearly here is the germ of a theory of poetry as knowledge, which as formulated by Hulme one need not be very far gone in idealism to question. In the first place, he assumes that all sensory images are visual:[14] an assumption obviously false.[15] Second, and more important, he thoroughly confuses poetry and life. If poetry is a substitute for consciousness itself, by which we intuit things and experience, on what ground can poetry exist? It can in that case only do poorly what we ourselves can do supremely well. A word is not, after all, equivalent to a thing.[16]

The implications of this theory of imagery are that poetry should occupy itself with objects: small objects, with definite limits, so as to present a minimum of difficulty to perception. Hulme predicts that the new poetry will "be cheerful, dry and sophisticated,"[17] in keeping with the finite quality of its subject matter.

It is noticeable that Hulme's distaste for Romanticism is in some measure due to what he regards as its Monism.[18] The classicist will not seek to impose a factitious unity upon the natural world. In the brilliant series of detached aphorisms collected under the name of "Cinders" he declares that there is no cosmos, that all is flux, and that "only in the fact of consciousness

14. "Each word must be an image seen, not a counter."—*Ibid.*
15. See above, p. 5 [ch. I].
16. See above, pp. 5-6 [ch. I].
17. *Speculations*, p. 137.
18. It seems needless to protest at length against the arbitrariness of Hulme's definition of Romanticism at this date, when we are all if anything too conscious of the difficulty of determining its essence.

is there a unity of the world." Taken together with his explicit utterances upon imagery, this pronouncement suggests an artistic preoccupation with the single image and a relative indifference to the unity of the whole, in keeping with his general *Weltanschauung.*[19]

III   Hulme expresses an attitude and a set of beliefs about Romanticism, poetry, and imagery which recur in a greater or less degree in the criticism of all his successors. His attitude toward the Romantics, for example, his love of definiteness and concreteness in imagery, and his desire for "a period of dry, hard, classical verse," are all apparent in the essays of T. S. Eliot.[20]

This attitude is faithfully reproduced in Eliot's superbly supercilious judgment:

. . . the only cure for Romanticism is to analyze it. What is permanent and good in Romanticism is curiosity . . . a curiosity which recognizes that any life, if accurately and profoundly penetrated, is interesting and always strange. Romanticism is a short cut to the strangeness without the reality, and it leads its disciples only back upon themselves . . . there may be a good deal to be said for Romanticism in life, there is no place for it in letters.[21]

In Eliot is the same narrowness of definition, the same epigrammatic brilliance, the same over-aweing certainty that one finds in Hulme. So confident is the tone, so nervous and close-packed the expression, that one is inclined to take this statement for far more than it

19. See *Speculations*, pp. 220-22.
20. For the literary relationship between Hulme and Eliot see F. O. Matthiessen, *The Achievement of T. S. Eliot*, pp. 56, 70.
21. *The Sacred Wood*, pp. 31, 32.

actually is. Mr. Eliot has failed to inform us what, where, and how extensive is the Romanticism of which he is thinking.

His preference for hard precision and concreteness in imagery is evident in such a comparison as he makes between Morris's *The Nymph's Song to Hylas* and Marvell's *The Nymph and the Fawn:*

> . . . the effect of Morris's charming poem depends upon the mistiness of the feeling and the vagueness of its object; the effect of Marvell's upon its bright, hard precision. . . . A curious result of the comparison of Morris's poem with Marvell's is that the former, though it appears to be more serious, is found to be the slighter.[22]

Akin to Hulme's demand for poetry which shall be "cheerful, dry, and sophisticated" is Eliot's defense of wit, a quality without which he deems poetry incomplete. "It involves, probably, a recognition, implicit in the expression of every experience, of other kinds of experience which are possible, which we find as clearly in the greatest as in poets like Marvell." Wit furnishes an "internal equilibrium" not to be found in the poets after the seventeenth century; particularly not to be found in the great Romantics.[23]

Eliot's greatest contribution to the New Criticism, "the unified sensibility," is, however, a complete departure from the ideas of Hulme.[24] In his important essay on "The Metaphysical Poets" Eliot suggested a view of literary history and a standard for poetry which have

22. *Homage to John Dryden*, p. 41.

23. *Ibid.*, pp. 45, 46.

24. It would seem to be related to Coleridge's theory of the secondary or poetic imagination, although with a different emphasis.

been extended and systematized by others. The metaphysical poets of the seventeenth century, along with many of the late Elizabethan and Jacobean dramatists, possessed a unity of sensibility, "a mechanism of sensibility which could devour any kind of experience." Through the influence of two powerful poets, Milton and Dryden, this unity was lost.[25] The metaphysicals, however, were in the direct current of English poetry, not those who followed. Judged by this standard of sensibility, the eighteenth and nineteenth centuries were found wanting. Thought and feeling were separated. "The poets revolted against the ratiocinative, the descriptive; they thought and felt by fits, unbalanced; they reflected."[26] To a poet like Donne, however, "A thought . . . was an experience; it modified his sensibility."

At this point Eliot proposes a definition of the poet's psychology which we find reflected again and again in later critics:

When a poet's mind is properly equipped for its work, it is constantly amalgamating disparate experience; the ordinary man's experience is chaotic, irregular, fragmentary. The latter falls in love, or reads Spinoza, and these two experiences have nothing to do with each other, or with the noise of the typewriter or the smell of cooking; in the mind of the poet these experiences are always forming new wholes.[27]

Closely allied to this statement is his shrewd remark on Johnson's condemnation of the metaphysical poets for

25. See also Basil Willey, *The Seventeenth Century Background*. Mr. Eliot has recently modified his view of the responsibility of Milton and Dryden for the "dissociation of sensibility."—"Milton," *Sewanee Review*, LVI, 185-209.

26. *Homage to John Dryden*, p. 31.

27. *Ibid.*, p. 30.

"yoking the most heterogeneous ideas by violence together."

> The force of this impeachment [says Eliot] lies in the failure of the conjunction, the fact that often the ideas are yoked but not united. . . . But a degree of heterogeneity of material compelled into unity is omnipresent in poetry.[28]

He observes of the poetry of the future that it will probably be difficult and complex:

> Our civilization comprehends great variety and complexity, and this variety and complexity, playing upon a refined sensibility, must produce various and complex results. The poet must become more and more comprehensive, more allusive, more indirect, in order to force, to dislocate if necessary, language into his meaning.[29]

Poetic imagery, then, is likely to be heterogeneous in material, comprehensive, and difficult, but unified by the amalgamating power of the poet's mind.

Mr. Eliot has offered a number of acute and suggestive generalizations, which have taken deep root in modern criticism. But the merely tentative and suggestive quality of his pronouncements contrasts remarkably with the rigidly dogmatic structures which have been reared upon them. The notion of "the unified sensibility," for example, of which its creator has modestly said that it has had a success in the world astonishing to him,[30] seems a slender basis for a new and revolutionary theory of the history of English poetry. On the one hand, to a reader of the Romantics it looks like a streamlined modern version of Coleridge on the Imagina-

28. *Ibid.*, p. 26.
29. *Ibid.*, p. 31.
30. "Milton," *op. cit.*, pp. 193, 194.

tion, or Wordsworth on the Poet in the 1800 *Preface;* and therefore, since it obviously is intended to exclude Romantic poetry, needs to be more fully differentiated from Romantic theory. On the other, since Mr. Eliot has invoked psychology, he does not sufficiently psychologize. The heterogeneity of the poet's materials emerges very clearly, but the assumption of the amalgamating power which unifies them remains shadowy.

Given the superior unifying power of the poet, how more precisely is it to be differentiated from the unification of experience which, as Hulme noted,[31] we are all able to achieve through consciousness itself? And in what way does this unity appear in poetic imagery? "In Chapman especially," declares Mr. Eliot, "there is a direct sensuous apprehension of thought, or a recreation of thought into feeling, which is exactly what we find in Donne."[32] This fusion of categories needs more elucidation: the unification is too swift to be comprehended. The passage from Chapman which glosses the statement, for one reader at least fails to clarify it:

> . . . in this one thing, all the discipline
> Of manners and of manhood is contained;
> A man to join himself with th' Universe
> In his main sway, and make in all things fit
> One with that all, and go on, round as it;
> Not plucking from the whole his wretched part
> And into straits, or into naught revert,
> Wishing the complete Universe might be
> Subject to such a rag of it as he:
> But to consider great Necessity.[33]

31. And as Coleridge had earlier noted in his Primary Imagination.
32. *Homage to John Dryden*, p. 29.
33. Quoted from Eliot, *ibid.*

Chapman's lines vigorously express an abstract idea; but to call them sensuous is to follow the example of Mr. Eliot's poet, who forces and dislocates language into his meaning. "Join," "plucking," and "rag," where we should expect to find the imagery, have little imaginal force. And the relation of part and whole, Man and Universe, which is the core of the passage, is an abstraction without sensuous and imaginative realization.

Mr. Eliot's apologia for the metaphysical poets performed a valuable service in helping to return to favor a poetry which had suffered long and undeserved neglect. Unfortunately, in so doing he suggested a whole aesthetic and theory of literary history, insecurely based and dangerously narrow and intolerant in its implications. And his stimulating but tentative pronouncements harden into dogma as the New Criticism proceeds.

IV   The doctrine of poetry and of imagery which appears in Eliot as "unified sensibility" or "heterogeneity of material compelled into unity by the operation of the poet's mind" is more elaborately formulated by I. A. Richards, to whose work all of the New Critics are indebted. Mr. Richards divides poetry into the "Synthetic" and the "Exclusive," a classification roughly corresponding to the "unified" and "dissociated" sensibility of Eliot. In Synthetic Poetry there is an "equilibrium of opposed impulses, which we suspect to be the ground-plan of the most valuable aesthetic responses." The distinction between Exclusive and Synthetic Poetry runs thus:

A poem of the first group is built out of sets of impulses which

run parallel, which have the same direction. In a poem of the second group the most obvious feature is the extraordinary heterogeneity of the distinguishable impulses. But they are more than heterogeneous, they are opposed. They are such that in ordinary, non-poetic, non-imaginative experience, one or other set would be suppressed to give as it might appear freer development to the others.[34]

From this distinction Richards evolves his theory of Irony. Exclusive Poetry is sentimental poetry, incomplete in its view of life and open to attack by Irony. Synthetic poetry, being itself ironic, is invulnerable:

Irony in this sense consists in the bringing in of the opposite, the complementary impulses; that is why poetry which is exposed to it is not of the highest order, and why irony itself is so constantly a characteristic of poetry which is.[35]

This principle of irony is apotheosized under the name of synaesthesis as the ultimate aesthetic experience, as Beauty itself, in *The Foundations of Aesthetics*. Synaesthesis is an equilibrium and harmony of various impulses, bringing into play all the faculties. By this equilibrium and harmony "we are enabled to appreciate relationships in a way which would not be possible under normal circumstances. Through no other experience can the full richness and complexity of our environment be realized."[36]

Richards, then, elaborates a conception of poetry and of poetic imagery which is parallel to the more tentative and fragmentary notions of Eliot. Although he is not concerned to assay individual poets, his illustrations are so chosen as to be implicitly damaging to the Romantics,

34. *Principles of Literary Criticism*, p. 250.
35. *Ibid.*
36. See Richards, *Coleridge on Imagination*.

especially to Shelley. His views in general support the
conception of English literary history proposed by Eliot.

Richards' Irony is deeply indebted to Coleridge's
theory of the Imagination, in which opposite or discordant qualities are reconciled, a more than usual state
of emotion is conjoined with more than usual order,
and judgment and self-possession are combined with enthusiasm and feeling.[37] There is, however, a significant
difference of emphasis. Coleridge would reconcile opposites in an organic synthesis of emotion and order, judgment and feeling. In Richards the synthesizing agent is
slighted, the discordant and opposing materials stressed.
It is the opposition and heterogeneity itself upon which
his attention is focussed, and the balancing and harmonizing are in the main left to take care of themselves.

The concept of Irony, or heterogeneity, or "unified
sensibility," is a basic tenet for most of the New Critics,
and I believe accepted in practice even when, as by John
Crowe Ransom, the theory itself is repudiated. Richards'
semantic emphasis upon the flexibility and variety of
words according to their context and situation has had
a like effect.[38] Richards also, like Hulme and Eliot,
prefers verse to be urbane, social, and easy in tone: a
preference which has had its influence upon later critics.
I think I do not distort his intention in saying that this
urbanity of tone is with him at least implicitly a standard of judgment. It is very close to Eliot's "wit," and
closely linked also with the theory of irony. It implies
a certain dandyism and imperturbability, a refusal to be

---

37. Coleridge, *Biographia Literaria*, ch. XIV.

38. See *The Philosophy of Rhetoric;* and "The Interactions of Words," in *The Language of Poetry*, ed. Allen Tate.

disturbed by inconvenient emotions. Like Eliot, Mr. Richards finds this quality absent in the Romantics.[39]

V   In the criticism of John Crowe Ransom and Allen Tate one finds the same general view of literary history as Eliot's; the same love of heterogeneity as in Eliot and Richards; the same demand for dry urbanity of tone. One finds in them also, however, a preoccupation with form unexampled even in Eliot, an exclusive and intransigent aestheticism. Poetry to them is an absolute substance, related to the affairs of the world only at several removes.[40] It "finds its true usefulness in its perfect inutility."[41] It is "the art of apprehending and concentrating our experience in the mysterious limitations of form."[42] The objective reality of poetry is in its formal qualities, which it is therefore the chief business of the critic to examine.[43] Poetry, however, gives us the only complete knowledge of the world, "that unique and formed intelligence of the world of which man alone is capable."[44]

To Ransom and Tate Romantic poetry is imperfect poetry because it attempts to communicate ideas;[45] be-

39. See, *e.g.*, *Practical Criticism*, p. 176.

40. "There is yet no general recognition of the possibility that an aesthetic effect may exist by itself. . . . But the modern poet is intensely concerned with this possibility, . . . He has performed a work of dissociation and purified his art."—Ransom, *The World's Body*, p. 59.

41. Tate, *Reactionary Essays*, p. 112.

42. *Ibid.*, p. ix.

43. "From my point of view the formal qualities of a poem are the focus of the specifically critical judgment. . . ."—Tate, *Reason in Madness*, p. 110.

44. *Ibid.*, p. 19. Cf. Ransom, *The World's Body*, p. 157: ". . . imagination is an organ of knowledge whose technique is images."

45. "I am attacking here the fallacy of communication in poetry. . . . It is no

cause it employs mass language, the only effective means
of communication; and because it is "associationist,"
vaguely musical, cloudy, and "pretty."[46] The best poetry, and the best imagery, is complex and ironic, "metaphysical." In the words of Tate, "The poet attains to a
mastery over experience by facing its utmost implications. There is the clash of powerful opposites."[47] Ransom approves of the deliberate obscurity of Tate's poem,
Death of Little Boys.[48] A poem is "nothing short of a
desperate ontological or metaphysical manoeuvre."[49]
The antithesis of this poetry is Romanticism. "The
poetry I am disparaging is . . . the poetry written by
romantics, in a common sense of that term."[50] Romantic
poetry is also to be condemned because it is "Platonic."
It is "allegory, a discourse in things, but on the understanding that they are translatable at every point into
ideas."[51]

Applied specifically to the problem of poetic imagery,
the theories of Ransom and Tate correspond roughly to
the ideas of Hulme and Eliot, and in a lesser degree to
those of I. A. Richards. Their view of Poetry as Knowledge is very close to Hulme's "poetry of things," and
would seem to be open to the same objections.[52] Ransom,

less a fallacy in the writing of poetry than of critical theory. . . . I suppose one may
say that it began to prosper after 1798; for on the whole nineteenth century English
verse is a poetry of communication. The poets were trying to use verse to convey ideas
and feelings that they secretly thought could be better conveyed by science."—Tate,
Reason in Madness, p. 65.

46. Ransom, *The World's Body*, p. 281.
47. *Reactionary Essays*, p. 12.
48. *The World's Body*, pp. 59, 60.
49. *Ibid.*, p. 347.
50. *Ibid.*, p. ix.
51. *Ibid.*, p. 122.
52. Fred H. Stocking, in Poetry as Knowledge: the Critical Theory of John Crowe

in commenting upon Aristotle,[53] declares, like Hulme, that the accurate description of things is enough for poetry, that the end of art is an infinite degree of particularity.[54] The realism of technique thus to be employed is not "photographic," but "psychological." The value and the distinction of the artistic process lie in the pains lavished by the artist upon technique.[55] But this technique, by Mr. Ransom's account of it, is an isolated entity related neither to subject or object. He tells us nothing either of the mind of the artist by which the thing is perceived or in what manner words are able to express the thing itself. Tate comparably asserts that poetry is *complete* knowledge, knowledge of whole objects, unlike the limited knowledge which science offers us, but also fails to furnish a psychological or metaphysical rationale.[56]

The flaw in the criticism of Ransom and Tate, in their approach specifically to Romanticism and particularly to Shelley, is its absolutism. They transform a set of interesting but incompletely grounded and provisional

---

Ransom and Allen Tate (an unpublished dissertation), gives a sympathetic and thorough account of this theory. The present study can apply neither virtue to this particular question.

53. *The World's Body*, pp. 193-211.

54. See F. X. Roellinger "Two Theories of Poetry as Knowledge." *Southern Review*, VII, 690-705.

55. *The World's Body*, pp. 208, 209.

56. *Reason in Madness*, pp. 60, 61. Ransom declares that the imagery of poetry should be "true in the commonest sense of true: verifiable, based on observation."— *The World's Body*, p. 157. But we would here seem to circle back to the problem of verification: how shall we distinguish the verifications provided by poetry from the verifications of "science"? And if they are distinguished how establish the "verifiability" of poetry? I take the "shock of recognition" to be capable of empirical proof on psychological grounds, but in this instance Mr. Ransom seems determined to abstain from using any information later in date than Aristotle.

insights into critical absolutes. They mistake[57] their own speculations, acute but limited in validity, for truths of universal application. They establish categories, and these categories suddenly become independent, fixed, and permanent.[58] They generalize with astounding haste. Like T. E. Hulme, they formulate a definition of Romanticism, for example, which is at first limited to a single context, but which is later applied indiscriminately to vast tracts of poetry and legions of poets. Consequently they are at their worst, in spite of their skill in close reading, when they are dealing with the individual phenomenon of a poem by a poet to whom they are theoretically and temperamentally opposed, and who in addition had the misfortune to be born in the wrong period.

VI   Thus when Mr. Tate sets himself to pass upon Shelley's *When the Lamp Is Shattered* one cannot but feel that the verdict has preceded the trial, and the judge has put on a black cap before summoning the witnesses. Of the last stanza he remarks:

> We can have a multiple meaning through ambiguity, but we cannot have an incoherent structure of images. Shelley, in confusion, or carelessness, or haste, could not sustain the nest-bird metaphor and say all that he wished to say; so, in order to say it, he changed the figure and ruined the poem.[59]

57. It is not certain that Mr. Ransom makes this mistake; one sometimes feels that his Olympian dogmatism is a kind of dramatic device. This study necessarily is unjust to his full critical position as amplified in *The New Criticism* and in recent articles in the *Kenyon Review*. What he has said, however, he has said; and concerning Romanticism and Shelley he shows no symptoms of repentance.

58. See Tate, "Three Types of Poetry," *Reactionary Essays;* Ransom, "A Note in Ontology," *The World's Body.*

59. *Reason in Madness,* p. 97.

The stanza in question runs thus:

> Its [Love's] passions will rock thee,
> As the storms rock the ravens on high:
> Bright reason will mock thee,
> Like the sun from a wintry sky.
> From thy nest every rafter
> Will rot, and thine eagle home
> Leave thee naked to laughter,
> When leaves fall and cold winds come.

The root question is clearly what to Mr. Tate is Shelley's failure to sustain the metaphor. The objection assumes that this design is Shelley's design, which he has been unable to execute. This is of course not so; Shelley is being condemned for violating a law of which he has never heard. It may be argued that ignorance of the law is no defense. This argument, however, depends upon the validity of the law itself, and if we carry the case to the supreme court, the great critics from Aristotle on, I think we shall find that the statute is unheard of— it is not in Aristotle, it is not in Longinus; it is not in Johnson, it is not in Coleridge. The lack of historical precedent admittedly does not damn it, but it does afford a strong presumption against its authority.

In other words, Mr. Tate is judging Shelley's poem by an external and irrelevant standard. One may certainly say that the "intention" of a poem has nothing to do with its ultimate value.[60] On the other hand, a correct evaluation depends upon a correct perception of the object, which Tate's method prevents him from attaining. To paraphrase Coleridge, it is pointless to

60. For the argument against "intention" see M. C. Beardsley and W. K. Wimsatt, "Intention," *Dictionary of World Literature*, ed. J. T. Shipley, and Wimsatt, "The Structure of the Concrete Universal in Literature," PMLA, LXII, 272n.

criticize a leopard for being an inferior type of bear.
The method might work very well for one of Donne's
poems, or Mr. Tate's own poems (although it can be
manipulated to damn any poem whatever), but it is
inappropriate to Shelley, and to all poetry outside the
"metaphysical" tradition. To recur to the legal metaphor, which in this special connection comes inevitably
to mind, Mr. Tate is trying to stretch a city ordinance,
or at best a state law, into nationwide validity. The
metaphor involves, it may be said, the admission that
there *are* Federal laws. Quite so: coherence is a law of
"nationwide" application; order is a value; and one
must agree that poetry should be an organizer of diverse
materials into unity. But Mr. Tate would petrify a
critical principle into a rule, would permit only his own
structure of order; and this rule has the authority only
which Johnson assigns to the neoclassical unities. The
passage, though familiar, is too apt not to quote:

> . . . a play written with nice observation of critical rules is
> to be contemplated as an elaborate curiosity, as the product of
> superfluous and ostentatious art, by which is shown rather what
> is possible than what is necessary.
> He that without diminution of any other excellence shall pre-
> serve all the unities unbroken, deserves the like applause with the
> architect who shall display all the orders of architecture in a citadel
> without any deduction from its strength. But the principal beauty
> of a citadel is to exclude the enemy, and the greatest graces of a
> play are to copy nature and instruct life.[61]

Having rejected Mr. Tate's implied order, at least as
prescriptive upon Shelley, we should to be candid demonstrate the design which he has so thoroughly failed

61. *Preface to Shakespeare.*

to see. But to do so we must cite the remainder of the poem, the first three stanzas:

I

When the lamp is shattered,
The light in the dust lies dead;
When the cloud is scattered,
The rainbow's glory is shed:
When the lute is broken,
Sweet tones are remembered not;
When the lips have spoken,
Loved accents are soon forgot.

II

As music and splendor
Survive not the lamp and the lute,
The heart's echoes render
No song when the spirit is mute:—
No song but sad dirges,
Like the wind through a ruined cell,
Or the mournful surges
That ring the dead seaman's knell.

III

When hearts have once mingled,
Love first leaves the well-built nest;
The weak one is singled
To endure what it once possessed.
O Love! who bewailest
The frailty of all things here,
Why choose you the frailest
For your cradle, your home, and your bier?

The "basic image" of *When the Lamp Is Shattered* appears to be the light and its containing vessel, a form of the "veil image."[62] This is a speculation about the

62. See above, pp. 230-39.

genesis of the poem, and need not be accepted; it is certain, however, that the relationship between light and vessel, expressed in the images of the lamp, the lute, the heart, and the nest, is the poem's core. It is the relationship between soul and body, spirit and matter, and it remains constant throughout, embodied in a regular progression of images. Thus in I the lamp and the lute predominate; in II they are generalized as "music" and "splendor," and the heart is introduced. In III it becomes the nest, and in IV the attention is turned to the wintry day to which the nest is exposed.

To elaborate, Shelley's lyric explores the poetic implications of a metaphysical relationship. On the level of metaphysics the relationship poses the nagging problem of the idealistic Monist—the unavoidable dualism of his terms, the stress between unity and duality. I appraises the possible relationships; on the one hand the ominous suggestion that the death of the body is also the death of the soul, and counterpointed against it the implicit and inherent suggestion that the light and the music are immortal and return to their source.

In II *music* and *splendor* gather together the paired images of I and connect them specifically with the heart. But the heart image has connotations more complex and emotional, and the poetic situation develops accordingly. The element of inharmony is added to that of extinction—there is a kind of ghostly survival in memory, but of harmony destroyed by its association with a ravaged instrument (ll. 13-16). The "ruined cell" and the "dead seaman" are both matter or flesh devoid of spirit, and with them enters a new suggestion of disease and decay.

In III Love—the spirit, the light, the music—becomes a wasting rather than a divine fire, which the stronger organism casts off but the weaker must endure as it may (17-20). The next four lines contrast Love as an eternal value, the "never-shifting mark," let us say, of the affirmations of Shakespeare's sonnets and the Petrarchan tradition in general, with love as it may come to be experienced by the imperfect individual.

In IV the shift to *thee* adds immediacy. *Thee* is ambivalent, suggesting both the *weak one* of the previous stanza and the weakness of all when overcome by love. This stanza tells of decay, disharmony, exposure. Love is a force banishing reason, a wasting disease, an exposer of weakness, a cause of disharmony. The light itself now shatters the lamp, the lute is broken by its sound, the soul destroys its fleshly covering.

The poem, then, consists of a single relationship whose implications are explored in a number of different images, of which Mr. Tate would more or less arbitrarily emphasize one. This distortion leads him into a number of misreadings of the final stanza; insisting upon the primacy of the nest-bird image, he falls into a deliberate literalness of which he would never be guilty if he were judging another type of poetry. Thus he objects that "The ravens in the second line are eagles in the sixth." The ravens, however, occur within a simile; they are equated neither with "thee" nor "thine eagle home." "I pass over," says he, " 'Bright reason'. . . . Are we to suppose that other birds come by and mock the raven (eagle), or are we to shift the field of imagery and see 'thee' as a woman?" This needs little comment: the dominant image of the last stanza is inclusive—a

blustering winter day, as was suggested above—and the single images are in harmony with it. The storms rock the ravens; "Bright reason" mocks like the sun from a wintry sky; "thine eagle home" ("eagle" because exposed) is open to wind, cold, and the chill sunlight of reason.

The strictures of F. R. Leavis upon the *Ode to the West Wind* are in much the same vein. He takes for his text the lines

> Thou on whose stream, mid the steep sky's commotion,
> Loose clouds like earth's decaying leaves are shed,
> Shook from the tangled boughs of Heaven and Ocean,
> Angels of rain and lightning: there are spread
> On the blue surface of thine aery surge,
> Like the bright hair uplifted from the head
> Of some fierce Maenad, even from the dim verge
> Of the horizon to the zenith's height,
> The locks of the approaching storm. . .

Mr. Leavis's general objection is that the imagery is vague. "In what respects," he asks, "are the 'loose clouds' like 'decaying leaves'?" The correspondence is "only the vague general sense of windy tumult." But his critique is so exhaustive that it must be reproduced in full. He continues:

. . . accordingly, the appropriateness of the metaphor 'stream' in the first line is not that it suggests a surface on which, like leaves, the clouds might be 'shed,' but that it contributes to the general 'streaming' effect in which the inappropriateness of 'shed' passes unnoticed. What again, are those 'tangled boughs of Heaven and Ocean'? They stand for nothing that Shelley could have pointed to in the scene before him; the 'boughs,' it is plain, have grown out of the 'leaves' of the previous line, and we are not to ask what the

tree is. Nor are we to scrutinize closely the 'stream' metaphor as developed: that 'blue surface' must be the concave of the sky, an oddly smooth surface for a 'surge'—if we consider a moment. . . . Then again, in what ways does the approach of a storm ('loose clouds like earth's decaying leaves,' 'like ghosts from an enchanter fleeing') suggest streaming hair? The appropriateness of the Maenad . . . lies in the pervasive suggestions of frenzied onset, and we are not to ask whether her bright hair is to be seen as streaming out in front of her) as, there is no need to assure ourselves, it might be doing if she were running before a still swifter gale: in the kind of reading that got so far as proposing to itself this particular reassurance no general satisfaction could be exacted from Shelley's imagery.[63]

To Mr. Leavis's objections to the comparison of "loose clouds" with "decaying leaves" one can only assert that there are quite adequate resemblances between them. The clouds and the leaves are carried in precisely the same fashion by the power of the wind. Furthermore, the resemblance holds for shape and color as well as movement. Swift-flying clouds may present the same angularities as leaves, and leaves flying horizontally through a gray sky will take the hue of their surroundings. But to attempt to defend in turn the visual particularity of each image is to miss the true point: that the controller, organizer, and unifier of the scene is the power of the west wind, which is also the point of the poem. Mr. Leavis appears to be isolating some archetypal cloud and leaf from their relationships with the wind and with the composition of the scene. "The kind of reading" which he would evidently apply is inappropriate to the poem, obscures its true design,[64] and if

63. *Revaluation*, pp. 204-7.
64. See I. J. Kapstein, "The Symbolism of the Wind and the Leaves in Shelley's

employed in this spirit would demolish any poetry whatever.

The "tangled boughs of Heaven and Ocean," as
Leavis says, "stand for nothing that Shelley could have
pointed to in the scene before him." It is quite true—in
fact self-evident—that there are no "boughs" in the
sky, no boughs in the sea. But the clouds derive from
these "tangled boughs"—tangled because Heaven and
Ocean intermingle, boughs because the clouds derive
from the sky and sea in just such an organic process as
causes the leaves to grow on the tree. Surely it is safe to
assert that this is an entirely justifiable development of
the implications of the figure, grounded on true and
rich resemblances. In any event, we may agree with I. A.
Richards that the criterion of imagery is meaning, significant relationship; not strong visuality in itself. Mr.
Leavis seems actually to be questioning the legitimacy
of the principle of metaphor. And if we accept his
grounds and take it that Shelley's verses are equivalent
somehow to a scene before Shelley's eyes—and take it
also that somehow it is not merely possible but also
obligatory to place it unaltered before ours—Mr. Leavis
is still applying a false standard. He takes each image
in turn as an absolute, cut off from its compositional
relationships. Shelley is describing the influence of wind
upon objects of nature, which are shaped and modified
by its action. He is describing objects in motion, framed
by the dome of the sky. But the critic would have him
elaborate in sculptural fashion a visual image which
would destroy his whole effect.

Ode to the West Wind,' " PMLA, LI, 1069-79; R. H. Fogle, "The Imaginal Design
of Shelley's 'Ode to the West Wind,' " ELH, XV, 219-26.

With a like disregard for the poet's intentions and methods, John Crowe Ransom, comparing nineteenth-century, or "Platonic," poetry unfavorably with metaphysical poetry, remarks scornfully that "Shelley is about as vigorous as usual when he says in *Adonais:*

> Thou young Dawn
> Turn all thy dew to splendour . . .

But splendor is not the correlative of dew, it has the flat tone of a Platonic idea, while physically it scarcely means more than dew with sunshine upon it."[65] Mr. Ransom would profit by re-examining the status of "splendour" in the light of a concordance and a volume of Shelley's poetry. Despite his acuteness, his method of calling upon Shelley to stand and deliver at sight is, to speak with moderation, inadequate. If he had been seriously inclined to come to grips with *Adonais* he might have avoided the unfairness of isolating this figure from the design of the whole.

VII   In Cleanth Brooks' *Modern Poetry and the Tradition*[66] the doctrines of the New Criticism become a developed and explicit system. The true "tradition," as one might guess, is the tradition of metaphysical wit and complexity. Like Eliot and Basil Willey he traces its downfall to Hobbes and the scientific rationalism of the late seventeenth century[67] and hails

65. *The World's Body*, pp. 137, 138.
66. Chapel Hill, N. C., 1939.
67. More like Willey, perhaps, than like Eliot, since Eliot placed the responsibility for the "Dissociation of sensibility" primarily upon two poets, Milton and Dryden. See above, p. 249.

its resurgence in the moderns of the twentieth.[68] Romanticism he finds unsatisfactory, both in theory and in practice. The Romantics attempted to break loose from the bonds of eighteenth-century neoclassicism, but failed to go far enough. Instead of repudiating completely the eighteenth-century belief in the inherent beauty and poetic value of certain types of objects, they merely substituted other objects.[69] By denying the importance of the intellect in favor of emotion and spontaneity they fell into the fallacy of dissociating the elements of poetic sensibility.[70] The modern poet and theorist, on the other hand, reposes his confidence in the power of his imagination, which fuses and harmonizes disparate, incongruous, and apparently unattractive materials into unity.[71] He does not make the error of distinguishing Fancy from Imagination, wit from high poetry.

In a separate essay Mr. Brooks joins Ransom and Tate in condemning "the fallacy of communication." the poem itself is "the linguistic vehicle which conveys the thing most clearly and accurately"; therefore it is fallacious to abstract its ideas in order to understand it.[72] The poet employs the methods characteristic of po-

68. *Modern Poetry and the Tradition*, pp. 11, 33-35.

69. *Ibid.*, pp. 5-10.

70. *Ibid.*, p. 32.

71. "It is his making, his imagination that gives the poem the poetic quality, not some intrinsic quality (beauty or truth) of the materials with which he builds his poem. The metaphysical poet has confidence in the power of the imagination. His is constantly remaking his world by relating into an organic whole the amorphous and heterogeneous and contradictory."—*Ibid.*, p. 43. Cf. Eliot, "Tradition and the Individual Talent," *The Sacred Wood*, p. 55: ". . . it is not the 'greatness,' the intensity of the emotions, the components, but the intensity of the artistic process, the pressure, so to speak, under which the fusion takes place, that counts."

72. "What Does Modern Poetry Communicate?" in *American Prefaces*, p. 25.

etry: indirection, "the use of symbol rather than abstraction, suggestion rather than explicit pronouncement, metaphor rather than direct statement."[73] In a later article he declares that paradox is the very stuff of poetry.[74]

Since Mr. Brooks applies specifically to Shelley his strictures against Romantic theory in general, it is appropriate to examine them a little more at length. He attributes to the Romantics a doctrine of the inherent beauty of poetic objects which he has found in Addison, relating it to Romanticism on the strength of a statement from Wordsworth: "Fancy depends upon the rapidity . . . with which she scatters her thoughts and images; trusting that their number, and the felicity with which they are linked together, will make amends for the want of individual value."

Now the phrase "poetic objects" presents its difficulties: it seems to suggest a confusion of life and art which one cannot believe has ever been literally accepted by any group; in any event, the citation from Wordsworth will hardly support its implications, since his "thoughts and images" are psychological, and related to "objects" only at many removes. Mr. Brooks does, however, hit at a vital issue. One may confidently repel the suggestion that any Romantic poet has believed that good material makes good poetry by some simple transference from life to paper; it is highly probable, on the other hand, that the great majority of poets of every period and allegiance have believed that some objects were more beautiful than others, and some subjects more

73. *Ibid.*, p. 27.
74. "The Language of Paradox," in *The Language of Poetry*.

promising to poetry. The greatest source of possible confusion lies in the meaning of "beauty." Mr. Brooks, if I interpret him properly, is in this context thinking of beauty as sentimentality, as false and oversimplified idealization; and for him it is a reproach to the Romantics that they desired to express the beautiful. The general imputation, of course, I flatly deny; but it would be senseless and humorless to attempt a systematic rebuttal.

One might, however, suggest that Mr. Brooks has fallen into the very trap he has prepared for Romanticism; that he proposes an absolute distinction of content and form, material and art. Thus by a shift from the theory of Romanticism to its poetry he has it performing the easy task of molding inherently beautiful materials into what one supposes must be beautiful poetry. Metaphysical poetry is more virtuous; apparently it deliberately sets itself a more difficult problem, on the theory that it is less laudable to shoot a bear than to kill it with your hands. Yet it could be considered that with successful execution the result will be the same; while by the second method the chance that the bear may win is largely increased. The imagination of the poet may be concerned with the choice of subject as well as the shaping of it; psychologically it may be that the two processes are simultaneous and indistinguishable. Mr. Brooks, like other New Critics, is deeply concerned to find trustworthy, objective standards of value. Will he then, when he judges the finished statue, estimate the cost of the stone, and have a preference for the cheapest?

If one accepts the implications of the literary history sketched in *Modern Poetry and the Tradition*, to which I presume most New or Metaphysical Critics would as-

sent, the eighteenth century becomes a kind of poetic nadir, above which the Romantics strove to rise with poor success. The underlying reason for this failure is not wholly clear. Mr. Brooks sometimes seems to feel that if they had taken thought, had been better men, had read more Donne, they too might have been Metaphysicals, and that their failure to be so was a flat dereliction of duty. One wonders by what mysterious providence the twentieth century has been blessed, that its poets alone have been privileged to see the light long lost; and why this providence so signally ignored meanwhile so many. One wonders further what justice can condemn the Romantic and Victorian outcasts; how in this case the ways of God shall be justified to the errant. Could this providence be named the Time Spirit? And if so, what becomes of our absolute, objective, and universal standards?

Mr. Brooks conceives of metaphysical poetry as a norm, or as a whole compared to which Romantic poetry is an imperfect part. Romantic poetry is the product of a divided; metaphysical of a unified sensibility. I suggest that this may well be a fallacy. Speaking frankly as a Romantic partisan, I am yet unwilling to attempt a reversal, to suggest that Mr. Brooks has confused the terms and should put them in their proper places. On the other hand, I am quite willing to assert that the Metaphysical whole is not less but more confined than the Romantic whole; that the area of reality governed by it has shrunk, and not expanded.

On such issues as this it is useless to argue at length; no one will be converted, and the chapter-and-verse would be another book. But let us take as a part of the

argument what may stand as an emblem of the whole. That is, the statement of Mr. Brooks that the Romantics dissociated the elements of poetic sensibility by stressing the importance of emotion and spontaneity.

The Romantics were fully aware of the problem, and considered themselves not to be over-stressing, but rather reinstating emotion, as a real factor in the poetic complex which had been badly neglected. Wordsworth, defining poetry as "a spontaneous overflow of emotion," continued immediately, ". . . . Poems to which any value can be attached were never produced on any variety of subjects but by a man who, being possessed of more than usual organic sensibility, had also thought long and deeply."[75] His "emotion recollected in tranquillity" epitomizes a psychological theory of poetic creation which strives to do justice to conscious and unconscious, intellect and emotion, idea and sensation. The *Prelude* is the fullest examination ever made of the organic unity of the poetic mind, an immense and subtle synthesis of widely differing forces. It is almost superfluous to speak of Coleridge's theory of Imagination, the unifying power in which all faculties are reconciled and none are slighted.[76] Shelley, with his Platonic Inspiration theory, manages to employ an extremely acute intellect in the substantial bulk of his considerable poetry. As a matter of fact Mr. Brooks himself, with his doctrine of imaginative as opposed to logical unity, might by fault-finding critics be charged with having effected this baneful separation.[77] He may very well plead that in his use of the

75. *1800 Preface.* See *Modern Poetry and the Tradition*, p. 18.
76. *Biographia Literaria*, ch. XIV.
77. See *Modern Poetry and the Tradition*, p. 66.

terms he has intended no simple opposition or dissociation; but then so with at least equal reason may the Romantics absolve themselves.

The application of these statements to Shelley follows. Shelley, in the opinion of Mr. Brooks, occupies much too high a place in the ranks of the English poets.

The traditional historian hardly sees Shelley as a very unsatisfactory poet greatly inferior to Keats. A more considered view must surely hold him so.

Shelley is not merely guilty of poor craftsmanship—slovenly riming, loosely decorative and sometimes too gaudy metaphor. Consideration of the two poets on the basis of tone and attitude will reveal more important differences. Keats is rarely sentimental, Shelley frequently so. Keats is too much the artist to risk Shelley's sometimes embarrassing declarations—'I die, I faint, I fail,' or 'I fall upon the thorns of life! I bleed!'[78]

Two charges in this passage are possible to discuss—Shelley's "loosely decorative metaphor" and his sentimentality. They may be translated into the assertion that he fails to measure up to Mr. Brooks' basic poetic standards—organic unity and irony. Irony Mr. Brooks has most recently defined, in the terms of Eliot, as "that which the mind of the reader can accept as coherent, mature, and founded on the facts of experience," and alternatively from I. A. Richards as

. . . 'poetry of synthesis'—that is, it is a poetry which does not leave out what is apparently hostile to its dominant tone, and which, because it is able to fuse the irrelevant and discordant, has come to terms with itself and is invulnerable to irony.[79]

Organic unity, or "the concept of the poem as organ-

78. *Modern Poetry and the Tradition*, p. 237.
79. "Irony and 'Ironic' Poetry," *College English*, IX, 234.

ism," which for Mr. Brooks is of such importance that "the best hope that we have for reviving the study of poetry and of the humanities generally" rests upon it, means that "Each part—image, statement, metaphor—helps build the total meaning of a poem and is itself qualified by the whole context."[80]

Now, insofar as Mr. Brooks has made it possible to measure Shelley by these standards, I should maintain that of the two poems which he cites *The Indian Serenade* is "sentimental" but possesses organic unity, while I should passionately deny that the *Ode to the West Wind* is either sentimental or inorganic.[81] In regard to the *Indian Serenade*, Mr. Brooks has so underrated the poet that he supposes him to be talking quite literally about himself; if the lover, the "I" of the lyric, is to be translated as it were bodily into Shelley, this lyric is indeed open to irony. But the title itself would indicate that this is not so, that the love affair is a matter of imagination and in a sense dramatic.[82] *The Indian Serenade* is slight and quite frankly of no great consequence. It seems to me artistic and well integrated in design. Robert Penn Warren is fairer to it than is Mr. Brooks in using it as an example of excessively "pure" poetry.[83]

80. *Ibid.*, p. 237; see also "The Poem as Organism," *English Institute Annual.*

81. See Fogle, "The Imaginal Design of Shelley's 'Ode to the West Wind,'" *op. cit.*

82. ". . . we meet the poet, even in the most personal lyric poetry, only in a strained and ambiguous sense. But we can go much farther than this. It is, in fact, quite impossible that the character represented in the poem should be identically the same with that of the poet. The character represented is that of a man in the grip of this or that emotion: the real poet is a man who has already escaped from that emotion sufficiently to see it objectively—I had almost said to see it dramatically—and to make poetry of it."—C. S. Lewis, in E. M. W. Tillyard and C. S. Lewis, *The Personal Heresy*, p. 9.

83. "Pure and Impure Poetry," *The Kenyon Review*, V, 230f.

Here we must note an important difficulty in using the concept of organic unity as a critical weapon. If one commences, as does Mr. Brooks, by speaking of the poem as "organism," one makes a statement about the nature of poetry and poetic creation. This statement has nothing to do with judicial or evaluative criticism; it is descriptive and leads to explanation rather than judgment. Criticism which begins with the assumption of the organic will not question the existence of meaningful relationships within the poem, but will proceed to look for them, in the full confidence that they are there to be found. Such a criticism will look for the master-principle of the organism within the poem itself; it will regard the importation of principles from without as irrelevant. As soon, in fact, as judicial criticism commences, the concept of the poem as organism ceases to have validity.

The practical consequences of this position are extensive. They lead me from my point of view to reject organic unity as a tool of evaluation, on the grounds that with good will one can find it in any poem whatever. It is not a reliable criterion, and if used as a criterion can be manipulated at will. If organic unity itself becomes a critical absolute, the grounds for distinction are wiped out. All poems which possess organic unity are equally good—if my contention is correct, and all poems may be shown to have organic unity, the result is soul-destroying.

A comparable, although perhaps a lesser source of difficulty, occurs in the use of the concept of irony. One can accept it as a standard for poetry, defined as does Eliot as "that which the mind of the reader can accept

as coherent, mature, and founded on the facts of experience," or in the Coleridgean formulation of "the
reconciliation of opposites"; but the application must
vary with the critic. Whether rightly or wrongly, I
cannot permit the decision as to what constitutes coherence and maturity in the individual work to be made
for me; I must make it myself, and will resist any formulation which seems to me to be arbitrary, distorted,
tactless, ignorant—in any way incomplete, in fine. I am
likely, then, to find Mr. Brooks's descriptions of the
Ironic unsatisfactory, as presumably he would mine. His
irony I am likely to find a mere attitude without a
situation, or a rigid, predetermined formula, or sometimes a new invention to enable you to go wading without getting your feet wet. I find irony, within the
present meaning of the term, in the studious under-
statement of the conclusion of *Michael*, in the self-real-
ization which underlies the apparent breaking-off of
Khubla Khan, in the breadth of understanding beneath
the excitement of the *Ode to the West Wind*. Mr. Brooks
would be unlikely to agree.

    In his most recent book, *The Well Wrought Urn*,[84]
Mr. Brooks has devoted an appendix to an eloquent
and persuasive defense of absolutist criticism. Here he
avouches the very worthy aim of applying a single objective standard to poetry of every age and type. The
explications with which he illustrates his method and
point of view are often distinguished and always interesting. One may hazard the opinion, however, that the
method, which accentuates the similarities between
good poems of all ages and ignores the differences, fails

84. New York, 1947.

to complete the process of criticism. For the essential qualities which make good poetry can only be adequately discussed after the differences have been accounted for, after the poems have been identified in their uniqueness. To use the metaphor of organic unity, by his method we get too quickly from the parts to the whole; we are likely to be overhasty in passing judgment and slight the complexity of the relationship.

In his appendix Mr. Brooks maintains that by standards alone can we avoid a disastrous relativism in which all judgments are dissolved and the study of literature itself is doomed.[85] And we may safely agree. But it does not follow that we must accept a single standard; still less does it follow that this standard must be that of Mr. Brooks. Alternatives presumably are possible. One might suggest that, to use terms differently employed in an earlier chapter, the ideal criticism is composed of the "participant" *plus* the "spectator" attitude. Observe the poem in its own terms and its own relationships, and only then proceed to evaluation by external standards.

Standards are undoubtedly essential; without them we cannot have rational or even intelligible criticism. We can be grateful to Mr. Brooks for many skilful and illuminating explications, and understand their bases from his statements of principle. Only thus, of course, can we hope to agree or disagree with judgment, and come at last to whatever truth we are qualified to see. But if he asks us to accept, let us say, "metaphysical poetry," as a norm, forsaking all others, we must reply that he has not sufficiently considered other poetry to

85. *The Well Wrought Urn*, p. 198f.

convince us that he has really examined all its possibilities; that we must combat our own limitations,
attempt to transcend them, and arrive at our own synthesis. Mr. Brooks has somewhere expressed the fear
that critical relativism may lead us to confuse Edgar A.
Guest and Shakespeare; critical absolutism, one may
feel, has already confused Edgar A. Guest and Shelley,
in an almost equal failure of values.

BIBLIOGRAPHY

INDEX

BIBLIOGRAPHY

I. TEXTS

Keats, John. *The Complete Works of John Keats*. Edited by H. Buxton
Forman. Glasgow: Gowans and Gray, 1900, 1901. 5 vols.

———. *John Keats: Complete Poems and Selected Letters*. Edited by
Clarence DeWitt Thorpe. New York: Doubleday, Doran,
and Company, Inc., 1935.

———. *The Letters of John Keats*, 3rd edition. Edited by Maurice
Buxton Forman. London and New York: Oxford University
Press, 1947.

———. *Poems of John Keats*. Edited by G. Thorn Drury, with an
introduction by Robert Bridges. London: George Routledge
and Sons, Ltd.; New York: E. P. Dutton and Co. 2 vols.

———. *The Poems of John Keats*, 5th edition, revised. Edited with
an introduction and notes by E. de Sélincourt. London:
Methuen and Co., Ltd., 1926.

———. *The Poetical Works of John Keats*. Edited by William T.
Arnold. London: Kegan Paul, Trench and Company, 1884.

———. *The Poetical Works and Other Writings of John Keats*. Edited
with notes and appendices by H. Buxton Forman; revised
with additions by Maurice Buxton Forman; with an introduction by John Masefield. New York: Charles Scribner's
Sons, 1938-39. 8 vols.

Peacock, Thomas Love. *Peacock's Memoirs of Shelley: with Shelley's
Letters to Peacock*. Edited by H. F. B. Brett-Smith. London:
Henry Frowde, 1909.

Shelley, Percy Bysshe. *The Complete Poetical Works of Percy Bysshe
Shelley*. Cambridge Edition. Edited by George E. Woodberry. Boston and New York: Houghton Mifflin Company,
1901.

———. *The Complete Works of Percy Bysshe Shelley*. Edited by Roger

Ingpen and Walter E. Peck. London: E. Benn Limited; New York: C. Scribner's Sons, 1926-30.

———. *Poems of Shelley.* Selected and arranged by Stopford A. Brooke. London: Macmillan and Co., Ltd., 1926.

———. *Shelley's Literary and Philosophical Criticism.* Edited with an introduction by John Shawcross. London: Henry Frowde, 1909.

———. *The Works of Percy Bysshe Shelley in Verse and Prose.* Edited by H. Buxton Forman. London: Reeves and Turner, 1880. 8 vols.

White, Newman I. (ed.). *The Best of Shelley.* New York: Thomas Nelson and Sons, 1932.

II. SCHOLARSHIP AND CRITICISM

Abel, Darrel. "Intellectual Criticism," *American Scholar*, XII (1943), 414-28.

Arestad, Sverre. A Study of Keats's Use of Imagery. Unpublished Ph.D. dissertation, University of Washington, 1938.

Aristotle. *The Poetics of Aristotle*, 4th edition. Edited and translated by S. H. Butcher. London: Macmillan and Co., 1936.

———. *The Rhetoric of Aristotle: a Translation* by Sir Richard Claverhouse Jebb. Edited by J. E. Sandys. Cambridge: at the University Press, 1909.

Arnold, Matthew. *Essays in Criticism.* 2nd Series. London: Macmillan and Company, Ltd., 1915.

Babbitt, Irving. *The New Laokoon: an Essay on the Confusion of the Arts.* Boston and New York: Houghton Mifflin Company, 1910.

Bailey, John. "The Poet of Stillness," *The John Keats Memorial Volume*, q. v.

Bate, Walter Jackson. *Negative Capability: The Intuitive Approach in Keats.* Cambridge, Mass.: Harvard University Press, 1939.

———. *The Stylistic Development of Keats.* New York: Modern Language Association, 1945.

Bates, Ernest Sutherland. "Mad Shelley: a Study in the Origins of English Romanticism," *The Fred Newton Scott Anniversary Papers.* Chicago: University of Chicago Press, 1929.

Beach, Joseph Warren. *The Concept of Nature in Nineteenth Century English Poetry*. New York: The Macmillan Company, 1936.
———. *A Romantic View of Poetry*. Minneapolis: The University of Minnesota Press, 1944.

Beardsley, Monroe C., and W. K. Wimsatt, Jr. "Intention," *Dictionary of World Literature*, q. v.

Bernbaum, Ernest (ed.). *Anthology of Romanticism*, 3rd edition. New York: The Ronald Press Company, 1948.
———. *Guide Through the Romantic Movement*, 2nd edition. New York: The Ronald Press Company, 1949.

Beyer, Werner. *Keats and the Daemon King*. New York: Oxford University Press, 1947.

Blackmur, R. P. *The Expense of Greatness*. New York: Arrow Editions, 1940.

Bradley, A. C. *Oxford Lectures on Poetry*. London: Macmillan and Co., Ltd., 1917.

Brooke, Stopford A. "Inaugural Address to the Shelley Society." *The Shelley Society's Papers*, Series 1, No. 1, Parts 1-2, 1888-91.
———. *Naturalism in English Poetry*. New York: E. P. Dutton and Company, 1920.

Brooks, Cleanth. "Irony and 'Ironic' Poetry," *College English*, IX (February, 1948), 231-37.
———. "The Language of Paradox," *The Language of Poetry*, q. v.
———. *Modern Poetry and the Tradition*. Chapel Hill: The University of North Carolina Press, 1939.
———. "The Poem as Organism: Modern Critical Procedure," *English Institute Annual*. New York: Columbia University Press, 1940.
———. *The Well Wrought Urn*. New York: Reynal and Hitchcock, 1947.
———. "What Does Modern Poetry Communicate?" *American Prefaces* (Autumn, 1940).

Brooks, Cleanth, and Robert Penn Warren (eds.). *Understanding Fiction*. New York: F. S. Crofts and Company, 1943.

Brooks, Cleanth, and Robert Penn Warren (eds.). *Understanding Poetry*. New York: Henry Holt and Co., 1938.

Brooks, Cleanth, J. T. Purser, and R. P. Warren (eds.). *An Approach*

to *Literature*, revised edition. New York: F. S. Crofts and Co., 1946.

Buck, Philo M., Jr. *Literary Criticism: a Study of Values in Literature*. New York and London: Harper and Brothers, 1930.

Bush, Douglas. *Mythology and the Romantic Tradition in English Poetry*. Cambridge, Mass.: Harvard University Press, 1937.

Caldwell, James Ralston. *John Keats' Fancy: The Effect on Keats of the Psychology of His Day*. Ithaca, New York: Cornell University Press, 1945.

Cameron, Kenneth N. "A Major Source of *The Revolt of Islam*," *PMLA*, LVI (1941), 175-206.

Campbell, Olwen Ward. *Shelley and the Unromantics*. London: Methuen and Co., Ltd., 1924.

"The Character of Shelley," *Quarterly Review*, CLXIV (1887), 285-321.

Clutton-Brock, Arthur. "Keats and Shelley—a Contrast," *The John Keats Memorial Volume*, q.v.

———. *Shelley: The Man and the Poet*. London: Methuen and Co., Ltd., 1909.

Coffin, Robert P. Tristram. *The Substance That Is Poetry*. New York: The Macmillan Company, 1942.

Coleridge, Samuel Taylor. *Biographia Literaria*. Edited with his Aesthetical Essays, by John Shawcross. Oxford: The Clarendon Press, 1907. 2 vols.

———. *Coleridge's Shakespearean Criticism*. Edited by Thomas Middleton Raysor. Cambridge, Mass.: Harvard University Press, 1930. 2 vols.

———. *Essays and Lectures on Shakespeare*, . . . Everyman edition. London: J. M. Dent and Co., Ltd.; New York: E. P. Dutton and Co., Inc., 1907.

Colvin, Sir Sidney. *John Keats: His Life and Poetry, His Friends, Critics, and After-Fame*. New York: Charles Scribner's Sons, 1917.

Courthope, W. J. *A History of English Poetry*. London: Macmillan and Company, Ltd., 1913. 6 vols.

Crane, R. S. "Cleanth Brooks; or The Bankruptcy of Critical Monism," *Modern Philology*, XLV (May, 1948), 226-45.

Darbishire, Helen. "Keats and Egypt," *Review of English Studies*, III (1927).

de Ullmann, Stephen. "Romanticism and Synaesthesia: A Comparative Study of Sense Transfer in Keats and Byron," *PMLA* (1945), 811-27.

DeVries, Louis P. *The Nature of Poetic Literature*. Seattle, Wash.: University of Washington Press, 1930.

Dictionary of World Literature. Edited by Joseph T. Shipley. New York: The Philosophical Library, 1943.

Dodds, Mrs. E. P. See Powell, A. E.

Downey, June Etta. *Creative Imagination: Studies in the Psychology of Literature*. New York: Harcourt, Brace, and Company, 1929.

————. *The Imaginal Reaction to Poetry*. Laramie, Wyo.: University of Wyoming Dept. of Psychology Bulletin No. 2, 1911.

————. "Literary Synesthesia," *The Journal of Philosophy, Psychology, and Scientific Methods*, IX (1912), 490-98.

Edgar, Pelham. *A Study of Shelley: With Special Reference to His Nature Poetry*. Toronto: William Briggs, 1899.

Eliot, T. S. *Homage to John Dryden: Three Essays on Poetry of the Seventeenth Century*. London: The Hogarth Press, 1927.

————. "Milton," *Sewanee Review*, LVI (Spring, 1948), 185-209.

————. *The Sacred Wood: Essays on Poetry and Criticism*. London: Methuen and Co., Ltd., 1920.

————. *Selected Essays, 1917-1932*. New York: Harcourt, Brace and Company, 1932.

————. *The Use of Poetry and the Use of Criticism: Studies in the Relation of Criticism to Poetry in England*. Cambridge, Mass.: Harvard University Press, 1933.

————. "What Is Minor Poetry?" *Sewanee Review*, LIV (Winter, 1946), 1-18.

Elliott, G. R. *The Cycle of Modern Poetry*. Princeton, N. J.: Princeton University Press, 1929.

Ellis, Frederick Startridge. *A Lexical Concordance to the Poetical Works of Percy Bysshe Shelley*. London: Bernard Quaritch, 1892.

Empson, William. *Seven Types of Ambiguity*, 2nd edition, revised. London: Chatto and Windus, 1947.

Fairchild, Hoxie N. *The Romantic Quest*. New York: Columbia
       University Press, 1931.

Fausset, Hugh I'A. *Keats: A Study in Development*. London: Martin
       Secker, 1922.

Finney, Claude Lee. *The Evolution of Keats's Poetry*. Cambridge, Mass.:
       Harvard University Press, 1936. 2 vols.

Fletcher, John Gould. *Goblins and Pagodas*. Boston and New York:
       Houghton Mifflin Co., 1916.

Foerster, Norman. "The Esthetic Judgment and the Ethical Judg-
       ment," *The Intent of the Critic*, q. v.

Fogle, Richard Harter. "The Imaginal Design of Shelley's 'Ode to
       the West Wind,' " *ELH*, XV (September, 1948), 219-26.

————. "A Recent Attack upon Romanticism," *College English*,
       IX (April, 1948), 356-61.

Garrod, H. W. *Keats*. Oxford: The Clarendon Press, 1926.

Gilbert, Katharine Everett, and Helmut Kuhn. *A History of Esthetics*.
       New York: The Macmillan Co., 1939.

Gingerich, Solomon Francis. *Essays in the Romantic Poets*. New York:
       The Macmillan Company, 1929.

Grabo, Carl. *The Magic Plant: The Growth of Shelley's Thought*. Chapel
       Hill: The University of North Carolina Press, 1936.

————. *The Meaning of the Witch of Atlas*. Chapel Hill: The Uni-
       versity of North Carolina Press, 1935.

————. *A Newton Among Poets: Shelley's Use of Science in Prometheus
       Unbound*. Chapel Hill: The University of North Carolina
       Press, 1930.

Havens, Raymond D. "Concerning the 'Ode on a Grecian Urn,' "
       MP, XXIV (November, 1926), 209-14.

————. *The Influence of Milton on English Poetry*. Cambridge, Mass.:
       Harvard University Press, 1922.

Haydon, Benjamin Robert. *The Autobiography and Memoirs of Benjamin
       Robert Haydon (1786-1846)*. Edited from his journals by Tom
       Taylor, with an introduction by Aldous Huxley. New
       York: Harcourt, Brace and Company. 2 vols.

Hoffman, Harold Leroy. *An Odyssey of the Soul: Shelley's Alastor*.
       New York: Columbia University Press, 1933.

Hornstein, Lillian H. "Analysis of Imagery: a Critique of Literary
       Method," *PMLA*, LVII (September, 1942), 638-53.

Housman, A. E. *Last Poems*. London: The Richards Press, Ltd., 1930.

———. *The Name and Nature of Poetry*. New York: The Macmillan Company, 1933.

Hughes, Glenn. *Imagism and the Imagists: A Study in Modern Poetry*. Stanford University, Calif.: Stanford University Press, 1931.

Hulme, Thomas Ernest. *Notes on Language and Style*, edited by Herbert Read. Seattle, Wash.: University of Washington Book Store, 1930.

———. *Speculations: Essays on Humanism and the Philosophy of Art*. Edited by Herbert Read. London: K. Paul, Trench, Trubner, and Co.; New York: Harcourt, Brace and Co., 1924.

Hungerford, Edward B. *Shores of Darkness*. New York: Columbia University Press, 1941.

Huxley, Aldous. *Point Counter Point*. New York: The Modern Library, 1928.

The Intent of the Critic. Edited, with an introduction, by Donald A. Stauffer. Princeton: Princeton University Press, 1941.

Jack, Adolphus Alfred. *Shelley: an Essay*. London: Archibald Constable and Co., Ltd., 1904.

Jeans, Sir James. *The Stars in Their Courses*. Cambridge: The University Press, 1931.

Jennings, J. G. *An Essay on Metaphor in Poetry*. London and Glasgow: Blackie and Son, Ltd., 1915.

The John Keats Memorial Volume. Edited by G. C. Williamson. London and New York: John Lane, February 23, 1921.

Kapstein, I. J. "The Symbolism of the Wind and the Leaves in Shelley's 'Ode to the West Wind,' " *PMLA*, LI (1936), 1069-79.

Kazin, Alfred. *On Native Grounds: an Interpretation of Modern American Prose Literature*. New York: Reynal and Hitchcock, 1942.

Kellner, L. "Shelley's *Queen Mab* und Volney's *Les Ruines*," *Englische Studien*, XXII (1896), 9-40.

Knight, G. Wilson. *The Starlit Dome: Studies in the Poetry of Vision*. London and New York: Oxford University Press, 1941.

Langfeld, Herbert S. *The Aesthetic Attitude*. New York: Harcourt, Brace and Co., 1920.

The Language of Poetry. Edited by Allen Tate. Princeton: Princeton University Press, 1942.

Larrabee, Stephen A. *English Bards and Grecian Marbles: The Relationship Between Sculpture and Poetry, Especially in the Romantic Period*. New York: Columbia University Press, 1943.

Leavis, Frank Raymond (ed.). *Determinations: Critical Essays*. London: Chatto and Windus, 1934.

————. *Revaluation: Tradition and Development in English Poetry*. London: Chatto and Windus, 1936.

Lee, Vernon [Violet Paget]. *The Beautiful: An Introduction to Psychological Aesthetics*. Cambridge: at the University Press, 1913.

Lee, Vernon [Violet Paget], and C. Anstruther-Thomson. *Beauty and Ugliness: And Other Studies in Psychological Aesthetics*. London and New York: John Lane, 1912.

Lewis, C. S. *Rehabilitations*. London and New York: Oxford University Press, 1939.

Lotze, Hermann. *Microcosmus: an Essay Concerning Man and His Relation to the World*. Translated by Elizabeth Hamilton and E. E. Constance Jones. New York: Scribner and Welford, 1886. 2 vols.

Lovejoy, Arthur O. *The Great Chain of Being: a Study of the History of an Idea*. Cambridge, Mass.: Harvard University Press, 1936.

Lowell, Amy. *John Keats*. Boston and New York: Houghton Mifflin Company, 1925. 2 vols.

Lowes, John Livingston. "Moneta's Temple," *PMLA*, LI (1936), 1098-1113.

————. *The Road to Xanadu: A Study in the Ways of the Imagination*. Boston and New York: Houghton Mifflin Company, 1927.

Lucas, F. L. *The Decline and Fall of the Romantic Ideal*. New York: The Macmillan Company, 1936.

Lynch, Arthur. "John Keats," *The John Keats Memorial Volume*, q. v.

Marsh, George L. "The Early Reviews of Shelley," *MP*, XXVII (1929-30), 73-95.

Matthiessen, F. O. *The Achievement of T. S. Eliot: an Essay on the Nature of Poetry*, 2nd edition, revised. London: Humphrey Milford, Oxford University Press, 1947.

Murry, John Middleton. *Countries of the Mind: Essays in Literary Criticism*. 2nd Series. London: Humphrey Milford, Oxford University Press, 1931.

————. *Keats and Shakespeare: a Study of Keats's Poetic Life from 1816 to 1820.* London: Humphrey Milford, Oxford University Press, 1925.

————. *Studies in Keats: New and Old,* 2nd edition. London and New York: Oxford University Press, 1939.

Pear, T. H. "Imagery and Mentality," *British Journal of Psychology,* XIV (January, 1924), 291-99.

Perry, Bliss. *A Study of Poetry.* Boston and New York: The Houghton Mifflin Company, 1920.

Pottle, Frederick A. *The Idiom of Poetry.* Revised edition. Ithaca, N. Y.: Cornell University Press, 1946.

Powell, A. E. (Mrs. E. P. Dodds). *The Romantic Theory of Poetry: An Examination in the Light of Croce's Aesthetic.* London: Edward Arnold and Co., 1926.

Praz, Mario. *La Carne, la Morte e il Diavolo nella Letteratura Romantica.* Milan and Rome: Societa Editrice "La Cultura," 1930.

Price, Hereward T. "Function of Imagery in Venus and Adonis," *Papers of the Michigan Academy of Science, Arts, and Letters,* XXXI (1945), 275-97.

Proust, Marcel. *Remembrance of Things Past.* Translated by C. K. Scott Moncrieff, introduction by Joseph Wood Krutch. New York: Random House, 1934. 4 vols.

Ransom, John Crowe. "Criticism as Pure Speculation," *The Intent of the Critic,* q. v.

————. *The New Criticism.* Norfolk, Conn.: New Directions, 1941.

————. *The World's Body.* New York: Charles Scribner's Sons, 1938.

Read, Herbert E. *In Defense of Shelley and Other Essays.* London and Toronto: William Heinemann Ltd., 1936.

Richards, I. A. *Coleridge on Imagination.* London: Kegan Paul, Trench, Trubner and Company, Ltd., 1934.

————. "The Interactions of Words," *The Language of Poetry,* q. v.

————. *The Philosophy of Rhetoric.* New York and London: Oxford University Press, 1936.

————. *Practical Criticism: A Study of Literary Judgment.* New York: Harcourt, Brace and Company, 1929.

————. *Principles of Literary Criticism.* New York: Harcourt, Brace and Company, 1924.

Rickert, Edith. *New Methods for the Study of Literature*. Chicago:
University of Chicago Press, 1927.

Riding, Laura, and Robert Graves. *A Survey of Modernist Poetry*.
London: William Heinemann, Ltd., 1927.

Ridley, M. R. *Keats' Craftsmanship: A Study in Poetic Development*.
Oxford: the Clarendon Press, 1933.

Roberts, Michael. *Critique of Poetry*. London: Jonathan Cape, 1934.

Roellinger, Francis X. "Two Theories of Poetry as Knowledge,"
Southern Review, VII (Spring, 1942), 690-705.

Rylands, George. "English Poets and the Abstract Word," *Essays
and Studies by Members of the English Association*, XVI (1931).

Salt, H. S. *A Shelley Primer*. London: Reeves and Turner, 1887.

Sélincourt, E. de. "The Warton Lecture on Keats," *The John Keats
Memorial Volume*, q. v.

Shaw, Bernard. "Keats," *The John Keats Memorial Volume*, q. v.

Sherwood, Margaret. *Undercurrents of Influence in English Romantic
Poetry*. Cambridge, Mass.: Harvard University Press, 1934.

Shipley, Joseph T. *The Quest for Literature: A Survey of Literary Criticism
and the Theories of the Literary Forms*. New York: Richard
R. Smith, Inc., 1931.

Shuster, George N. *The English Ode from Milton to Keats*. New York:
Columbia University Press, 1940.

Smith, C. Willard. *Browning's Star-Imagery: The Study of a Detail in
Poetic Design*. Princeton: Princeton University Press, 1941.

Solve, Melvin T. *Shelley: His Theory of Poetry*. Chicago: University
of Chicago Press, 1927.

Spurgeon, Caroline F. E. *Shakespeare's Imagery: And What It Tells Us*.
New York: The Macmillan Company, 1936.

Stauffer, Donald. *The Nature of Poetry*. New York: W. W. Norton
and Company, Inc., 1946.

Stocking, Fred H. Poetry as Knowledge: the Critical Theory of
John Crowe Ransom and Allen Tate. Unpublished Ph.D.
dissertation, University of Michigan, 1946.

Stoll, Elmer Edgar. "Symbolism in Coleridge," *PMLA*, LXIII
(March, 1948), 214-33.

Strong, Archibald T. *Three Studies in Shelley*. London: Humphrey
Milford, Oxford University Press, 1921.

Sweet, Henry. "Shelley's Nature Poetry," *The Shelley Society's Papers*. Series 1, No. 1, Parts 1-2, 1888-91.

Symonds, John Addington. *Shelley*. English Men of Letters Series. New York: Harper and Bros., 1879.

Tate, Allen. *Reactionary Essays on Poetry and Ideas*. New York: Charles Scribner's Sons, 1936.

————. "A Reading of Keats," *The American Scholar*, XV (Winter-Spring, 1945-46; Spring, 1946), 55-63, 189-97.

————. *Reason in Madness: Critical Essays*. New York: G. P. Putnam's Sons, 1941.

Thompson, Francis. *Shelley*, 3rd edition. London: Burns and Oates, 1909.

Thorpe, Clarence DeWitt. "Empathy," *Dictionary of World Literature*, q. v.

————. "Keats's Interest in Politics and World Affairs," *PMLA*, XLVI (1931), 1228-45.

————. *The Mind of John Keats*. New York and London: Oxford University Press, 1926.

————. "Some Notices of Empathy before Lipps," *Papers of the Michigan Academy of Science, Arts, and Letters*, XXIII (1938), 525-33.

Thorpe, Clarence DeWitt, and Norman E. Nelson. "Criticism in the Twentieth Century: A Bird's-Eye View," *College English*, VIII (May, 1947), 395-405.

Tillyard, E. M. W., and C. S. Lewis. *The Personal Heresy*. London and New York: Oxford University Press, 1939.

Titchener, Edward B. *Lectures on the Experimental Psychology of the Thought-Process*. New York: The Macmillan Company, 1909.

Todhunter, John. *A Study of Shelley*. London: C. Kegan Paul and Co., 1880.

Trelawny, Edward John. *Trelawny's Recollections of the Last Days of Shelley and Byron*. Introduction by Edward Dowden. London: Humphrey Milford, 1931.

Trowbridge, Hoyt. "Aristotle and the New Criticism," *Sewanee Review*, LII (Autumn, 1944), 537-55.

Tuve, Rosemond. "Imagery and Logic: Ramus and Metaphysical Poetics," *Journal of the History of Ideas*, III (October, 1942), 365-400.

Valentine, C. W. "The Function of Images in the Appreciation of Poetry," *British Journal of Psychology*, XIV (1923), 164-91.

Van Ghent, Dorothy B. Image-Types and Antithetical Structures in the Work of Keats. Unpublished Ph.D. dissertation, University of California, 1942.

von Erhardt-Siebold, Erika. "Harmony of the Senses in English, German, and French Romanticism," *PMLA*, XLVII (1932), 577-92.

————. "Synaesthesien in der englischen Dichtung des 19 Jahrhunderts," *Englische Studien*, LIII (1919), 1-157, 196-334.

Warren, Robert Penn. "Pure and Impure Poetry," *The Kenyon Review*, V (Spring, 1943), 228-51.

Weaver, Bennett. *Toward the Understanding of Shelley*. Ann Arbor: University of Michigan Press, 1932.

Wellek, René. "The Mode of Existence of a Literary Work of Art," *Southern Review*, VII (Spring, 1942), 735-54.

White, Newman Ivey. *Shelley*. New York: Alfred A. Knopf, 1940. 2 vols.

Whitehead, Alfred North. *Science and the Modern World*. New York: The Macmillan Company, 1925.

Willey, Basil. *The Seventeenth Century Background: Studies in the Thought of the Age in Relation to Poetry and Religion*. London: Chatto and Windus, 1934.

Wilson, Edmund. *Axel's Castle: A Study in the Imaginative Literature of 1870-1930*. New York and London: Charles Scribner's Sons, 1942.

Wimsatt, W. K., Jr. "The Structure of the 'Concrete Universal' in Literature," *PMLA*, LXII (March, 1947), 262-80.

Winstanley, Lilian. "Platonism in Shelley," *Essays and Studies by Members of the English Association*, IV (1913).

Yeats, William Butler. *Ideas of Good and Evil*. London and Stratford-Upon-Avon: A. H. Bullen, 1914.

INDEX